Education in Germany
since Unification

Edited by David Phillips

Oxford Studies in Comparative Education
Series Editor: David Phillips

SYMPOSIUM
BOOKS

Symposium Books
PO Box 65, Wallingford, Oxford OX10 0YG, United Kingdom
www.symposium-books.co.uk

Published in the United Kingdom, 2000

ISBN 1 873927 93 2

This publication is also available on a subscription basis
as Volume 10(1) of *Oxford Studies in Comparative Education*
(ISSN 0961-2149)

Typeset in Monotype Plantin by Symposium Books
Printed and bound in the United Kingdom by Cambridge University Press

Education in Germany since Unification

Contents

The Legacy of Unification

DAVID PHILLIPS

On one point commentators on German affairs are in general agreement: the fall of the Berlin Wall, the collapse of the German Democratic Republic (GDR), and the unification of the two Germanies, East and West, took almost everyone by surprise. Even the closest observers have had to admit their failure to anticipate events of such world-historical significance, despite their detailed knowledge of the socio-political scene in which they occurred (Garton Ash, 1999, p. xiii).

Between the opening of the border on 9 November 1989 and unification as early as 3 October 1990, visions of a future Germany had to be imagined on the basis of almost no previous planning, not even at the highest levels. Indeed, although lip service had long been paid to the notion of an eventual bringing-together of the two Germanies, political leaders remained sceptical about its actually being realised: Margaret Thatcher, for example, was apprehensive about the possibilities, believing that:

> *a truly democratic East Germany would soon emerge and that the question of reunification was a separate one, on which the wishes and interests of Germany's neighbours and other powers must be fully taken into account. (Thatcher, 1993, p. 792)*

She was not alone among Western leaders in taking this line, and she thought that Chancellor Kohl had initially shared her view. Pulzer (1995, p. 157) argues that Kohl could be seen as 'a prisoner of the two-state theory', with 'no contingency plan for the collapse of the GDR regime'. Even in his Ten-Point Programme of 28 November 1989, Kohl had envisaged an interim confederation arrangement, with a gradual development of relations dependent upon conditions like free elections, the release of political prisoners and the abandoning of a command economy in favour of free market conditions (Bahrmann & Links, 1994, p. 147). The swift developments that led to unification in the autumn of 1990 took place in far from ideal conditions: insecure GDR administrations, economic confusion [1] and hastily concocted legislation.

As far as education was concerned, there was, on the one hand, a sudden freedom and opportunity to rethink educational philosophies and, on the other, an unremarkable state of normalcy, with institutions simply continuing their day-to-day work. Indeed, it is salutary to remember the sheer ordinariness of much that happens in education, despite what appear to be huge changes at high political levels. Visitors to educational institutions in the GDR (and in other eastern bloc countries) would often be surprised at the mundane familiarity of much that they observed. The reality was that, for the most part, here were ordinary teachers teaching ordinary things to ordinary children in unextraordinary circumstances.

But the changed political circumstances after the opening of the border enabled those concerned with education in the GDR to begin the process of envisaging reform, and there were some early initiatives, including several under the auspices of the *Akademie der Pädagogischen Wissenschaften* [2], which were quickly overtaken by events (Hörner, 1990; Anweiler, 1990; Neuner, 1996, p. 292). Once unification was accepted as a political inevitability, steps had to be taken to create a proper framework in which it could realistically be implemented. Monetary union from the beginning of July 1990 – remarkably, at a time when the GDR was still a sovereign state – 'had all the hallmarks of a West German takeover' (Kettenacker, 1997, p. 204) and helped to seal the decision to implement full unification. Further impetus was provided by the Unification Treaty (*Einigungsvertrag*) of 31 August 1990, which included much mention of education, among other things reaffirming the power of the *Länder* to reshape educational provision within their jurisdictions. Article 37 of the Unification Treaty also guaranteed recognition of qualifications gained in the GDR, but this was of little comfort to those who had graduated from school or university in the east who quite naturally feared that formal parity of recognition was one thing, while equality of actual treatment (or parity of esteem) would be quite another. Many young enough opted to take further parallel qualifications in the west.

An early imperative for the parliaments of the new *Länder* was the promulgation of school laws, and this too was accomplished remarkably swiftly, with little regard to the possibility of radical departure from West German norms. Garton Ash recalls Adenauer's catchphrase, 'No experiments!' (*keine Experimente!*), to characterise the election campaign of March 1990:

> *They had experienced enough experiments to last several lifetimes: Hitler's experiments, Stalin's experiments, Ulbricht's and Honecker's. They'd had quite enough of being guinea pigs. (Garton Ash, 1999, p. 13)*

And this was to be the case with the development of educational policy, despite the feeling that there was a missed opportunity to retain, albeit experimentally, some promising features of the old GDR system.[3] Between April and July 1991, draft school laws were prepared (Rust & Rust, 1995, p. 189), pre-empting any recommendations that might emerge from various processes of evaluation of the educational scene in the former GDR (such as the lengthy and thorough investigations undertaken by the *Wissenschaftsrat* [4]). Civil servants were seconded from western ministries to help with the drafting of legislation (Boeger, 1998, 1999).

Western academics were quickly on hand to offer wisdom to eastern universities desperate for advice after decades of isolation. Some eminent figures gave generously of their time and contributed a great deal (see Becker, 1991, for example), but others were not always the most suitable or well qualified. A lot of material support was provided, though by no means enough to cope with the actual needs.[5]Retraining programmes were instituted to convert teachers of Russian – somewhat unrealistically in many cases – into teachers of English.

What could not be prepared for was the trauma caused by unification for the GDR population as a whole and especially for those charged with educating the young. As one observer put it:

> the mood and attitudes in Germany … have shifted from short-lived euphoria after the fall of the Wall, to … resignation, anxiety, bitterness and fear on the East side to resentment, fear and condescension on the West side. (Macrakis, 1992, p. 73)

Pritchard identifies similar problems:

> The fall of the Wall was greeted with almost universal joy and relief. When the euphoria had died down, however, many Easterners experienced a feeling of loss, almost of bereavement, for the passing of their state and their socialist principles. The ideas and ideals which had guided their lives for so long were discredited. The result was a feeling of profound sadness and anomie. The Wende was a shock to the whole personality structure. (Pritchard, 1999, pp. 18–19)

The discrediting of what the GDR had stood for was compounded by the fact that the economic transformation hoped for following unification did not materialise. To be sure, there was much outward evidence of the new order (the western banks and insurance companies, for example, moved in with astounding speed), but the material circumstances of individual citizens were not changed overnight, and the east was quickly made aware of the realities of unemployment. Salaries in the east were pegged at a lower rate than those in the western *Länder*. Many teachers lost their jobs.

What did all this mean for ordinary teachers remaining in post? For the vast majority who had been pursuing a professional occupation competently within the limitations of the state's expectations of them, the sudden doubt cast on their competence was at the very least disorienting in its effect. The undermining of their presumptions about their role as educators and the function of the institutions in which they taught – through extreme criticism from the west of all aspects of education in the GDR – was particularly unfortunate at a time when there was a willingness to adapt to new ideas and to seize the opportunities that greater freedom would offer. In the event, east German teachers accepted the structural transformations 'with great acquiescence' (Weiler et al, 1996, p. 58).

Of course, it was not of itself unacceptable to believe in the ideals of the 10-year polytechnical school. With the political imperatives of its curricular provision removed, it could still have provided an educationally defensible model as a 'comprehensive' school. But teachers had to suffer the assumption on the part of policy-makers that such a school type was fundamentally unacceptable, while West German models were automatically to be adopted in various forms, despite repeated criticisms levelled over many years at the tripartite system of secondary education so firmly rooted in the western *Länder*. We should not lose sight of the reality of this judgement of the GDR model: effectively it was saying, as far as east German teachers were concerned, that institutionalised equality of treatment of the pupil population was not acceptable.

Some 10 years on there are still considerable problems facing the teaching profession in the eastern *Länder*. Teachers can still feel neglected and isolated, despite the advances in the material conditions of schools (though many buildings are still way below the standards of those in the west) and the assimilation of the teaching profession into the western framework. They are bitter about assumptions on the part of western critics that all their work in the GDR was without worth; they feel that much that was good in their former practice has been abandoned without sufficient thought. It will clearly take some considerable time yet before the psychological damage caused by the hastiness of post-unification reform can be healed.

* * * * * *

The chapters which make up this present volume are concerned in various ways with the issues raised here. E.J. Neather, basing his chapter on a series of interviews with east German teachers and academics, analyses problems of continuity and change in education since the *Wende*. Stephanie Wilde and Bernhard Streitwieser have undertaken detailed studies of teachers' views of the situation with which they are now having to cope and the circumstances which have led up to it. Karen Galtress-Hörl describes on the basis of personal experience the difficulties involved in retraining teachers of Russian during the period 1992–96. Nina Arnhold deals with the transformation of higher education and research within the context of the role of the Science Council (*Wissenschaftsrat*), a subject to which I return in a contribution describing my experience of a working group set up by the *Wissenschaftsrat* in the autumn of 1990 to report on the future of teacher education in eastern Germany. As with Karen Galtress-Hörl's chapter, this account is by way of a record of personal experience, informed by commentary with the benefit of hindsight. Hubert Ertl looks at the background to current problems in vocational education and training, and Rosalind Pritchard contributes a chapter on the development of what was a new subject for schools in the east – religious education.

Taken together, the chapters reflect the many concerns that still have to be addressed in assessing what has been achieved over the past 10 years of educational development in the eastern *Länder*.

Notes

[1] The East German Mark was changing hands at a rate of up to 15:1 with the *Deutschmark* before currency union on 1 July 1990 (Nicholls, 1997, p. 321).

[2] The Academy of Pedagogical Sciences was abolished at the end of 1990. In that year, it had produced a publication series (*Bildungswesen aktuell*) which made many proposals for reform of the existing GDR education system. The pages of the *Deutsche Lehrerzeitung (DL)*, previously little more than a propaganda sheet of the regime, were filled with enthusiastic debate about future provision in education from an early point following the events of November 1989 (see, for example, 'Thesen zur Schulreform', *DL*, 51, 1989).

[3] I had argued in an early paper, for example, that an opportunity was missed to conduct a real experiment with comprehensive schooling, using the GDR's 10-year school as a basis. In retrospect, it appears that this idea would not have been technically feasible, given guarantees in the *Grundgesetz* (Basic Law) about parental freedom of choice (Phillips, 1992, pp. 115–116).

[4] I was a member of the *Arbeitsgruppe Lehrerbildung*, appointed by the *Wissenschaftsrat* in 1990 to report on teacher education in the former GDR. We found when we visited Ministries of Education in the new *Länder* in early 1991 that it was too late for any recommendations we might make to have implications for systemic change, since decisions had already been taken on such matters as the future shape of the school system and the pattern of teacher education (two-phase rather than one-phase) to be introduced.

[5] For example, the initiative *Schulbuchhilfe für die neuen Länder* ('textbook support for the new *Länder*' of the Federal Ministry of Education provided some 2.5 million books in history, politics and German (Bundesministerium für Bildung, Wissenschaft, Forschung und Technologie [BMBF], 1995, p. 25).

References

Anweiler, Oskar (1990) Die 'Wende' in der Bildungspolitik der DDR (Dokumentation), *Bildung und Erziehung*, 43, pp. 97–107.

Bahrmann, Hannes & Links, Christoph (1994) *Chronik der Wende. Die DDR zwischen 7 Oktober und 18 Dezember 1989*. Berlin: Ch. Links Verlag.

Becker, Johannes M. (1991) *Ein Land geht in den Westen. Die Abwicklung der DDR*. Bonn: Dietz.

Boeger, Wilhelm (1998) *Der Leihbeamte*. Halle: Mitteldeutscher Verlag.

Boeger, Wilhelm (1999) *Der Leihbeamte kehrt zurück*. Halle: Mitteldeutscher Verlag.

Bundesministerium für Bildung, Wissenschaft, Forschung und Technologie (BMBF) (1995) *40 Jahre Bildungs- und Forschungspolitik*, 1955–95. Bonn: BMBF.

Einigungsvertrag (1990) *Der Einigungsvertrag: Vertrag zwischen der Bundesrepublik Deutschland und der Deutschen Demokratischen Republik über die Herstellung der Einheit Deutschlands*. Bonn: Goldmann.

Garton Ash, Timothy (1999) *History of the Present*. London: Allen Lane.

Hörner, Wolfgang (1990) *Bildung und Wissenschaft in der DDR. Ausgangslager und Reform bis Mitte 1990*. Bonn: Bundesminister für Bildung und Wissenschaft.

Kettenacker, Lothar (1997) *Germany since 1945*. Oxford: Oxford University Press.

Macrakis, Kristie (1992) Wissenschaft and Political Unification in the New Germany, in Kurt-Jürgen Maas (Ed.) *From Two to One. US Scholars Witness the First Year of German Unification*, pp. 72–85. Bonn-Bad Godesberg: Alexander von Humboldt Foundation.

Neuner, Gerhart (1996) *Zwischen Wissenschaft und Politik. Ein Rückblick aus lebensgeschichtlicher Perspektive*. Cologne: Böhlau.

Nicholls, A.J. (1997) *The Bonn Republic. West German Democracy 1945–1990*. London: Longman.

Phillips, David (1992) Transitions and Traditions: educational developments in the new Germany in their historical context, in Maurice Whitehead (Ed.) *Education and Europe: historical and contemporary perspectives*, *Aspects of Education*, 47, pp. 111–127.

Pritchard, Rosalind O. (1999) *Reconstructing Education. East German Schools and Universities after Unification*. New York: Berghahn.

Pulzer (1995) *German Politics, 1945-1995*. Oxford: Oxford University Press.

Rust, Val D. & Rust, Diane (1995) *The Unification of German Education*. New York: Garland.

Thatcher, Margaret (1993) *The Downing Street Years*. London: Harper Collins.

Weiler, Hans N., Mintrop, Heinrich A. & Fuhrmann, Elisabeth (1996) *Educational Change and Social Transformation. Teachers, Schools and Universities in Eastern Germany*. London: Falmer Press.

Change and Continuity in Education after the *Wende*

E.J. NEATHER

The scale and diversity of the changes experienced by the citizens of the former German Democratic Republic (GDR) during the period following the collapse of the regime in 1989 present formidable difficulties to the writer who wishes to provide not just a chronicle of events but some sense of the ways individuals responded to and lived through such an upheaval. In the field of education, as in every aspect of society, one can provide names and dates, one can give an account of significant legal and organisational change and refer to key documents, but such essential factual records still fall short a reality which emerges from every conversation. And the perception of that reality is so varied; no two people have the same story to tell about their reaction to the *Wende*, of their response to events and developments during and since the autumn of 1989. Oral history would appear to offer some possibility of getting at historical reality as experienced by individuals, though there are potential weaknesses to an approach based on individual interviews because of faulty or selective memory, and because of the relationship of the interviewer to the subject. On the side of the interviewee, there may well be self-justification and special pleading. On the side of the interviewer, there may be a tendency to become only the voice of the subject and a need to refrain from objective criticism or analysis. What must remain clear to the interviewer is that past reality does not allow itself to be reconstituted *only* by the accumulation of individual experiences. The interview, or the personal document, such as a diary, can only have a representative quality, which needs to be set against the larger picture revealed by written records, if they exist. Nevertheless, as Thompson makes clear:

> *once the life experience of people of all kinds can be used as its raw material, a new dimension is given to history … Reality is complex and many-sided; and it is a primary merit of oral history that to a much greater extent than most sources it allows the original multiplicity of standpoints to be recreated. (Thompson, 1978, pp. 4–5)*

However, the 'multiplicity of standpoints' leads Fulbrook to sound a warning about possible distortions:

> *a continuing stream of selective and partial revelations, often reflecting more on the interests of the present than the realities of the past, continually serves to transform*

both the interpretative framework and the ostensible 'knowledge base' on which any
overall historical interpretation is constructed. The interests of journalists and
politicians may both coincide and collide with those of the former subjects and alleged
victims of history, or of historians from a wide range of theoretical and methodological
traditions. Memories challenge reconstructions; personal experience queries
documentary evidence; the sands on which any new interpretation is to be constructed
are constantly shifting. (Fulbrook, 1995, p. 7)

So, a sense of balance is necessary to assess personal testimony, particularly in a historical context where the politics of the recent past may lead to accusations of guilt. The unveiling of some Stasi connections has led to causes célèbres even for writers of otherwise unchallenged integrity such as Christa Wolf. But Fulbrook herself, a little later in her book, writes, 'whatever its potential pitfalls, the possibility of oral history provides potential avenues for social historical investigation' (1995, p. 13). Oral history also offers the possibility outlined in Niethammer's statement; 'A democratic future requires a past in which not only the ruling classes are heard' (Niethammer, 1985, p. 7). This statement echoes Thompson:

Since the nature of most existing records is to reflect the standpoint of authority, it is
not surprising that the judgement of history has more often than not vindicated the
wisdom of the powers that be. Oral history by contrast makes a much fairer trial
possible: witnesses can now also be called from the underclasses, the unprivileged, and
the defeated. It provides a more realistic and fair reconstruction of the past, a challenge
to the established account. (1978, p. 5)

This particular historical bias may, however, seem particularly appropriate to the circumstances of the GDR's 'revolution'. In the GDR, the new patterns were imposed from outside. Individuals had limited say in shaping the structures within which they would live and work. Within the particular context of education, how did individuals cope with such change, draw on the past they had known and adjust their lives to the unknown future of the upheaval?

The approach adopted in the following interviews was to establish no hard law about the *type* of information required. Apart from the interviewer's knowledge of the background situation, and, in many cases, the personal circumstances of the interviewee, each case was treated as a unique as well as a representative life-story. The interviewer asked few questions, giving the interviewee plenty of time to range freely. This was, therefore, the very opposite of the positivist interview, with its concern for objectivity and where the interviewer keeps control and sticks to a protocol of questions. The pattern was free-flowing dialogue, following just a few basic principles in sequencing the topics and phrasing the questions. This process was aided by the fact that nearly all the participants were well known to the interviewer. It might be argued that such bonds of friendship weaken the validity of the evidence, in that the interviewer would not wish to risk a critical confrontation. But the counter-arguments are stronger; personal knowledge of background and circumstances meant that the interviewer could, in almost all cases, vouch for the truth of statements made. Finally, the internal evidence for truth and lack of attempt to cover up the past is evident from the nature of the interviews and the readiness of the subjects to speak openly.

It could certainly be argued that the case studies presented here can lay no claim to being representative. For example, all the subjects have personal experience of education to university level, so that there are no accounts by disaffected or unmotivated students. All could rank among the educational successes of the GDR. It is also true that there is a majority of female subjects rather than an attempt to balance the sexes. The following criteria also played a role in the final selection of subjects.

- A range of ages should be represented to provide evidence from all phases of the GDR. Thus, the two oldest subjects started school during the Nazi period, and the youngest was born in 1970 and experienced the *Wende* as a university student.
- There should be both Party members and non-Party members, to draw some conclusions about the place of Party membership both in pursuing a career during the GDR and in the effect on subsequent careers after the *Wende*.
- There should be examples of supporters and opponents of the GDR system.
- There should be representatives of a range of occupations within the education system.
- There should be examples of those who prospered and those who suffered as a result of the *Wende*.

The interviews were all conducted during the period May 1997–May 1998.

Wilfried

Wilfried, a teacher trainer in a university department, saw the rise of groups opposed to the government in Leipzig in the months leading up to the events of October 1989. The Church, of course, played a significant role at the time. But the general response among the population to calls for change was limited. Until the build-up of the situation in the summer of 1989, opposition was largely limited to small groups of like-minded intellectuals. Based in Leipzig, Wilfried was at the epicentre of the coming earthquake, and joined the demonstrations in the days following the National Day on 7 October:

> *On the following Monday, the 9th, there was a first big mass demonstration, more than 50 or 60,000 people, I think, and I was one of the demonstrators. From the outset, it wasn't at all clear whether the police and the battle groups who had taken up position in the side streets leading off the* Leipziger Ring … *whether they would open fire or not.*

Despite the fears, there was no shooting, and the freedom from that fear brought out greater numbers than ever onto the streets. Wilfried comments on the fact that within the universities at this time, there was little sign of the coming revolution. Whereas in most revolutions it seems that the students are part of the motor of revolution, that was not the case in the GDR.

As far as developments in education were concerned, the reformers at this time, as in other aspects of GDR society, were thinking in terms of a reformed socialist GDR, not of a merger with the Federal Republic:

The general expectation was certainly that the GDR would continue to exist but ... with a fundamental reform of the system, both political and economic. That would certainly have entailed the retention of the unified, so-called unified education system.

There had been positive aspects of school and university in the GDR which were disregarded by the new authorities, who proceeded to put in place the system as it existed in the west, regardless of criticisms which even West Germans themselves made:

Basically, we were passive, we had to follow the flow. We could do scarcely anything to resist the process. I sent a flood of protest letters to the new Minister for Science, not only about my own case but more generally on behalf of the subject area. None of the letters was answered. We were faced with unalterable facts and, in the last analysis, this system was, if you like, thrust upon us.

Some of the new developments at school level were demanded by the public. Wilfried singles out the introduction of the *Gymnasium* and the extended teaching of English:

There was a very marked tendency to put in place the Gymnasium and then, of course, the other school types. Then, at the outset, there was a very marked boom in English studies. English has now taken over the role that Russian held earlier.

He welcomes the new spirit which has entered schools but regrets the fact that many teachers remain 'servile', too influenced by their years of subordination and conformity. It is also partly a result of the concern of teachers about their jobs in the reorganisation.

Wilfried then talks about the process of reform within the University; in particular, the key decisions about the future of staff and departments:

It all started off, within a relatively short period of time, I think by the end of '91, with the abolition of certain Sections that had become superfluous, for example, in all universities the dominant Sections for Marxism–Leninism. The sections for Philosophy as well ...

As regards staff, he feels there were many injustices; in particular, the fact that key figures from the former regime, such as Party Secretaries, have managed to gain professorial chairs in the new system:

So there are turncoats who knew, from the very beginning, just how they could, without apparent contradiction, serve the new masters just as they had served the old ones. And there were others who had made protests previously, and couldn't hold their tongue during later developments and who came out of this process badly.

How was it possible that the rigorous process of staff selection could allow supporters of the discredited regime to survive? What criteria were applied in reviewing staff appointments?

> *Evaluation was made on the basis of three criteria. The first was collaboration as an informer or in some honorary position for the Stasi. The second was a marked association with the former regime and conduct in some function such as Director of an Institute, Rector, Dean, Party Secretary of an institution or something similar. The third point was subject aptitude or need. So, one could be given notice if there was no further need for the post. Most of these cases were fairly handled, but there were also many cases where there was a good deal of manipulation. I personally had that sort of experience.*

Wilfried was asked by the interviewer to expand upon his own experience of the staff selection processes. He had actually broken with the Party in 1986, when such a move required a certain amount of 'civil courage'. He had therefore imagined himself to be well placed before any tribunal judging his acceptability in the new University. To his surprise, objections were raised on the third of the criteria he outlined, aptitude, as he had taken his doctorate in a different area from the one in which he now practised. Since the doctorate was in American Studies and his post was in the training of teachers of English, this might be seen as a minor point at a time when major political issues were being considered.

> *I took my doctorate in the area of American Studies, and in teaching and research my position is in the methodology of the teaching of English. And so a decision was reached by a commission, the composition of which remains, to this day, very obscure, that I was not sufficiently qualified for this subject and for this post. And they wanted, at that time, to sack me and remove me from the University, but that didn't in fact happen, because of my own serious objections and also the objections raised by academic colleagues, especially those in the old* Bundesländer, *who knew me and my activities far better than the members of this commission. That probably saved me.*

So Wilfried survived, although his chair was ranked at a lower point in the civil service scale than his seniority demanded. He pursued his case for some years, without success, and can only explain the bias shown against him by the existence of powers from the earlier regime, who had always wanted to get rid of him:

> *So there must be powerful figures somewhere who date back to the earlier regime, and who had already wanted to get rid of me – I mean professionally, not physically. And such figures have discovered how to disappear from view and survive the period of the* Wende. *They have managed to adapt so well to the new system that they can continue to have a sort of subliminal effect.*

Nevertheless, Wilfried is one of those who was a university professor before and after the *Wende*. It was not normal to gain a chair in the GDR unless one was 'reliable'. How does he interpret his personal fate?

> *Q: But there has been a certain continuity in your career, through all the political currents and educational changes. You have managed to survive.*
>
> *W: Yes, thank God, I managed to develop an attitude so that I didn't let these obvious intrigues and injustices affect me too deeply. Obviously, in the family circle or somewhere, you've got to be able to talk through your problems and be able to talk*

about things with others, with many of my friends too. So I was able to let off steam,
but for the most part, whether before or after the Wende, *I didn't allow myself to be*
deflected in my work. So I carried on with my teaching sessions and I've continued to
research, to publish, and so in this respect I've carried on as if there was nothing to
bother me.

There are still things that remain unanswered here, and it should be added that Wilfried had particular problems with the authorities after his wife fled the country in the 1980s to join her parents in the west. He used to meet up with her from time to time in Poland. Their meetings were observed by the Stasi, as he knows from reading his Stasi file. Yet, he always kept his university post. Unlike some other GDR citizens, he has no nostalgia for the past. 'I shed no tears for the GDR'. He does, however, regret some of the wasted years:

When I'm abroad, it naturally makes me think and when I compare myself with
academic colleagues from the old Länder, *who had completely different chances*
earlier in their careers – they could go and pursue part or all of their studies abroad, in
England or the USA or wherever they wanted.

Ursula

Ursula (also a teacher trainer) began this part of the interview by responding to a question about the *Pädagogischer Kongress* of May 1989. This was a moment when teachers and all participants in the education system hoped for signs of change from the top. But nothing changed, and Margot Honecker trotted out the usual clichés:

The Party was stuck in a sort of permafrost. At that Pädagogischer Kongress
practically the whole of the Politburo of the Party was present. So they had nothing to
do all day long except sit at the PK and basically so much was already on the move in
universities and HE [higher education]. So it was with a sort of hunger that
everybody took note of what was happening over in the Soviet Union and thought that
something similar should be happening here, that certain questions had to be asked,
and they were quite simply afraid to set something in motion which they would not be
able to control. But sadly, sadly, nothing moved at the official level.

And when the *Wende* finally did arrive, the hopes in education were for a socialist reform. Ursula was never a member of the Party, but like many GDR citizens, her roots were socialist and she hoped for a transformation of the rigid GDR into something more resembling democratic socialism.

I was never in the Party, but this ideal of socialism was always fascinating. Of
course, it was utopian and it was never realised in any of the countries of the eastern
bloc, but we did hope that perhaps socialism could become a reality if it was reshaped,
reformed.

When the idea of a unified Germany was first launched at the demonstrations, when the cry 'Wir sind das Volk' ('We are the people') was replaced by the cry 'Wir sind ein Volk' ('We are one people'), Ursula had 'a really uncomfortable feeling'.

This had not been her personal intention in hoping for change. Like many GDR citizens, she was aware of the negative side of the capitalist west, the crime rate, the drugs culture, aspects which were undeveloped in the authoritarian GDR.

> *And now we've got the whole thing with all its negative aspects as well, which we've got to live with. And we are often quite misunderstood by colleagues and people from the west when we criticise this state, because their argument straight away is 'You just want to have your old GDR back again'.*

For Ursula, 1989–90 'were certainly the most marvellous years of our life', because of the speed of events, the sense of being caught up in history. The scale of the changes, and the effects of 'colonisation' then tempered the enthusiasm at the way the revolution was going. In education, the senior figures in the new Ministry were all from the west:

> *And what we had hoped for, that there would be new developments in education or new moves to restructure education here in Saxony, such hopes were very quickly removed, because the inclination of the civil servants from the west was just to copy their own system as precisely as possible and set it up here. So there was no evaluation of our school, of our education. So we had absolutely no influence on the restructuring of the educational system.*

If this influence of the west was so strong, Ursula was asked, how can one explain the evident desire of the GDR public for some of the west's institutions, such as the *Gymnasium*? It is true, she says, that there was a desire for more selection in the school system, for a move away from the *Einheitsschule*:

> *But perhaps not in the form which was characteristic of the old* Länder *where children were already sorted out by the end of four years of primary school. Not at such a tender age, when talents and inclinations have just not begun to show themselves and children who are very protected in primary school, partly without being graded and marked and who live with plenty of praise and recognition and then they are plunged suddenly into class 5 in the* Gymnasium *where there is pressure to succeed and marks rule the roost. Many children were obviously just not accustomed to such pressures.*

As parents adapted to the new schools, became aware of the importance of the *Gymnasium* and of gaining the *Abitur*, there was a rush to get their children into such schools, so that, in the first year, as many as 40% of children entered on selective education for which many were not really suited. It was also the case that many teachers in the newly-established *Gymnasien* were ex-*POS* (polytechnische Oberschule) teachers, with no experience of teaching at the required level. Most serious in Ursula's eyes, however, was the amount of valuable experience and advances in the GDR system that was simply dismissed and excluded from the new system. Ursula's comment here is worth quoting in full, as she draws from her own experience as a child given a way out of deprived circumstances by an education system which cared for her, and into which she had subsequently brought the same ideals of human concern and caring for her pupils. Her words about the

19

relationship of teacher and pupil certainly do not support some of the critical statements made about pupil control and surveillance in the GDR school:

> And then a great deal was discarded that was of great educational value. Of course, there was a political motive behind it all but the GDR teacher was responsible for her children, for the achievements, for the success of her children. She had to take the rap if children failed to reach the class objectives. It was not the children but the teacher who had to demonstrate how she had looked after these children, how she had helped them and so on. And now, the teachers quickly realised that this was no longer required. That they are now conveyors of knowledge and the educational virtues, the efforts on behalf of each individual child, that has largely been lost and the result is that the school and the job of the teacher have lost out as a result.

Ursula is someone for whom there has been a measure of continuity despite the change. She remains a trainer of teachers of Russian, although with far fewer students than previously. Her lack of a Party history helped her to make the transition without problems and even to gain the title of professor, which she could not have had in the GDR because of her determination to stay out of the Party. So, does she see herself as a winner or loser in the process? Some advantages are clear:

> Well, the Wende was a sort of liberation for me, and an opening up, even a revelation. Finally, we were able to try out alternative approaches and active forms of teaching and project methods. We couldn't do that before and so we imbibed these things like mothers' milk and tried to introduce such approaches into our teaching.

But there are also losses. One of these relates to the Marxist notion of the 'collective'. The word was commonly used in the GDR, to refer to any group working as a team, whether children in the crèche or colleagues at work. The concept means more than teamwork, as Ursula explains, and contrasts strongly with her present experience of isolated work at the University.

> We always swapped ideas, ideas about teaching. We shared advice about different approaches, we adapted them together. We developed a structure for in-service education of teachers together. We worked together on new teaching programmes. We were always working together for a common aim, and my most recent experience is that I'm in a team of one.

She feels that the greater individualism, the lack of the support of the collective, not only in education, is responsible for some of the psychiatric problems reported on in the new Länder.

Sigrid

Sigrid, as a researcher in one of the central institutes, was closely engaged in work on various reform projects in the months leading up to the Wende. Although not personally affected by the Pädagogischer Kongress of May 1989, she had been working on parallel projects:

> But it was clear that we started a good many initiatives in the years leading up to the Wende so as to stimulate discussions about reform. And our particular problem was

that the leader of this Institute for Vocational Education (where I worked) was only very marginally interested in new approaches.

Although there had been no sense in her institute that the educational system was in any danger of collapse, there was a feeling that the time was ripe for reforms:

In the field of education, we saw a real chance of carrying through a successful transformation of the system on the basis of the insights which we had gained, from international developments as well, and from the successful initiatives which we had observed.

What were her hopes at that time? The work at the Institute and also in an unofficial working group of researchers which established itself, was that they could draw on some of the international findings they had found in their work:

For example, now there might be a chance to seize the idea of the comprehensive school as it had widely established itself in Europe And in this way we might further develop our own Einheitsschule *with quality initiatives.*

Her professional view was not at all that the *Einheitsschule* was necessarily a socialist concept. She was impressed, for example, by the Swedish comprehensive school and the comparisons that could be drawn with the GDR schools. But the failing of the *POS*, as she saw it, was the failure to provide adequate incentives for individual advancement by bringing in more differentiation, and the inability to adapt flexible teaching and learning methods:

And the real failure of this GDR Einheitsschule *and our educational system was, in my opinion, the lack of opportunity for individual development, for differentiating according to personal inclination and ability and also the lack of an approach which starts with the learner, which shapes the educational process by taking the learner as a starting point. That is now becoming the norm in vocational education, in the project method, where the students have their own task ... and the teacher takes on more the role of adviser.*

The disappointment of the *Wende,* for her as an educational researcher, was the abrupt halt to all the reform projects for the future brought about by a completely unexpected event. And then, there was a ready-made educational system to hand in West Germany. The reaction of Sigrid and her research colleagues was amazingly pragmatic. Instead of bemoaning the fact that their projects were dead, their institutes disbanded and an educational system imposed, they developed their unofficial group of researchers into an independent research institute, offering expertise and services within the academic and educational market place. Instead of philosophising about an educational takeover, they accepted it as a *fait accompli* and decided to offer research into the developing new structures:

But I really want to make my point clear here. We were faced with clear practical problems in this whole process at the time of the Unification Treaty. Our institutes were all being disbanded in 1990. We had had the feeling for a long time that we wanted to carry on our work; we wanted to get involved with our ideas and with a realistic view of the next steps. And the next steps in the real world were the

restructuring of schools and other institutions on the pattern of the old Länder, *with
their existing legal structures. So we made a public group out of our unofficial working
group and we said, right, we are ready and willing to carry out research studies in
connection with the new processes. We didn't have any time to shed tears about the
reforms which we'd never succeeded in introducing. We just got on with it and said,
with our know-how, we see the chance of carrying out research.*

It was an impressive response, revealing the dedication of the true researcher and an
instant adaptation to political realities and the market economy. She is clear that in
the limited time for putting into place new structures of education, the only possible
approach was to take over the existing West German models:

*In this short space of time, no other way was possible except to take over the
functioning model, legal framework, rules and structures from the old* Länder.
*Simply because there was no way that the old GDR structures could fit into the new
system.*

It was not only a question of time. There was also public opinion. The public
wanted the *Gymnasium*, whatever the researchers said about it being old-fashioned.
The reform ideas that were debated during the Wende were just not practicable to
set against the two forces of rapid social change and public opinion. At least, there
were some changes and adaptations to the western pattern, with the introduction of
new school types in Saxony and Thuringia and with the alternatives proposed for
religious instruction.

How does Sigrid explain this demand for the *Gymnasium?* After all, GDR
parents had no personal experience of such a school. It was clear that West
Germany was a successful country. But they were also conscious of deep-seated
German traditions:

Yes, well, I think that the idea of the Gymnasium *is tied up with notions of higher
values. That has a long history. And I think that something of that kind is carried
forward, even through the whole history of the GDR, as an ideal that is really worth
striving for, and with new ambitions awakened, the best that could be offered to
children was seen to be the* Gymnasium.

At the time of the interview, Sigrid was doing some university teaching, as well as
her research work. She has strong views about the university system imported from
the west:

*I think that the present system which has been established here in educational studies
is chaotic in many aspects and impossible for students trying to see their way through
the system, as there is no structured course which is systematically built up to lead to a
satisfactory outcome in a manageable period of time. In this case, the system of
university training in the GDR, which had some similarities with the English pattern,
was significantly more efficient and more effective.*

She believes that there are far better examples in other countries, not only with
regard to the structures but also styles of working with students. Her main criticism
is the lack of teamwork, the individualism of the lecturers and professors:

> *And I think that the teaching styles and the ways in which the professors operate are incredibly individualistic. There is no teamwork, no sense of common purpose, and very few examples of working together.*

Most depressing for her as a researcher is that these 'chaotic' institutions are now responsible for research, following the abolition of the GDR research institutes. So, her view that the *Gymnasium* was welcome because of its good reputation does not extend to higher education:

> *That so many students just don't finish their courses; that a course lasting four years in England takes seven years or more here. That is just not competitive on a European level.*

The single gain, in her view, is that the freedom and individualism does mean greater flexibility in planning one's courses, so that she is able to pursue her own ideas about project work and autonomous learning.

Brigitte

Brigitte, at the time of the *Wende,* had a successful career in vocational education behind her, still limited by her unwillingness to join the Party, but strongly committed to her work, her colleagues and her society. She describes the sense of uncertainty amongst her colleagues, particularly those with Party associations who might fear for the future. In this situation, she is the one who is seen as fair to both sides:

> *During this period of collapse there was a very great sense of uncertainty amongst the teaching colleagues who were Party members. There were fears as to what might happen to them. How would they be treated by colleagues who were not Party members? They were often in despair. And there were certain decisive moments when you held back, where you only spoke openly to a very small circle of friends, where you hid behind a façade. At that time I spoke with my colleagues a great deal, with Party members as well as the others. I was suddenly aware that among my colleagues there were people who had opposed the regime, and I had never been aware of that. So we talked, and I found it interesting that Party members came to me and said, you're not in the Party, but it would be a good thing if you could sign our appeal for a GDR on a different basis.*

Brigitte gives a graphic account of what life must have been like within such a 'Kollegium' during the *Wende*; colleagues who emerge as dissidents; Party members who fear that others may turn on them. The appeal that colleagues wanted Brigitte to sign was a call for a 'new' GDR, maintaining the socialist system but improving it. She was faced with a conflict. This system of the GDR, for all its faults, was the place where she had developed professionally and personally. At every stage of her life, she was concerned to achieve the maximum but remain true to herself. How does the individual maintain their integrity in this system and at a time of such fundamental change?

> ... *whether you can remain true to yourself, whether you can find your own way, so that you can say, this is my way, because I know it fits in with my own ideas and I can look anybody in the eye and tell them so. And my husband said to me, do we want the GDR back again? Well no, we didn't want it back. Because we had also experienced things in our family which were really bad. At those times it was important to have your family close around you and supporting you. And here I was approached by people looking for help from somebody who was not in the Party. That was a conflict for me which only I myself could solve. But I signed the appeal because the people concerned were important to me.*

She had no wish to save the old GDR, but in such a situation, where the system was already *kaputt*, she felt her responsibility was to use her freedom from political taint to help colleagues who had made different, possibly wrong, choices in the past. But, as with other interviewees, there is a distinction made between individual members of the Party, and the key factor is not membership but whether that membership has been used to cause harm to others:

> *Amongst our group of colleagues, nobody had been abused. And no student had suffered or been thrown out of the institution. Those were all things which I had to weigh in the balance.*

Of course, this was one conflict involving a small number of people in a single institution, and, in any case, the demand for a 'new' GDR was a dead letter. But the whole incident serves as an example of many similar conflicts and trials at that time.

The decision was taken that Brigitte's institution was to be disbanded. On 19 May 1990, she attended a meeting in Berlin of the professional association for teachers in vocational education. She was convinced that membership of this union was an important step in the new politics, and she returned, called a meeting and founded a new branch which quickly grew from 50 to 300 members throughout the *Land* Brandenburg.

Brigitte emerges from these interviews as someone who will not sit around while others take the initiative. She established contacts with West German representatives, and she called meetings to be addressed by officials from the new *Land* authority; and she discovered that nobody from the authority could speak with knowledge of vocational education. So it was that a new career opened up before her, and she was asked to join the newly formed team responsible for administering vocational education in Brandenburg. She says that it helped that she was herself from Brandenburg, and also that she was a woman, but it is clear that with her experience and character, and with her freedom from Party associations, she was ideally placed to take on her new role.

In 1992, she joined a political party for the first time, the Social Democratic Party of Germany (SPD). For her it was socialist in intention and it was a *Volkspartei* (people's party). She swiftly moved to become leader of a section concerned with secondary education in the Potsdam area. She has had other offers, but has seen enough of politics to know that she would not wish to become a full-time politician.

How does she now assess the vocational education of the GDR, in which she spent all her professional life until the *Wende*?

An important criterion for an evaluation of the vocational school of the GDR was, in my opinion, the following. Teachers in these schools in the GDR had either followed an apprenticeship and then pursued their studies, or they studied after a spell of practical work on the job. That is to say, they had always had professional experience and were firmly anchored in socialist reality. And so, whether teaching in a community school or in a works school like myself, you had direct experience of the world of work. And you couldn't make great claims for yourself because the youngsters could see if there was no cement ready or if materials had been taken home. You couldn't tell tall stories, and you had to be aware of that if you wanted to be credible as a teacher. I think that was an important factor in the vocational school.

She is also impressed by the way the GDR-trained teachers of the *Berufsschule* have tackled the problem of retraining and re-education. It may be that they experienced a more radical change in their work practices than other teachers, because of their necessary links with industry, and because of the changing technology in their work. For the students themselves, there have been massive changes as a result of the change in attitudes to employment and the introduction of competition in the workplace:

In the GDR vocational school there was a basic principle drawn from the philosophy of the state, that everybody is eligible for training and therefore for some certainty about the future working life. That included handicapped and disadvantaged students. That was a socially positive aspect of the GDR. It also removed personal responsibility because it removed the necessity of personal concern. Nor could you study anything you liked.

So there have been losses on the human side despite the gains in terms of self-confidence and autonomy. The greater thrust of individualism has also brought the negative aspects of Western capitalist society.

Ingrid

Ingrid was different from the other interviewees in that she left the GDR around 1976 and, apart from family visits, did not return to live in her home town of Dresden until 1990. She tells how she experienced the *Wende* at a distance, 'with great joy and excitement'. She obtained a post at a school which was in the process of transforming from an Erweiterte Oberschule (*EOS*) to a *Gymnasium*, and experienced the whole process of change. The headteacher had been a hard-line Party member, and she had already been replaced by someone who, although also a Party member and teacher of *Staatsbürgerkunde*, was regarded as more flexible. The first conflict Ingrid encountered was whether this transitional head should be voted in as permanent. Her account reveals some of the tensions both within the staffroom and within society at large:

Many colleagues were in favour of his staying in post. It was also the case that they were all a bit afraid of what might happen if they got a West German head, and what sort of atmosphere there would then be. So the feeling was, we'd rather have one of us, somebody we know, perhaps even somebody of whom we could say, yes, we know what he said in the past. Because then at least you knew where you were, people could also say to him, don't try and tell us any stories, we all know about your past. For that reason, it's certainly true that many would have been prepared to see him continue, perhaps also because they themselves had a past which they had to live with. And it would have been comforting for them to say, well yes, you were a Party member as well.

In the event, he was voted out and the post advertised. His replacement was a *Wessi* (West German), although he was allowed to carry on as a teacher in the school. In his case, and in others, the evidence from participants is that there were actually very few cases of teachers losing their jobs. The unforgivable was to have a past Stasi connection. Otherwise, even after receiving notification, most teachers appealed and their appeals were allowed. Ingrid recounts the story of another teacher of *Staatsbürgerkunde* (abbreviated as Stabü):

One teacher became a famous case. Herr Ritter was a very popular teacher of history and Staatsbürgerkunde, a valuable member of the teaching staff. I've heard mixed opinions about him. He was very cultured, knew a great deal and he was sacked with very little notice, because he had been a teacher of Stabü *and Party Secretary, but he had nothing to do with the Stasi. Then he was promptly given a job at another school and carried on working. So somehow, he made a successful appeal.*

As far as the restructuring of the school was concerned, that was conducted entirely from higher authority. Teachers were not involved, even in matters, for example, of unsatisfactory school buildings. This was reform by decree. At the school level, the main virtue for teachers was to be flexible in a time of change and improvisation:

That was a period of improvisation, and people were relatively willing to teach subjects that they had never actually studied, or to teach different age groups. It was actually, from a teacher's point of view, a positive time, because people were very flexible, and because the majority agreed that a good many things should be done differently.

Among the problems of adjustment for teachers was the need to come to grips with a whole new legal and bureaucratic system. It was this that sapped the enthusiasm of many:

The teachers who had got themselves ready to accept a great deal of change suddenly noticed that the formalities were more important than big new ideas. It gradually proved to be an everyday disappointment, that everything was handled in such a dogmatic and bureaucratic way.

Many things had actually been less bureaucratic in GDR times. Also new to the teachers were the parental demands. As far as the question of 'colonisation' is concerned, Ingrid puts an alternative point of view, and praises the solidarity of their partner *Land*, Baden-Württemberg:

So Baden-Württemberg was our partner Land, *and they advanced enormous sums of money to pay for in-service training for books and school contacts. This was a sort of solidarity, that must be said.*

In any case, the citizens of Saxony voted overwhelmingly for a Christian Democratic (CDU) government. They can hardly complain if they don't like the educational policies of the CDU. It was also the case, as Sigrid recounts, that things had to happen quickly. The GDR was, to all intents and purposes 'an empty space', and development had to happen straight away. Of course, there were those who objected to the takeover and had other ideas. But Ingrid believes that they were, in fact, a minority:

> *Of course, there were murmurs from those who had imagined things differently, but they weren't the majority. There were groups of idealists and I think that can be compared with peace movements in the West or with environmental groups. They don't necessarily have a great say in major political decisions either.*

With the background of her own time in the GDR, Ingrid is quite unsentimental when she looks back, and has little time for those who claim to be nostalgic for the good old days of the GDR:

> *My own opinion is that when people go into raptures, for example, about social cohesion in the GDR, they are certainly very often seeing the past through rose-coloured spectacles, in the same way that people are nostalgic about the War. Nobody would wish to hand back the freedoms that have been gained in exchange for their nostalgia. People really want the best of both worlds, the comfy sense of belonging and being protected and a guaranteed job, and the cheap bread rolls and all the rest.*

As far as her students are concerned, the *Wende* is old history, and they have adapted to the new conditions with astonishing rapidity:

> *At the time of the* Wende, *there was a great deal of talk about politics and also a great enthusiasm for the new freedoms. Then, quite soon, there was cynicism and it was OK to be rather blasé. That was also because often their parents were unemployed. And then the way of thinking of the consumer society arrived. What had been a cause of great excitement at first quite quickly became rather ordinary.*

Bärbel

Bärbel was a successful young headteacher in the GDR, but her short history of service as Party Secretary of her school seems to have been the reason for her to be made a special case and required to give further proofs of her competence to serve the new regime. In fact, as will be seen in the subsequent account, she decided to give notice before being dismissed, but her story is a graphic illustration of personal and professional tensions during the period of change in 1989–91. She is proud of the fact that her school did not experience the bitterness and ill-feeling which, she claims, was common in other schools:

> *And in a lot of schools there were rows and bitterness between colleagues. That led to confrontations and because, I think, there was a more open climate in our school, we had discussions and expressed our different opinions, but as a school, we remained unified as far as parents and children were concerned.*

She and her staff engaged in discussions with the parents, and avoided some of the stress in other schools, where children were moved, or where parents refused to have their children taught by particular teachers. During this time of change, in a school with a good and positive atmosphere, there was a sense of euphoria about the possibilities of change. And for Bärbel personally, the movement and change gave her the first real sense of how closed her mind had been earlier, and how unready to criticise the system:

> *That was 89–90, a year with a great deal of élan and enthusiasm. And slowly my eyes were opened and I said to myself, you really ought to have been more critical.*

She threw herself into the new tasks, feeling that if there was anything in her past that might be challenged, she certainly had a clear conscience and could prove, by her current work, that her concerns lay with the school, with children and with her colleagues. There were plans to make the school special in some way, to create a foreign language centre. Then the political changes started to take shape. The schools were required to establish school conferences on the West German model, where parents, teachers and pupils had their representatives and their votes. Even this was no hindrance to Bärbel, who was confirmed as headteacher by the school conference, with only one vote cast against her.

She felt that she was safe in her job at this point, even when the CDU were voted into government in Saxony, and the West German education system established, a process which she sees as a takeover:

> *And things moved quickly in a direction which was really a takeover of the systems of the old* Länder. *After the unification, that was quickly settled.*

She embarked upon a major course of professional development as a headteacher, run by the partner-*Land*, Baden-Württemberg. Looking back at her subsequent fate, she is amazed that so much time and effort was invested in her future career, if she was to be challenged about her background.

> *For us then there was a very pleasant period of further training. They acquainted us with all sorts of things which very quickly became part of our professional lives. I had a very positive attitude to all that was going on, as a result of this further training, and could show my colleagues, to some extent, what the pattern of developments would be.*

But the wheels of political judgement were slowly grinding and teachers were gradually being notified if anything in their past was considered doubtful. We have already seen some of the criteria in interviews with Wilfried and Ingrid. Above all, there was a certainty that teachers with a Stasi background should go. But also, doubt was cast on those who had been too close to the Party and therefore, by association, too closely concerned with support for the regime.

Bärbel still had no sense that she was in danger, even though she handed in her questionnaire with full details about her past. But a further round of enquiries named teachers who were required to take a special examination because of something thrown up by the earlier questionnaire:

> *That must have been in the spring of 1991, the information about which teachers had
> to be further investigated and possibly reckon on getting the sack. Teachers who had
> been in positions of responsibility, teachers of history and* Stabü.

Bärbel found herself in the unenviable position of having to serve these notices to members of her staff, while knowing that she herself was under review. She remains sceptical about the whole process. It seemed that nothing would halt the inexorable process of the authorities, whatever support was offered by her colleagues and others:

> *Parents wrote letters, and there were student demonstrations and parents wrote
> petitions. Every member of the School Conference wrote letters in support of me.*

So she was facing dismissal for political reasons, but with no clear idea of what her crime was:

> *I think that I was given notice because I didn't just fulfil my official function as
> headteacher, but at the same time, for a period of a year and a half, held the honorary
> post of Party Secretary for the school. That's what I assume, although nobody has
> actually told me.*

So, on 9 January 1992, she received her notice of dismissal. There were many avenues of appeal, and many teachers who received such notices were subsequently reinstated. But Bärbel had had enough. She was still only 33, she had devoted her whole life so far to education, but she was young enough to start a new path, and she decided not to fight the battle right through to the courts.

In fact, she says that officials in the *Kultusministerium* (Ministry of Education) did not agree to her dismissal and recommended that the whole process should be repeated:

> *But I drafted a letter to the commission saying that I would not take the final test and
> that I wished to end the process for reasons of health.*

Given the experience of other teachers and headteachers, it seems highly likely that Bärbel would have been reinstated. But it is not difficult to imagine the personal toll of living through these months of uncertainty, and Bärbel had two young children and was coping with all the other stresses and strains of that period. She has no regrets about making her decision, even if it seemed premature and meant turning her back on her career. She was lucky to gain a place on a retraining course and to be very happy in her present job. So, her regrets only amount to an occasional sadness when she meets former pupils or colleagues. And in the new Germany, she sees the main gain for her personally in her increased self-confidence and independence:

> *Mainly, I have learned to assert myself. Former colleagues who are still teachers have
> tended to stay at the same school. They have just changed the master they serve. They
> have nearly all stayed put. But I have learned of the need to put oneself to the test, to
> apply for jobs, to be able to sell oneself and also to learn just exactly what you can do.
> If I'd stayed in school, I expect I would have just gone along in my little rut.*

29

In these words, she confirms a view repeated a number of times. The schools may have changed their structure but the personnel remain largely the same.

Gabriele

Gabriele is a case in point of a teacher who continued teaching in the same school throughout the period of the *Wende*, only changing schools when she had the chance to move to a newly established *Gymnasium*. Her story is of particular interest for this reason.

At a time of such upheaval, one wonders how the pupils reacted in school. Gabriele tells how pupils came to her when the Stasi headquarters in Dresden was stormed by the citizens. They wanted to be excused their afternoon optional English lesson to join the demonstration. Not willing to take the decision herself, she asked the headteacher on their behalf, but the request was rejected. In the atmosphere of the time, such a refusal was pointless, and the pupils went anyway, knowing that they had the support of their parents, and beginning to feel the pulse of revolutionary change. The headteacher was, in any case, increasingly isolated, with pupils boycotting lessons, particularly in *Staatsbürgerkunde*, and her own teaching staff turning against her. Issues of her behaviour in the past were raised; how she had, for example, actively penalised teenagers who refused to engage in the youth initiation ceremony of *Jugendweihe*. The headteacher called a meeting and demanded a vote of confidence in her actions, which was refused. A popular colleague was voted in as head by the *Kollegium*, and his unpopular predecessor was relegated back to the classroom for a short time, and then left altogether, as more came out about the past, including the fact that her husband had been an active officer of the Stasi. Such anecdotes about pupils and staff give some idea of what life must have been like for teachers at this time. Gabriele had no problems in her teaching. She welcomed the changes that were coming and she threw herself into the discussions which all the pupils demanded:

> *Lessons with the students were real fun. We had so many discussions. That was a terrific time. I had absolutely no problems with my teaching. The students continued to accept me and many of the other teachers. Lessons just carried on, except that we had a great deal more to talk about.*

Gabriele was taken aback when, in November 1989, the crowds started to chant their slogan 'Wir sind ein Volk'. Unification had not been part of her own expectations or hopes. With her contacts to *Neues Forum*, the main news opposition party, she was part of the debate that looked for changes towards a more open GDR.

The start of the Round Table discussions opened up further possibilities for the direction of change, and still hopes were focused on the possibilities of change within the socialist society. Still, according to Gabriele's view, a unification of the two German states was not a credible option. Meanwhile, she continued teaching as society changed around her and her school. Her particular combination of subjects did not offer many problems. English gained in status and in German, she found that she could still use some of her earlier materials. For teachers of history and more 'ideological' subjects, the situation was no doubt more problematic. She was only aware of a sense of freedom in her teaching:

> *I didn't find it a problem. In fact, I really enjoyed it, it was a sort of liberation, just because one could think and say whatever one liked.*

She stayed at the same school until the advent of the structural reforms brought in by the new CDU government of Saxony. There was then a debate among the staff as to whether they should apply for status as one of the new *Gymnasien*. The result was a divided staff, the departure of many teachers, including Gabriele, and, finally, the closure of that school. She moved to a newly established *Gymnasium* in another part of town. Despite this later change of school, however, she is an example of someone who was acutely aware in her personal life of the revolution she was living through, and yet who stands as an example of continuity, one of the very many teachers who remained teachers:

> *For me there was not really a definite break, either in my own personality or in my work, and I quite quickly grew accustomed to new ways of living.*

As far as her pupils are concerned, she is conscious that many of them, although they come from relatively privileged social backgrounds, are pessimistic about the new society and the chances it offers them:

> *What strikes me is that many students ... go along with this sense of having no future. They are clever, they are young, they usually come from good homes and have good prospects but they just allow themselves to cruise, to say, I won't get a job, and I don't want to go on studying. That wasn't the case earlier, at least, that is the way it seems to me.*

Like so many citizens of the former GDR, she is ambivalent about what has been lost, particularly the close personal relationships.

And yet, she is still clear in her mind that she remains an 'Ossi'. Her experience of West Germans who have moved to Dresden is not good, and she feels that they will never understand the experience of living in GDR society. She is in no doubt that a clear difference still exists, but the next generation, of course, will not be conscious of this history:

> *And I think that my children's generation won't be aware of any difference between east and west. That will be gone, but I'm pleased personally to have lived in both worlds.*

Lorna

For Lorna, 1989 was the year she entered *Pädagogische Hochschule* in Dresden to start on her chosen career as a teacher of mathematics and geography in the GDR, with the intention certainly of joining the Party and of teaching in an *EOS* and perhaps even at university level. Within a month of her starting her course, Dresden erupted with the demonstrations of October 1989. Astonishingly, Lorna seems to have been strangely untouched by the revolutionary movement around her. There were so many changes in her private life that the world outside seemed not to impinge on her:

> *But everything was on the move, I hadn't really settled properly in Dresden, my course had not really begun, and everything was so new. New people, new love-life, everything was on the move and the* Wende *was just one more thing to add. I was hardly aware of the day when the wall was opened up, I had different worries, and anyway we didn't have access to a newspaper, so that it wasn't until the weekend that I became part of the wider world. We had no TV, just a radio in our room, if that, in the very beginning. So yes, we were living there in our own little world and were astonished when the troubles started in Dresden.*

Her concerns when trouble started on the streets were for her personal safety rather than for any idea of participating in the rebellion. She never imagined that the state was approaching its end, and assumed that, even if the leadership were to be overthrown, the society would continue. There were some changes to their courses, and the political subjects were dropped, which came as something of a relief. Lorna seemed so much to represent the student body who 'slept through the Revolution' that the question was put to her: was that the case, and, if so, how did she explain such a phenomenon? For Lorna, the answer is clear. Anybody with dissident tendencies was already identified at school, and was unlikely to get further with a career of study.

> *People who held that point of view were naturally rebellious, and that would have been clear at school. Anybody who had drawn attention to themselves in this way would have had problems in getting a place as a student or going on to the EOS. Or if the family was already noted (for such attitudes) then the children were steered accordingly and just not allowed entry to the EOS ... so that anyone who had followed a line at school that was critical of the regime, well that would certainly develop during student life, so that there were not many of them left by the start of higher education.*

There could be no clearer statement of the politicisation of the GDR school. Students with 'unreliable' tendencies found their path to further education blocked. Lorna accepts this fact without criticism. But although she took no part in the demonstrations, and waited to see what society would bring, she does not feel that there were major changes in her own outlook. The fact is, she would still become a teacher, and still teach the subjects she had chosen. So, although there were fundamental changes all around her, she sees her own life pattern as maintaining a relatively direct course:

> *There was no point at which I needed to change anything. In my course of study everything fitted together very well. There was suddenly a possibility to take the decision whether or not to teach in a* Gymnasium. *That really appealed to me, and I was pleased about that. That actually got rid of a problem for me, that I would have had to work myself up to a post in the EOS.*

She welcomed the consumer benefits that came with the *Wende*, and the freedom to travel, but it still did not lead her to criticise the society which had been unable to offer these freedoms. So what does she feel as she looks back at the GDR? For her, the great advantage was the certainties of life in the GDR:

> *Well, the good thing was that one could be quite certain about the path one would follow. That is no longer the case. I would have been quite clear when I started my university course. You just had to keep reasonably close to the political line, which I wouldn't have found difficult, and get the academic results. Then you'd get your job, the first two years might have been anywhere, but then you could certainly move. That was all very secure and you could plan a long way in advance. And because I'm the sort of person who likes planning and wants to know how things are going to work out, that would have suited me, and I had already fixed in my own mind how it would be.*

Does she have no sense that it was an authoritarian society, and that the security offered was also a type of social and personal control? Her only comment here is that she did not personally encounter any of the negative side of such a society. Seeking to push her further in her views on the negative side of GDR society, the interviewer asked her about information which has emerged since the *Wende*, particularly about Stasi activities. Her reply is again surprising, since, even here, she has doubts about whether the stories are true, or elaborated. Even if true, she does not know of anybody who was actually harmed by such activity. It is worth quoting this answer in full, as it shows how Lorna has managed very successfully to maintain a set of beliefs from the past while adapting perfectly to the new society:

> *Among my own circle of acquaintances, nobody suffered. And as long as I don't have a personal example where I can actually say, you were really unlucky, I'll continue to be convinced that all this has been blown up out of proportion. Yes, of course, there were informers, but one should also recognise that it was often laughable, that people were trying to find out things that were of absolutely no importance. And my opinion is that as long as nobody was harmed, one shouldn't make such a thing of it. And the people who acted as informers shouldn't all be subjected to the same judgement. For some young people it may have been tied up with their career, like the cases of young sportsmen you hear about. We're talking here about young people who had their own personal plans, and if somebody said to them, you can do this but only if you sign here, who is going to bother when they are 18 or 19?*

Perhaps alone among the interviewees in this study, Lorna does not seem to question the past, or adopt a critical attitude to what she describes here. Since completing her studies, crossing over from her beginnings at the *Pädagogische Hochschule* to a West German style course at the university, she completed her probationary period and then, because of her high marks, gained one of only two posts in Saxony to teach her subjects at a *Gymnasium*. She is complimentary about the system of training and about the way in which the *Leistungsprinzip* is applied to ensure that those with the best marks gain the posts. She is able to make some interesting comparisons between the *EOS*, such as she attended, and the *Gymnasium*:

> *In the old GDR perhaps the best 10–12% got to the EOS, and now it's the best*
> *third of students who get to the Gymnasium. That means that in our present*
> Gymnasium, *only the top third of students are at the level we were used to in the old*
> *EOS, to prepare for the Abitur. And the Gymnasium begins in Class 5, so the*
> *whole climate of the school is different from the old EOS, which didn't start until*
> *Class 9. That means that there was certainly more sense of community.*

The teaching force is also different. In the GDR, the *EOS* was staffed either by older teachers who had gained their posts through experience, or by political appointees:

> *Or there were some who had perhaps been very committed politically, and who had*
> *pushed through the system somehow, and they tended to be the younger ones.*

Lorna's whole professional life will be spent in a unified Germany. She is able and likely to succeed, and has entirely accepted the society which was thrust upon her so unexpectedly. But she remains deeply marked by her commitment to the society of the GDR and by the Party influences which shaped her. She has no wish to bring back the GDR, no pointless nostalgia, but she is unwilling to view the society critically, even with the knowledge of that society which has since emerged.

The *Wende* and after – conclusions

From the variety of experience recounted in the interviews of this chapter emerges some picture of the events unfolding during the autumn of 1989, and the ways in which these individuals adapted to the subsequent changes in their professional and personal lives. Most of the individuals speaking here were clear that there had to be change of some kind, and were aware of the gathering storm even if unable to predict the consequences. Lorna, the youngest of the group, seemed unaware of what was about to happen and even uninvolved when it was going on around her. She seems representative of the lack of student involvement remarked on by commentators. Those who hoped for change and sensed that it was coming thought largely in terms of some socialist renewal, as is expressed by Ursula and Gabriele. The genuinely socialist roots and formation of these citizens of the former GDR are remarkably clear. Ursula still clings to some utopian vision of a socialist society, and Brigitte joined the SDP because, in the new Germany, this is the party of someone who can say, 'I was always "red". My roots are in the working class'. One senses that if only the frozen intellects of the GDR leadership had been able to move earlier and more flexibly, there would have been popular support for a fairer and less authoritarian form of socialism. The change of emphasis by demonstrators from 'Wir sind das Volk' to 'Wir sind *ein* Volk' is commented on by Ursula and Gabriele as a shock, and as a development which they had not wished for. In Gabriele's case, and she was certainly not alone, she even considered that the unification of the two societies was out of the question: 'I always said one thing for sure, one thing I know, these two systems will never come together'.

The tensions and stresses of the restructuring of schools and universities is made clear by the accounts of Wilfried, Bärbel, Brigitte and Gabriele. Inevitably, at the personal level there were recriminations and accusations, promotions and demotions, bitterness, but also, as Brigitte shows, solidarity. The uncertainties of the situation among teachers were graphically reflected in the behaviour of pupils in school, as reported by Gabriele. They seem more anxious to get involved than do the students of Lorna's generation.

The attitudes to questions concerning a West German takeover or 'colonisation' of the GDR are very varied. They range from Wilfried's 'we just had to let them do what they wanted with us' and Ursula's 'I think that the concept of colonisation expresses a measure of truth' through to Sigrid's determination to get on with the job of shaping the new education system and Ingrid's tribute to the financial and moral support of Baden-Württemberg in setting up the new education in Saxony. This is an area in which there is certainly no sort of consensus.

All the interviewees welcomed the new freedoms, even Lorna who, although the youngest, seems most imbued with the philosophy of the GDR. Among the freedoms, that claimed by Bärbel is particularly interesting. Although she is the one person here who actually lost her job, she welcomes the new possibility to make her own way, demonstrate her personal initiative and sell her talents in the market place. The mirror image of this sort of personal freedom is Lorna's comment that a virtue of the GDR was knowing exactly where you were, and having your whole life organised and planned for you.

Among the elements of continuity amongst all the changes described here is the sense of distinction between *Ossi* and *Wessi*. Gabriele, who could not be more open-minded and outgoing, has had negative experiences of West German incomers. She feels that this distinction is bound to remain until her children grow up to form the new generation of 'unified' Germans. Even Ingrid, who had actually spent some 15 years out of the country before returning in 1990, is conscious that she remains an *Ossi*. This is not to imply that there is any particular nostalgia for the GDR. Brigitte and her husband talk it over at the time of change and ask themselves, 'Do we want to keep the GDR?' The answer is a clear negative. Ingrid is dismissive of those who long for secure employment and cheap bread rolls but who would not be willing to give up their new found freedoms. But there is regret for the loss of certain aspects of GDR society, largely based upon the sense of the collective, of working together and what Ingrid calls, even if half mockingly, 'diese gemütliche Geschütztheit' ('this comfy sense of belonging').

With regard to the changes in school and university, the fewest problems seem to have been in the area of *Berufsbildung*, as reported and explained by Brigitte. In schools, there is an acceptance of the *Gymnasium* linked to the general agreement by all, notably Sigrid and Lorna, that one of the failings of the GDR school was the lack of *Leistung*, the failure to push pupils to achieve. But there is a common expression of regret that selection of pupils starts at such a tender age in comparison with the former *EOS*. Ursula feels that something very special in the GDR school was concern for the individual pupil, and that has been lost. As regards the universities, Sigrid is scathing about the 'chaos' of the university system imported from the west, and Ursula deplores the isolation and individualism of the new university.

The individual experiences described in these interviews represent some glimpses of 'the "inner" events that are the most real, the most immediate experience of human beings' (Berlin, 1953, p. 15). The 'ordinary day-to-day succession of private data' (Berlin, 1953, p. 20) was gathered as a record, which, for all its partial nature, also represents a version of 'reality (which) is complex and many-sided' and which 'allows the original multiplicity of standpoints to be recreated' (Thompson, 1978, p. 5). The varied perspectives and points of view are, of course, personal and individual, but they are also, in a general sense, representative, and add a valuable extra dimension to our understanding of educational change in the territory of the former GDR.

References

Berlin, Isaiah (1953) *The Hedgehog and the Fox – an essay on Tolstoy's view of history*. London: Weidenfeld & Nicolson.

Fulbrook, M. (1995) *Anatomy of a Dictatorship*. Oxford: Oxford University Press.

Niethammer, L. (Ed.) (1985) *Lebenserfahrung und Kollektives Gedächtnis*. Frankfurt/Main: Suhrkamp.

Thompson, P. (1978) *The Voice of the Past:Oral History*. Oxford: Oxford University Press.

A Study of Teachers' Perceptions in Brandenburg *Gesamtschulen*

STEPHANIE WILDE

Introduction – background and description of research project

By 1999, many teachers in eastern Germany could look back upon almost 10 years of experience within the so-called new school systems introduced after unification with West Germany. Many of the same teachers could also look back upon decades of experience within the school system of the German Democratic Republic (GDR), as pupils, trainee teachers and teachers.

This time lapse offers an opportunity to study individual cases of adapting to such profound and rapid change. The experiences of these teachers and their perceptions of these experiences reflect both an ongoing and a retrospective process. The speed of events and the speed of change within the school system after 1990 left teachers little opportunity to ask questions of themselves or of the newly created ministries of education in the five reconstituted states of eastern Germany. The time to provide constructive answers to these questions was also in short supply. The transformation of eastern German education is still very much an ongoing process, even though the pressures of daily school life have long since gained the upper hand.

Indeed, it could be argued that different types of instability and uncertainty have replaced the high levels of instability and uncertainty associated with the time immediately after the fall of the Berlin Wall for the teachers in Brandenburg *Gesamtschulen*. There are two main sources of this instability and uncertainty. First, the dramatic fall in pupil numbers because of the drop in the birth rate after 1990 is affecting educational planning in Brandenburg. The teachers are currently facing a real threat to their work because of the dramatic fall in the birth rate in eastern Germany after the *Wende*, which has in turn led to falling rolls in schools. In 1990, 4074 pupils enrolled at Brandenburg *Gesamtschulen*. This figure fell to 3679 pupils in 1996, and 2877 in 1997. (Statistics from the Statistical Report on Schools 1997/1998, Statistisches Bundesamt, pp. 40–41.) Secondly, the level of inter-school competition is rising, both between *Gesamtschulen* and *Gymnasien* and *Realschulen* and between schools of the same type, fighting as they are for each pupil. This situation brings with it a further uncertainty, because these low pupil cohort numbers will not support the current three-school system in Brandenburg, and the competition between the *Gymnasium* grammar-school type, the *Gesamtschule* and the *Realschule* will become ever more fierce, as indeed it will between schools of the same type, and between teachers.

Research Aims

The aims of the research are broadly descriptive and exploratory. The research questions focus on the subjective understandings of the individual teachers and include the following.

- What are the current successes and the current problems of the *Gesamtschule* school type in the Brandenburg context, according to the teachers?
- Which aspects of the school system of the GDR do the teachers feel might have been worth preserving?
- Which aspects of the school system of the GDR did the teachers feel no regret to see disappear?
- Where did the teachers find strength and support during the ongoing transformation process?
- Which factors have hampered the process of transformation for the teachers?

The main research focus is on the teacher perspective because it is teachers who carry the weight of internal school reform, and who have had, and still have, the task of translating large-scale systemic change into a school reality in Brandenburg. Further, as Dirks et al argue (1995, p. 230), many of the teachers currently in post in eastern Germany will carry internal school reform for some time in the future, as the majority of the teachers are between the ages of 35 and 50.

The research involves interlinked themes, including personal professional development and professional identity, coping in the context of large-scale educational and societal change and structural issues such as the suitability of the *Gesamtschule* concept for the state of Brandenburg, the issues of educational financing in the economically weak area of eastern Germany, and both explicit and implicit comparisons between the current school type and the main school type in the GDR, the 10-year unitary *polytechnische Oberschule* (*POS*).

Methodology – justification of decisions

The research is conceived as a qualitative study of the subjective opinions of a sample of teachers currently professionally active in the *Gesamtschule* school type in the state of Brandenburg. As the focus of the research is these subjective opinions, the research design is qualitative in nature. The aim of the research is not to quantify the opinions of teachers in order to approximate to a 'typical' or 'dominant' set of opinions manifested by teachers in Brandenburg. Instead, the aim is to describe some *examples* of perspectives held by the teachers in the sample. There are no claims for either the representativeness of the sample or the generalisability of the findings. However, the research design attempts to achieve a broad perspective by examining schools within different contexts – urban, small-town and rural. The research aims to describe the parameters of opinion of a sample of teachers in some detail and to describe their perspectives and experiences. The research design aims to produce rich data from a small sample of teachers, with the aim of describing their experiences and perspectives in detail.

Data Collection

Data collection is based at a total of four *Gesamtschulen* in Brandenburg – a pilot study was conducted to test the research design and to sensitise the researcher to the research context, and, at the time of writing, data have been collected from two schools for the main study. The school sample includes an urban school, a small-town school and a rural school, in order to include different social environments, and to allow for some different patterns of competition faced by Brandenburg *Gesamtschulen*.

The three schools are all *Gesamtschulen*, but have different structures. The urban *Gesamtschule* has an attached primary sector and an attached secondary level 2 (Classes 1–13), the small-town *Gesamtschule* offers secondary levels 1 and 2 (Classes 7–13) and the rural *Gesamtschule*, where data have yet to be collected, offers primary level and secondary level 1 (Classes 1–10). The two schools with secondary level 2 are both facing a fight to retain these classes, in view of the competition with the *Gymnasien*. The rural school is almost certain to be given 'small primary school' status early in the 21st century, as the intake from the local area cannot support a secondary school. This means that many pupils may have to make long bus journeys to school.

The study examines a combination of teachers and schools. The teachers' perspectives on the realities of teaching in Brandenburg in the late 1990s cannot be separated from their current school experiences. The research therefore examines the current professional context of the opinions expressed by those teachers.

Studies of the Schools

I became familiar with the school organisation and the daily pressures upon teachers by participating in each school for a period of approximately 6 weeks. During this period, I was able to observe lessons for all class levels, and all subjects. It was also possible to participate in staff meetings and staff social activities. Further, informal staffroom conversations and exchanges with the teachers and pupils provided further perspectives.

In this sense, the aims of this phase of the research are those of an ethnographic study, as defined by Hammersley & Atkinson (1995, p. 1):

> *In its most characteristic form it involves the ethnographer participating, overtly or covertly, in people's daily lives for an extended period of time, watching what happens, listening to what is said, asking questions – in fact, collecting whatever data are available to throw light on the issues that are the focus of the research.*

Further, this time provided the opportunity to make contact and communicate with most of the teachers at the schools, so that it was possible to answer any questions about the research. In this way, the teachers were not taken aback if they were then invited to be interviewed.

Semi-structured Interviews

The teachers to be interviewed were chosen by random selection. Teachers were aware of the fact that each of them was equally interesting to the research project. No teacher declined the invitation to be interviewed. As the research focus is the subjective accounts of the teachers, the main advantage of using interviews as a method of data collection is the fact that it allows for reflexivity.

Each teacher participated in two interviews. The first interview focused on the teacher's professional biography, and the second interview focused on their perceptions of education policy in Brandenburg and the changes since 1990.

The aim of the research is describing, rather than measuring, and in this context, interviews offer scope for the teachers to express differentiated opinions in some depth. A semi-structured interview schedule was used, but for some of the teachers in the sample, a single opening question led to a narrative-style discussion of the issues relevant to the research. The interviews were open discussions, and the teachers had control over the direction of the interview, so that they could explore issues of particular interest or importance to them.

The interviews took place in the context of a wider communication between the researcher and the staff of the schools. The interview situation was certainly more formal than the other conversations held at the school, not least because formal appointments were made for the interviews, notes taken and the conversations also recorded in most cases, but the interviews did have something of the nature of a personal conversation. This was partly because many teachers took the opportunity in the school day to speak to the researcher, and in this sense, I was able to enter the interview situation in a pre-informed position. Thus, the interviews could begin on a personal note, and so there was no extended 'ice-breaking' phase. This was a positive factor for the atmosphere of the interviews, and for the readiness of the teachers to communicate, but there was a danger of overfamiliarity and overempathy, and I had to guard against this.

This was one of the ethical dilemmas of conducting the research. I had to deal with the various roles attributed to me by the pupils, teachers and headteachers. Despite the fact that my role was marginal in all contexts, be it observing a lesson, spending breaks in the staffroom or speaking informally to pupils and teachers, both pupils and teachers accepted me into their environments. This allowed for certain information to emerge that might not otherwise have emerged, but the level of analytic distance was reduced. This was particularly the case during interviews, when teachers adopted an informal or even conspiratorial tone.

Other ethical problems included how to deal with contradictory statements given by the teachers, and also how to deal with sensitive information regarding their professional biographies without damaging the open nature of the interviews.

Presentation of the Data

The following data emerged from the research periods spent at two Brandenburg *Gesamtschulen*. The data presented include: brief descriptions of the schools and selected data from the interviews conducted. The data presented is not the exhaustive picture of the data collected, but has been organised in order to offer some initial descriptive answers to the research questions outlined.

Urban Gesamtschule

This school is located in a city in the state of Brandenburg. The school has both an attached primary school sector and an attached *Abitur* (university preparation examination) preparation level, and therefore offers the full range of classes from 1 to 13.

The school had 950 pupils in the school year 1998/99, of whom 270 were in the primary school sector, 500 in secondary level 1 (Classes 7–10) and 180 in secondary level 2 (Classes 11–13). There were 71 teachers in total, of whom 58 were female and 13 male. The headteacher and his deputy were both male. Thirteen teachers worked exclusively in the primary sector.

The school comprises two buildings, one dating from 1907 and the other from 1909. Initially, the schools were separate *Gymnasien* and, during GDR times, they were both *POS*. The schools are separated only by a courtyard, which has trees and benches. This proximity means that it is not logistically difficult to run the two buildings as a single school unit, but there is nonetheless a sense of a 'split site' at the school. Urgent building work was being completed on the outer walls of the school, but many classrooms also needed painting and the heating system was in need of an overhaul. The sports facilities were cramped and dated. However, it had been possible to convert one small room into a French library and reading room, and the school newspaper has its own editorial office. Further, the school benefits from the presence of the local library on its premises. These elements have a decisively positive impact on the morale of the pupils and teachers, and are actively appreciated by both groups. The primary school classes are based in one of the buildings, while the secondary pupils move between the two. Some teachers almost never come into contact with each other, depending on the practicalities of their timetables.

At the time of research, the school leadership consisted of the headteacher and his deputy, but it seemed that running the two school buildings was a task for which more than two people would be required. The teachers' council therefore proposed an extension of the leadership, so that a further two teachers would take on leadership duties, in order to relieve some of the pressure from the current team, and to allow time for conceptual work, as well as organisational duties.

The presence of the secondary level 2 has a strong qualitative impact on the ethos of the school. The teachers were aware of the need to find a strong profile for the school, but this had so far not been successful. This was attributed to some extent to the overwork of the school leadership, and the teachers hoped for new developments once the leadership had been extended.

Many of the teachers at the school commented favourably on the level and intensity of cooperation between staff members, be it as co-tutors or as subject colleagues. There was a high level of willingness to work together on the part of the majority of the staff. Some of the teachers had been at the school for decades, but many teachers had joined in stages after the *Wende*, as smaller secondary schools became primary schools. This new constellation of staff members was stressful for both the teachers new to the school and for those who had grown accustomed to the previous situation.

Small-town Gesamtschule

This school is located in a small town some distance north of Berlin, close to the border with the state of Mecklenburg-Vorpommern. The population of the town is around 12,000. The school offers classes 7–13. The ethos of the school is strongly affected by the presence of secondary level 2, in place since 1993.

The school had some 700 pupils in the school year 1998/99, of whom 500 were in secondary level 1 (Classes 7–10), and 200 in secondary level 2 (Classes 11–13).

There were 52 teachers at the school, of whom 38 were female and 14 male. The school head and his deputy were both male.

The school consists of four separate buildings. The main building, called house one, was built in 1968, and is an H-shaped concrete building on three floors. House two is adjacent to the main building and is used for Class 7. Houses three and four are non-purpose built, and located some 10 minutes' walk away from the main buildings, an inconvenience for both teachers and pupils.

The quality of the classrooms diverged widely. There were new physics classrooms, and a new computer centre. However, elsewhere in the school, basic requirements were not being met. For example, two classrooms used by Class 7 were not properly insulated and, after heavy rain, pupils had to mop down their chairs and desks before lessons could begin. However, positive features included extensive and regularly changing displays of pupils' work, a school café designed and constructed by pupils and run by a retired teacher, and a pupil-designed courtyard.

The school leadership has a strong qualitative impact on the school, because the headteacher combines commitment to the school with a highly individual and charismatic approach to running the school. Teachers and pupils commented with regularity on his impact on the school, indicating that he places high demands on teachers and pupils. The leadership was perceived to be very strict, almost to the point of aggression, but this was outweighed by the fact that pupils and teachers felt that this approach had achieved a good deal at the school. The high demands were also placed into the context of his high level of commitment to his work and to his school. The two main areas emphasised by the leadership were teamwork at the school and public relations work in the surrounding area.

The provincial location of the school meant that many teachers knew each other's families, and those of some of the pupils. This created an atmosphere of intimacy at the school, and there is also continuity across the generations, as the older teachers have taught the parents of some of the pupils. Indeed, one of the older teachers even taught the current headteacher when he himself was a pupil at the school.

Selected Interview Data

The interviews with the teachers were characterised by both implicit and explicit comparisons between the education systems of the GDR and of Brandenburg within unified Germany. The teachers referred to aspects that might have been usefully retained, and to aspects the demise of which they did not regret. A number of contradictions arose, both within the opinions of the individuals and between the opinions of the teachers. These contradictions arose in subtle ways, as well as in clear mismatching of opinions and assessments. To a certain extent, the teachers were themselves aware of these contradictions, but were as yet not able to confront them fully, it seemed. The 10 years that had passed by did not seem to represent a long enough time span for teachers either to have fully completed the protracted leave-taking from the GDR education system, or to have fully embraced the education system of the state within unified Germany.

The data selected offer an initial exploration of the research questions. In some cases, specific perspectives of individuals are outlined, and in other cases, teachers' opinions are cited as examples of an opinion held by others in the sample.

Teachers' Views on the Gesamtschule *School Type: its potential and its problems*

The 14 teachers at the two schools were facing some of the same difficulties, since they teach in the same school type, operating under the legal, social and economic framework of the state of Brandenburg, even though the immediate contexts are very different. The hampering factors identified by teachers at both schools include:

- the perceived drop in standards of general knowledge and willingness to learn on the part of the pupils;
- the reduced motivation of the pupils and a perceived negative change in their behaviour patterns;
- perceived injustice in the treatment of East German teachers with regard to pay and recognition, and dissatisfaction regarding the question of civil servant status and the many different stages on the pay scale;
- the lack of examinations after Class 10 in Brandenburg, and dissatisfaction with the decentralised *Abitur* examination;
- the pressures of making their schools attractive to pupils in order to compete with other schools, and of producing effective publicity.

All of the teachers in the sample commented that they were in favour of the *Gesamtschule* school type in theory, but that the reality of the school situation in Brandenburg meant that the educational reality of the school type is far from satisfactory.

Many teachers commented on their dissatisfaction that some of the problems faced by the *Gesamtschulen* in western Germany regarding status and recognition had been imported into Brandenburg. Many also commented on the unsuitability of North-Rhine Westfalia as the role model state in western Germany, as this state is densely populated, and Brandenburg is sparsely populated.

However, the majority of the teachers in the sample viewed the potential of the *Gesamtschule* as high in the following areas: differentiation, possibilities for elective courses and greater social equality than in a system that separates pupils into different schools. However, they commented that Brandenburg *Gesamtschulen* are still affected by selection – namely, the choice of many of the more able pupils to transfer to the *Gymnasium* at Class 7, the so-called 'creaming' factor. For example, Ingrid B. of Urban *Gesamtschule* commented wryly on her initial enthusiasm for this school type, going on to say that the reality of the situation soon took over. In the school, she says, the *Kurssystem* (the division of pupils into ability groups for certain subjects) breaks down because most of the more able pupils transfer to the *Gymnasium* at Class 7. This means, she says, that the higher level *Erweiterungskurs* (extension course) is not really true to its name, while the *Grundkurs* (basic course) operates at an extremely low level, in her opinion. This view is shared by most of the teachers in the sample. Maria T. commented that she also felt that the system reduced the sense of solidarity amongst the pupils, as the class group is regularly split throughout the school day. The division of the classes also means that it is difficult for the class tutor to meet all of the class together, and sometimes may have to write a report on a pupil with whom she has had very little contact. However, Anna P. made a positive decision to transfer to the *Gesamtschule* from a *Gymnasium*. She commented that many of her colleagues could not understand her decision, as it is effectively viewed as a voluntary demotion because of the high status of the *Gymnasium*. She argues, however, that it was a good decision on her part, because the social climate, amongst teachers and pupils, in her opinion, is much better at the *Gesamtschule*.

Elements of the School System of the German Democratic
Republic which Teachers Believe Might have been Worth Preserving

Some teachers responded with surprise to this question, commenting that their recent experience had been that there was little interest in any positive aspects of the school system of the GDR. However, many were quick to temper enthusiasm for the previous system by indicating that the extreme political pressure on teachers and pupils more than outweighed the positive features of the school system. Indeed, Kathrin Q. of Urban *Gesamtschule* made a point of speaking to me the day after one of her interviews in order to emphasise the impact of the political pressure during the GDR, because she wanted to be sure that I was aware of the depth of her feeling, and she was concerned that it had not come across strongly enough during the interview.

However, Paul C. of Urban *Gesamtschule* pointed to a dilemma expressed by other teachers too – namely, a need or an instinct to leap to the defence of the

GDR, even though there was much with which he could not agree. He argued that the reality of life in the GDR is all too often reduced to the Socialist Unity Party of Germany (SED) regime and the *Staatssicherheitsdienst* (Stasi or secret service). He comments that these were indeed significant elements of the GDR, but that in his view debate regarding the GDR should not focus exclusively on these areas.

There was some consensus regarding elements of the school system of the GDR which the teachers viewed as worth preserving. All of the teachers interviewed in the sample mentioned the following aspects that they believed to be worth preserving from the GDR school system:

- examinations after Class 10;
- a centralised *Abitur* (broadly equivalent to the A- evel) examination;
- precise curriculum guidelines;
- a wide variety of extra-curricular activities;
- teaching in the class group;
- a higher level of knowledge acquisition;
- greater cooperation with parents;
- better discipline.

However, it is important to stress the comments made by many of the teachers in the context of their responses. For example, Dieter T. of Small-town *Gesamtschule* indicated that some of the elements he cites as worth preserving are inextricably linked to the elements of the current system he most welcomes. He commented, for example, that the more precise curriculum guidelines were an advantage, but that they restricted freedom in lesson planning, one of the aspects he most welcomes in the new system. Further, the reduced availability of extra-curricular activities is linked with the disappearance of the *Freie Deutsche Jugend* and *Pionier* youth groups, whose aim it was to begin training the socialist personality. Again, Dieter T. commented that more activities should be available for the pupils outside school hours, and that the GDR offered more possibilities in this area, but that the context of those activities was unacceptable. Karin B indicated the difficulty of reaching a clear conclusion regarding the extra-curricular activities and argued that:

> *many people complain about the* FDJ *and* Pionier *afternoons, but nowadays the pupils miss this opportunity to do things together. Of course, it was obligatory to spend one afternoon a month with the pupils but, as long as it was nothing overly political, the pupils seemed to enjoy it … It is important, too, that teachers get to know the pupil in a different context, and vice versa, this mutual understanding, so that the pupils realise, this person is not just a teacher who stands in front of them and asks them to do things, but is also a normal individual, who can have fun – in this way a much better foundation is laid.*

At Urban *Gesamtschule*, Emma B. stressed the positive features of the unitary structure of the GDR school system, with regard to administration and the freedom of movement of the pupils. She added that during the GDR it was possible for pupils to move to another city or town, and be able to continue their schoolwork with the same curricula and the same textbooks. Since unification, she argued, a pupil is faced with many new textbooks and new curricula if a school change is effected even within the same town.

Vera F. spoke for many of the other teachers when she stressed the importance placed upon education by the GDR. She said she had felt valued as a teacher during the GDR, and indicated a contrast with the status of teachers in unified Germany, where she feels they are often vilified in the press.

At Small-town *Gesamtschule*, Mark C. commented that he feels that the pupils in the school have become more ill-disciplined since the fall of the Wall. Most of the teachers in the sample shared this view, and some suggested that the reintroduction of the *Kopfnoten* (marks for behaviour at the top of school reports) might go some way to address this problem. During the GDR, marks were given for *Fleiß, Mitarbeit, Betragen und Ordnung* (diligence, cooperation, general behaviour and organisational skills). However, Julia F. commented on the subjective nature of these marks, and doubted whether they would be effective, a misgiving shared by some of the other teachers. A further factor to take into account is that of generational differences. Petra G. indicated that she was aware of colleagues, mostly older colleagues, struggling with discipline problems within the new school system, but she added that it was not easy to initiate a dialogue with them on this subject.

> *None of the teachers stands up and says, 'I cannot cope, or I cannot cope because I did not understand the* Wende*', nobody does that, but let's not pretend, one hears pupils, you do not need to ask them directly, they talk about it themselves ... quite simply the question of discipline is also a matter of survival.*

Indeed, at both schools, there were teachers who were often ill, or who had been ill for a long time. Teachers commented to the researcher that they suspected that some of the illnesses were stress-related.

With regard to pupil behaviour and increased discipline problems, Astrid P. referred to the influence of parental behavioural patterns. She claimed that, before the *Wende*, teachers reminded parents of their duties, whereas since then, parents remind teachers of their duties. The diminishing of a sense of cooperation with parents has made it more difficult for the teachers to cope, according to Astrid P. Julia F. also mentioned the concept of misunderstood freedom in this context. She indicated that, in her opinion, parents have taken the new freedom without understanding the implications fully, and this has had profound effects on the behaviour of the pupils.

Most of the teachers also argued that the level of knowledge acquisition had fallen since unification. Mark C. commented on the documented superior performance of GDR pupils in mathematics and science, adding that the methods used in the GDR schools must have had some value. Julia F., a teacher of languages and German, also shared this perception of a higher level of general knowledge and of subject learning during GDR times.

Elements of the School System of the German Democratic Republic
which the Teachers Feel No Regret to See Disappear

Most of the responses in this context focused on two issues: the political and ideological content of schooling in the GDR, and the regimented nature of schooling.

At Urban *Gesamtschule*, Vera F. commented on her relief that every minute detail of each lesson is no longer pre-programmed, and that she can be more flexible and spontaneous in her classes. Kathrin Q. stressed that she welcomes the fact that the extremely high levels of political pressure on pupils and teachers have gone, and that as a teacher, she is no longer required to justify her every move. Most of the teachers also mentioned relief at the disappearance of military instruction and the regular *Fahnenappelle* (official school assemblies).

Paul C. welcomed what he describes as the 'ideological unloading' of the GDR school system. He added his positive assessment of the fact that more pupils are now able to take the *Abitur* examination, commenting that during GDR times able pupils were prevented from continuing their education because of their so-called unsuitability on political grounds. In unified Germany, he said, the problem has been reversed because so many pupils have the right to continue their schooling, leading, he says, pupils of insufficient ability to attempt the *Abitur*.

At Small-town *Gesamtschule*, all the teachers commented on their dissatisfaction with the lack of elective subjects at the GDR school. Astrid P. commented on her relief that the 'regimented' nature of the school system of the GDR no longer exists.

Paul C. of Urban *Gesamtschule* commented that, in his view, the education system of the GDR had faults, and the education system of unified Germany has different faults, but that his level of personal dissatisfaction and disappointment with the current system is deeper, because his hopes for the renewal of the system had been so high.

Factors which Provide the Teachers with Strength and
Support during the Ongoing Transformation Process

The teachers in the sample identified a range of factors that have supported them during the ongoing transformation process. All teachers mentioned the support from the private sphere of family and friends. At both schools, the level of inter-staff support was often mentioned. Also, at Small-town *Gesamtschule*, all the teachers in the sample mentioned the positive support offered by the school leadership.

At Urban *Gesamtschule*, Emma B. commented that in her view, 'teaching skills are not dependent on the fall of the Wall' ('Pädagogisches Geschick ist wendefrei'). She argues that she can look back upon decades of experience of teaching her subjects, and views this subject competence as a source of confidence. She adds that the resonance she receives from the pupils supports her in her work.

For some of the teachers, the new opportunities the change brought with it were a source of strength and motivation. For example, Anna P. stresses the opportunities offered her by the change in the school system as a source of energy and support. As a teacher of French, she has now been able to set up an exchange with a school in France, organise study trips, make use of the new textbooks for teaching the language and use literature and films previously unavailable to her before the change in the system. Anna P. was not the only teacher to cite such fresh stimulus in the teaching of her subject as a source of support, but not all the teachers make this comment. It is perhaps significant that Anna P. is a highly committed and dynamic teacher, who was not yet 40 at the time of the fall of the Wall. She comments herself that she is not sure how she would have borne the change if she had been rather older in 1989. For Kathrin Q., a significant change was that she was able to train to teach a new subject – law – and was thus able to stretch herself intellectually.

For Paul C., the transformation process has been a period of personal uncertainty and disappointment. However, his main source of motivation is his pupils, and the pleasure he senses when the pupils have gained knowledge of value from his lessons. He commented that some of the events of the last 10 years, particularly his sense of unjust treatment, have been hard to bear, and asserted that it was important for him that he believe in his work as a teacher. He argued that if he did not have this belief, he would have no motivation at all: 'If I did not believe in my work as a teacher, I would have no motivation. It is not the pupils' fault. Sometimes it is really difficult'. In this example, Paul C. falls back upon his sense of his professional identity in order to support himself. He argues that his commitment to his work is not offered financial or professional recognition – he does not have civil servant status, fears the reduction of his teaching hours and feels that teachers as a professional group have been scapegoated – and so he must motivate himself via his professional identity and his relations with his pupils.

A de facto sense of pragmatism was present in many of the interviews with the teachers. However, at Small-town *Gesamtschule*, two teachers voiced this explicitly. Mark C. comments: 'Nobody knows how things would have been, if things had been different, so I just stop philosophising, and get on with the job'. Petra G. argues a similar point, stating that she simply had to come to terms with the changes, and respond to them actively, because the only way she can make a living is by teaching. In addition, Karin B. finds strength in her 20 years of professional experience, arguing that these cannot be taken away from her. She also adds that her earning power and standard of living are higher now that at any other point in her life.

Factors Identified by the Teachers as Hampering the Process of Transformation

The teachers referred to a variety of different factors that hampered the process of transformation, some relating to recognition and pay, and some relating to less tangible factors.

For example, Paul C. of Urban *Gesamtschule* pointed to the negative effect of the differing earning categories of the teachers at the school, and the divisive nature of these differences. He referred repeatedly to his sense of injustice, and summed up: 'I feel far more discriminated against now than during the GDR ... no promises have been kept in this system ... I have just been lied to and cheated by this system'.

He explained this sense of frustration with regard to the fact that he was deemed too old to apply for civil servant status and to his sense of job insecurity despite the fact that he undertook further training to be able to teach at secondary level 2. He added that he did not appreciate being 'told how [he had lived his] life during the GDR'. Many other teachers shared this view and some commented that, in their view, west German observers were both mis- and ill-informed regarding the education system of the GDR.

Ingrid B. spoke of frustrations and disappointments also described by most of the other teachers. She was bitter at her perceived classification as a 'second- or even third-class teacher', and at the frustration of her initial activities after the *Wende*: 'At first, naive as we were, we believed we could now put our ideas into practice, but we were only an annexed area, we were not supposed to bring anything with us, we just had to conform'. Emma B. commented that one of the main difficulties for her was accepting the fact of her own low level of criticism during the GDR. She said that she feels anger towards her university professors who taught only a partial reality, but accepts that her pupils would be justified in levelling similar criticisms at her.

With regard to the question of changes in teacher attitudes, Mark C. of Small-town *Gesamtschule* argued that:

> *The school is undergoing a transformation, and this transformation is very slow and will take a long time ... many aspects of the behaviour of teachers who trained under socialism will remain the same for the whole of their lives, they will stay the same. So a transformation will only occur when young teachers join the school, and gradually influence the school with their ideas.*

He added that his main source of dissatisfaction was a sense of unjust treatment, with regard to teacher pay in Brandenburg and the issue of civil servant status. He also referred to increased levels of bureaucracy, and the negative impacts of inter-school competition. Further, he argued that the lack of detailed information in the curriculum guidelines created unnecessary extra work.

Petra G. summarised the elements which make her professional life difficult in the following way:

> *that the young people are harder to deal with nowadays, since the border opened ...*
> *There is no meaning in their life, nothing to aim for. Their parents are unemployed*
> *and they bring the problems with them to school, then they become aggressive.*

Most of the teachers also expressed critical opinions with regard to the education ministry, and the education minister, Angelika Peter. (During the period of research, there was a good deal of publicity surrounding the call from the Brandenburg teachers' union for the resignation of the minister.) The main complaint from the teachers was a perceived lack of sufficient financing. However, Karin B. of Small-town *Gesamtschule* commented:

> *of course, everybody gets upset and feels disadvantaged or short-changed. We used to*
> *do that before too, we also complained about Mrs Honecker [GDR education minister*
> *and wife of Erich Honecker] but most people have forgotten that already.*

She also criticised the decision-making processes in Brandenburg:

> *sometimes it seems that there is no real, good concept, decisions are made from one day to the next and in such a half-hearted fashion – one cannot see a clear goal any more.*

Commentary on the Interviews

The views presented here demand respect because they are those of teachers who have worked through the ongoing transformation process. As Reh argues with regard to one of the teachers she interviewed, the purpose of the research is not to judge whether they are what they claim to be (Reh, 1997, p. 31). However, while according the teachers' subjective opinions appropriate respect, it is also important not to approach them uncritically. Some of the responses involved contradictions, be it of a deliberate nature or not. The pragmatic approach adopted by some of the teachers perhaps ignores some of the major issues still to be resolved within the eastern German teaching profession. Examples of such contradictions are the welcoming of differentiation in the school, whilst also complaining of the destruction of whole-class teaching, two incompatible approaches, and the criticism of the lack of precise information in the curriculum guidelines in conjunction with the welcoming of greater freedoms in their teaching.

The conflicting and ambivalent opinions expressed by the teachers highlight the difficulty of their situation. Many of the teachers in the sample are now teaching in a school building that was previously the school of an entirely different social system. The psychological pressures of this situation are high. The teachers also stress their view that the schools they have worked in and are working in are reflections of the given society. It might be possible to argue that the teachers try to view their professional work as distinct from the wider political and social framework of the school, and that in this way they cope with the fact that they have taught pupils within two opposing social systems.

With regard to comparisons between the GDR and West Germany, the emerging picture from the teachers echoes that offered by a teacher interviewed by Reh, that: 'It is not that the GDR is bad, and the FRG is good, nor is the reverse the case' (Reh, 1997, p. 32). Further, the responses of the teachers raise questions regarding the connections between school and society, and the question of where the responsibility for educating the next generation lies. Some of the problems at the schools are to do with the wider society, such as the bleak employment prospects for current school-leavers and the ongoing values crisis in eastern Germany. Also, there is a need for a discourse other than that of teachers criticising the ministry, and the ministry making increasing demands of teachers.

Analysis of the Data in the Context of Previous Research

The research findings emphasise a high level of differentiation between the perspectives, opinions and experiences of the teachers interviewed. This differentiation also expresses itself in the form of internal contradictions voiced by individual teachers. This emphasises the psycho-social complexity of the current situation for teachers in Brandenburg *Gesamtschulen* and serves to warn against drawing conclusions of a rigid nature. The temptation of painting a picture of the 'typical' teacher or of the 'typical' response to the *Wende* based on these data is dangerous, since each individual teacher is affected by so many differing factors, including the status of their current school, the status of their teaching subject and the nature of the team spirit amongst the staff of the school.

However, a 'typical' picture is not the aim of the research, nor does the research design make such conclusions possible. Instead, the research findings aim to be descriptive and exploratory in nature, citing *examples* of possible responses and positions, but not arguing that these responses are in any way generalisable or applicable to other teachers, schools or groups of teachers.

The research findings are by the nature of the research design highly subjective and qualitative, but they must also be analysed in the context of previous research, in order to see to what extent the data converge, and to what extent they diverge, with the conclusions reached.

The Gesamtschule *Concept*

The teachers interviewed were critical in their attitudes to the reality of the *Gesamtschule* in Brandenburg. The majority of the teachers argued that they were in favour of the theory behind the school, but felt that the reality left a good deal to be desired. This converges with research published by Reh, who quotes a teacher as saying that she had moved from one school type in desperate need of reform to another school type in desperate need of reform (Reh, 1994, p. 47).

The teachers interviewed also described, in different ways, some of the difficulties of being a *Gesamtschule* teacher. Public perception, they said, is increasingly that this school is the school available for those pupils who do not succeed in transferring to the *Gymnasium* at Class 7. This school type is viewed as the school for pupils who might achieve, and the perception of the *Gesamtschule* is increasingly becoming that of a 'sink school'. In conditions of competition, it is essential for the schools to develop a successful profile and to carry out effective public relations work. The teachers argue that they are hampered in this work by the so-called poor reputation of the *Gesamtschule*, its perceived inferior status compared with the *Gymnasium*, and also misconceptions regarding their school type in press reports and in public opinion.

These criticisms voiced by the teachers echo comments made by Kuhn in his assessment of the *Gesamtschule* in eastern Germany (Kuhn, 1996, p. 558). He argues that the provenance of the schools in Brandenburg was different to their provenance in West Germany, where this school type was the result of a move to initiate a more progressive approach to education. By contrast, in Brandenburg, the development of this school type was very much a political decision. In terms of the perceived battle for popularity of the *Gesamtschule*, as identified by many of the teachers in the sample, Kuhn comments that the school has effectively become the 'third-choice option', and in effect could be seen to have taken on the role of the lower track *Hauptschule* school type in western Germany (Kuhn, 1996, p. 560).

Rust & Rust also express the difficult position of the *Gesamtschule* in eastern Germany in their book on the unification of German education:

> One of the difficulties was that the Gesamtschule represented, in some respects, the closest type of school to the old polytechnical school (POS). This ought to have been an advantage, but in reality it contributed to great confusion and organisational dissonance because some teachers and parents wanted it to be patterned after the POS, while others wanted it to replicate the West German model of essentially three schools under one roof, and others wanted something quite new ... It appears that the comprehensive school in the new states has a future as dubious as in West Germany.
> (Rust & Rust, 1995, pp. 205–206)

Almost all the teachers also comment on their lack of direct involvement in the decision-making process. Indeed, Anna P. of Urban *Gesamtschule* refers to a sense of 'fake participation' in the decisions immediately after the *Wende* and in the intervening period.

With regard to pupil intake, all the teachers commented on the absence of the 'top third' of the pupils, who are able to transfer to the *Gymnasium*. This is a fundamental dilemma in the Brandenburg concept, in that the so-called school for all children was set up in a position of competition with the other two school types. Kuhn also argues that the teachers have difficulties adapting to the pupils who are actually at the schools – a difficulty mentioned particularly by those teachers in the sample who are active in secondary level 2 (Kuhn, 1996, p. 558).

Kuhn concludes the assessment of the *Gesamtschule* by placing the responsibility for making this school type effective firmly on the shoulders of the teachers. He argues that the fact that the *Gesamtschule* will almost certainly have to fight for its position in either a tripartite or at least a bipartite structure should be no cause for bitterness or resignation, but rather a motivating factor to improve actively the internal workings of the schools (Kuhn, 1996, p. 562). This assessment is shared by the teachers in the sample, most of whom displayed an extremely high level of commitment to their school and to their pupils. However, the teachers were also profoundly aware of the fact that some of the difficulties they are faced with on a day-to-day basis were either created or exacerbated by political decisions in which they were not directly involved. This attitude dovetails with that expressed by an interviewee of Reh, who comments that the ministry has good reform ideas, but that these reform ideas actually overburden those who are supposed to carry them out, namely the teachers (Reh, 1994, p. 49).

Two main areas of difficulty for schools dominate the discourse regarding Brandenburg *Gesamtschulen* – namely, the dramatic fall in the birth rate in eastern Germany since the *Wende* and the position of this school type compared with the *Gymnasium* and *Realschule*.

Pressures on Teachers

The sample of the teachers at the two schools indicated pressures that they must cope with on a day-to-day basis. Although some of these pressures are highly individualised, there was also consensus on difficult aspects of teaching in a Brandenburg *Gesamtschule* in the late 1990s.

In almost all cases, at least some of the aspects identified dovetailed with those listed by Hoyer (1996). He argues that not all of the sources of destabilisation of teachers in Brandenburg are rooted in the past, and contends that a greater pressure upon teachers is represented by the challenges of the present. These include:

- competition between the different school forms and the teachers within them;
- the non-recognition of examinations and qualifications gained before the *Wende*;
- pay differentials and the burden of requalifying;
- the sense of being 'second-class' teachers because of the pay differential between eastern and western Germany;
- perceived unjust treatment in comparison with west German teachers with regard to the conferring of civil servant status; and
- reductions in the need for teachers (Hoyer, 1996, pp. 14–15).

This last point is often mentioned by the teachers in the sample, who fear a poisoning of the cooperation between the teachers once the situation reaches the point where colleagues are aware that they are fighting for their jobs. The issues of recognition and professional identity are also addressed by Lenhardt & Wernet (1999).

However, the discourse cannot exclusively be one of pressures and problems, in spite of the intense difficulties faced by the teachers at these schools. The challenges of the last 10 years have been met with resilience and enthusiasm by many of the teachers. In the current context, teachers cannot be sure they will stay at the same school for any significant length of time, in view of the changes in pupil numbers. Therefore, the commitment shown to achieving internal school reform and organising school trips and extra activities for the pupils demands an extremely high level of motivation and professional commitment. Many of the teachers in the sample are aware that they are working at a level of commitment higher than their current professional situation would indicate in terns of pay and recognition, and some expressed a fear of the possibility that their level of frustration could expand until they were no longer prepared to do extra work, but would simply 'give their lessons and go home'. These teachers are already guarding against this potential development, but also empathise with other colleagues, particularly those close to retirement, who are unwilling to do anything more than the absolute minimum. This echoes with the comment made by Reh & Tillmann:

> *And who gets involved in a pedagogical new start at their school, when they are not even sure whether they will be able to continue to work as teachers in the following school year? (Reh & Tillmann, 1994, p. 237, present writer's translation)*

Concluding Remarks

The past 10 years have involved intense work for all of the teachers in the sample. They have been faced with trying to adjust to a new school type, in some cases a new school, new curriculum guidelines, in some cases new teaching subjects, new examinations, changes in the behaviour of the pupils they teach, increasing uncertainty regarding their employment, ongoing lower pay compared with western colleagues and continual criticism in the press and in the public domain.

However, most of the teachers in the sample displayed a high level of commitment to their work and enthusiasm for new methods. This was despite their perception that as a professional group they have become scapegoats for some of the problems in eastern Germany, and that they have been badly treated and misinformed by the ministry of education in Brandenburg. In this sense, I share the privilege described in the introduction to the Rust & Rust's 1995 book and the 'high regard for the professional and humane orientation demonstrated by these educators' (Rust & Rust, 1995, Introduction, p. xii).

The structural changes within the education system of the GDR involved, to a large extent, conforming to west German patterns. As Schubarth (1999) argues, the opportunity for a constructive, two-way dialogue between east and west regarding education structures was lost. However, the initial changes were only the start of the transformation process, which is ongoing, and will continue well into the next century. It will be important not to miss an opportunity for dialogue between eastern and western German teachers within unified Germany. Indeed, it can be argued that the responsibility for the transformation process within eastern German schools does not lie solely with teachers in eastern Germany, but rather that all teachers in Germany must face the challenge of adjusting to teaching in unified Germany.

Note

This chapter is a revised version of a paper presented at the Comparative and International Education Society annual conference, 1999, in Toronto, Canada and represents an initial account of research work in progress at the time of writing (April, 1999). The interview extracts are translations from the German by the writer, who conducted all the interviews.

References

Dirks, Una, Bröske, E., Fuchs, B., Luther, R. & Wenzel, H. (1995) LehrerInnenbiographien im Umbruch, in Martine Löw, Dorothee Meister & Uwe Sander(Eds) *Pädagogik im Umbruch*, pp. 229–252. Opladen: Leske & Budrich.

Hammersley, Martyn & Atkinson, Paul (1995) *Ethnography – principles in practice*, 2nd edn. London: Routledge.

Hoyer, Hans-Dieter (1996) *Lehrer im Transformationsprozeß*. München: Juventa.

Kuhn, Hans-Jürgen (1996) Der steinige Acker – Gesamtschule im Osten, *PÄD Forum*, December, pp. 558–562.

Lenhardt, Gero & Wernet, Andreas (1999) Lehrer und deutsche Einheit, *Die Deutsche Schule*, Heft 1, pp. 68–84.

Reh, Sabine (1994) Lehrer-Leben im Umbruch, *Pädagogik*, 46(7–8), pp. 45–49.

Reh, Sabine (1997) Fragwürdige Klischees, *Pädagogik*, 49(4), pp. 28–32.

Reh, Sabine & Tillmann, Klaus-Jürgen (1994) Zwischen Verunsicherung und Stabilitäts-Suche, *Die Deutsche Schule*, Heft 2, pp. 224–241.

Rust, Val D. & Rust, Diane (1995) *The Unification of German Education*. New York: Garland.

Schubarth, Wilfried (1999) 'Kulturschock' und Schulentwicklung, *Die Deutsche Schule*, Heft 1, pp. 52–67.

Statistisches Bundesamt (1998) *Allgemeinbildende Schulen: Schuljahr 1997/98*. Wiesbaden: Statistisches Bundesamt.

Memory and Judgement: how east German schools and teachers have been regarded in the post-unification decade

BERNHARD THOMAS STREITWIESER[1]

Introduction

Two images confronting the German public at the moment tell dramatically different stories about schooling in the former German Democratic Republic (GDR): one is a colour photograph in the country's leading news magazine, *Der Spiegel*, and accompanies an article entitled 'Anleitung zum Hass' (Instructed to Hate) (Pfeifer, 1999, pp. 60–66) on a recent study that finds the GDR's school system to blame for right-wing tendencies among youth; the other photograph is black and white and part of a series of photographs published in a thin hardcover booklet entitled *Fröhlich sein und singen: Schule vor der Wende* (Rejoice and Sing: school before the turn) (Döring, 1996). *Der Spiegel* has over one million readers each week; the publisher of the book managed 2000 copies for Berlin and some of the New Federal States.[2] In each photograph, the most noticeable object is a hand: the photograph in *Der Spiegel* shows five nursery school children lined up against a green, sterile bathroom wall, sitting on potties. While the expressions on their faces vary – eyes turned downcast in resignation, heads spun in shock, lips curled in defiance – depression is the prevailing emotion. The single arm above their heads sternly drills a pointed finger down at them. The other photograph also has a hand in it, but this time the person it belongs to is in the picture: a pleasant-looking teacher whose outstretched hand is gently raising a first grader's chin up to her eye level, a gesture of kind encouragement. In this picture, the students' faces evidence self-confidence. Both of these images could not contrast more sharply, and yet strikingly be speaking to the same theme concurrently. They also clearly show that the power of those to interpret and publicise the prevailing image of the GDR is unevenly distributed. The juxtaposition of both of these images illustrates the extreme ends of what remains 10 years after the *Wende* [3]: still very polarised viewpoints presented to the public about the GDR's education system and its teachers, and the legacy that their continued employment in schools will not allow to heal or be put to rest.

This chapter is an attempt to generally characterise some of the issues that have played an important role in shaping the atmosphere surrounding schools and teachers of the former GDR in this first post-*Wende* decade. The collage of opinions herein is based on some preliminary impressions gained over a year and a half long data collection period. The chapter precedes the deeper analysis of the collected material and its selection for presentation in a larger study. In this chapter, I will illustrate how the progress of the transformation process of former East German teachers has been judged in the educational research on the one hand, and in the sphere of the general public's understanding on the other. At the end of the chapter, I will illustrate how the research and the public debate have both impacted the daily work of a sample of eastern Berlin teachers.

A Decade of Retrospection

The past decade and particularly the most recent years leading up to the 10-year anniversary of the end of the GDR have witnessed an avalanche of retrospective publications both in the research and for the bookstore market in remembrance and judgement. Since 1990, more than 1000 works have been published and at present no fewer than 500 researchers of various disciplines are engaged in studies of all possible aspects dealing with East Germany and its legacy (Hartmann, 1999, pp. 14–15). In terms of books available to the general public (leaving out research studies appearing in academic journals for the moment), the best works admit that it is still too early to draw up an accurate balance sheet on the GDR's history of the *Wende* and post-*Wende* periods, cognisant that the vantage point of unemotional analysis will only come with the safe cushion of time. Instead, these works content themselves with the hope that their contribution may help complete a more expansive picture in time (Engler, 1999, pp. 8–9). Many of the early works instead are colourful and provocative, both in terms of their photographic content (see Rathenow & Hauswald, 1990; Billhardt & Hensel, 1999; Drommer, 1999) and their playful prose (see Ensikat, 1998, for example), while others cleverly blend bitter-sweet irony and self-deprecating humour to poke fun at GDR nostalgia and other divisive clichés that have grown out of the unification (see Andert, 1993, 1994; Röhl & Jankofsky, 1996, 1999). The overwhelming tenor, however, of the books written by or targeted for eastern German readers bespeak of a first decade of loss and disappointment, not only with the disappearance of a system that had given them an identity (even if they recognised its flaws), but also with the reality of life in a West German system that has been largely disappointing and perceived as swallowing them whole but hardly bothering to include them (see Maaz, 1991; Schönherr, 1992; Luft, 1994; Dahn, 1996, 1998; Gaus, 1998; Schorlemmer, 1998; among others). While a direct characterisation of 'colonisation' (Dömcke & Vilmar, 1996) or a 'relationship of dominance' (Händle, 1998a) is not expressed by everyone, there is an underlying bitter conviction, such as that expressed by a dismissed former education professor, Karl-Heinz Riemann, that their geographic territory was annexed but the enormous intellectual potential they had to offer – and were enthusiastic to share – was arrogantly cast aside (personal communication,

28 September 1999). Again and again, bitterly ironic interpretations have been made for what, arguably, have become the three most memorable phrases of the *Wende*: the incessant chant of 1998's east German demonstrators, 'Germany, one fatherland!' [4]; former-Chancellor Willy Brandt's call that 'What belongs together must now grow together' [5]; and then-Chancellor Helmut Kohl's promise to bring about 'flourishing landscapes' in the east. Also, every negative fatherland-configuration, from 'Hurried fatherland' (eilig Vaterland) (Dahn, 1998, p. 57) to 'Deceitful fatherland' (Lüg Vaterland) (Klier, 1990) to 'Not a united fatherland' (Kein einig Vaterland) (Gaus, 1998) has been argued. Among many, especially those who at the time of the *Wende* were in mid-career, there remains today a feeling of powerlessness and anger under the west German government. Teachers in large measure are no exception to this.

As an outsider assumed by the majority of east Germans to be less burdened with the stereotypes – real or perceived – between them and their west German counterparts, it is not difficult to engage either 'side' today in a conversation about life before and after the *Wende*. In most cases, one question usually opens a floodgate of memories and quickly drawn conclusions. While it may be true that as bookshop owner Thomas Junge argues, 'of the seventeen million East Germans at least ten million of them will tell you something different today' (personal communication, 6 October 1999), the clear perception among the majority of those asked is of collective frustration.

> *The majority of east Germans continue to feel like second class citizens and feel monopolized if not directly colonized. And the west Germans see this as the height of ungratefulness. Increasingly you can diagnose hate on both sides … 'Ossies' are in a bad position today. Through annexation with the 'Besserwessies' [6] not only has their self-confidence and identity left been left behind, but they have been reduced to humiliated, maybe even dangerous, losers. This is a time of heated emotions. An invisible Wall not only goes through minds but also through hearts. (Dahn, 1998, pp. 57, 65; my translation)*

The negation of the east Germans as a people that once had their own nation, coupled with the disqualification of their accomplishments, has led to cries for recognition. A new exhibit in Dresden's city museum calling itself 'Die andere Vergangenheit' (The Other Past) notes:

> *One fifth of today's citizens have a different background that was the result of living in the GDR for forty years … Some will argue that they don't have a different background, only the past that defines their individual lives. And yet, that life was determined by the circumstances and the possibilities and impossibilities in the GDR. (Brochure, Stadtmuseum Dresden, 1999; my translation)*

Peter Ensikat's book in its title rhetorically begs the question, 'Hat es die DDR ueberhaupt gegeben?' (Was There Even a GDR?); Hans-Joachim Maaz in his 1991 book title labels the east Germans 'Das gestuertzte Volk' (The Fallen People); in Schönherr's book, he wonders if the east Germans are perhaps 'Ein Volk am Pranger' (A People in the Stocks). And the litany of woeful titles goes on. When the GDR's achievements are recognised by west Germans, east Germans often seem to perceive a slap in the face – whether what is presented has been done so in a deliberately negative way or not. The clearest example is a recent art exhibition in Weimar entitled 'Rise and Fall of the Modern' in which the (west) German curator wanted to display the contrasting works of the Nazi and socialist dictatorships. Showered with hate mail and derision, the curator's defence that he was only trying to open up a dialogue met with what he could only see as 'politically motivated condemnation' (Cohen, in *International Herald Tribune*, 19 August 1999).

Voting trends in the new federal states have not helped the east Germans to move away from us–them, Communist–Capitalist characterisations either. The significant support for the PDS, a party founded out of the ashes of the SED (the former Communist ruling party in the GDR) as a new leftist alternative to the Social Democratic Party (SPD) [7], has grown in popularity in the east over the decade, almost doubling its voter strength between the 1990 and 1998 national elections. It currently maintains a 20% voter support base in each of the five new federal states and especially strong support in eastern Berlin. To point out the extreme differences in east–west voter preferences 10 years after the *Wende*, one need only compare an eastern and western state: in the 1998 elections to the German Bundestag (Parliament), the PDS in Mecklenburg-Vorpommern in north-eastern Germany received 23.6% of the vote, while for that same year in Bavaria, south-western Germany, it only received 0.7% (Statistisches Bundesamt). More recently, in the Berlin parliamentary and mayoral elections in October 1999, the PDS in the eastern districts of the city won 39.5% of the vote, in contrast to a mere 4.2% in the western districts (voter turnout was registered at 64%), clearly evidencing a still very divided city (*Berliner Zeitung*, 11 October 1999). Finally, the media's droning characterisation of the PDS as the 'successor party to the SED' (even if this is factually accurate) appears only to have helped it grow as an underdog party for those in the east who seem to recognise in it their voice at the national and local level and evidence that the core values and ideals of the GDR should find their place in a capitalist society still.

The Research Community and the Public Arena

Over the last 10 years since the collapse of the East German state, there has been a noticeable and wide disparity between how citizens of the former GDR, and particularly its teachers, are treated in the research literature, and in contrast, how they are judged in the public arena. Since early on in the decade, the terms 'continuity and change' in the study of the transformation process of former East German education [8] have been important keywords in the research on educational transition. The establishment early in the decade of these terms as important foci for the research set in motion a host of longitudinal, questionnaire-based empirical studies and carefully constructed qualitative research projects that have expanded our knowledge about the coping phenomenon of the east Germans and their educators. These studies have been conducted with as much objectivity and sensitivity as any well-carried-out analysis so closely following the emotional events of 1989 could expect. In the public sphere, on the other hand, matters have been handled quite differently: one cannot speak of analysis and reflection yet, but instead only of painful gut reaction and accusation. No shortage of highly-charged and emotionally-loaded terms [9], either created anew since the *Wende* or given creative interpretations beyond their original meanings, have taken the debate out of the careful hands of research and thrown it into a maelstrom of assumptions and reproaches such that the outside observer would do well to have a jargon dictionary just for orientation. In this discussion, the 'public sphere' includes everything from social commentators targeting a mass bookstore market to citizen groups bent on promoting some cause, to newspaper reporters looking to grab headlines, to agenda-driven civil rights speakers, to religious leaders. While researchers have to obey the conventions set by the scientific standards of their trade and thus in most cases shy away from making dangerous and inflammatory statements, these other groups have not restrained themselves from venting in many cases extreme positions and setting off what has not been a shortage of public firestorms involving the GDR's educational legacy over the decade. In the best sense, these debates have been the painful initial steps in a necessary healing process of coming to terms not only with the GDR's past, but also with how the reunification was handled. In the worst sense, these debates have given legitimacy and cause to those outposts of opposition that seek confrontation and revenge, whether against 'Wessies', 'Ossies', the investigation of the former State Security (Stasi) by the Gauck Commission [10], or against teachers.

Interestingly, while the research camp and the public sphere have both agreed in their observance of more continuity than change in the transfer of East German educational philosophy and methodology into the West German school system, it is in the nature of the characterisation*s* of the *kinds* of continuity where the divide between both 'groups' becomes clear. What research has mostly explained as an understandable, even natural coping strategy to rely on prior training and experience in times of upheaval, the public sphere has consistently characterised as a sinister, condemnable and even dangerous transfer of authoritarian behaviour. That is, what in the research is sometimes characterised as a positive transfer of some of the best elements of GDR pedagogy, the public sphere only sees as resistance to democracy and a stubbornness to change.

Research on Continuity and Change

Besides the research community's work on 'continuity and change' (see Benner et al, 1996; Tillman, 1996; Zedler & Weishaupt, 1996; Händle, 1998b among others), other publications, conferences and lectures sponsored by various interests and magazine and newspaper articles have all devoted considerable space to the discussion. However, in the absence of a standard and agreed definition for these terms, their use – and abuse – by individuals or groups with their own agendas is not surprising. This has especially been the case with the first term, 'continuity'. With great changes for teachers and the rest of east German society in the socio-economic and political situation since 1989, answers to the same question asked at different points in time clearly vary a great deal. It is in this sense especially that continuity has been defined and what specifically is argued to have been transferred from East German to West German schooling in the new federal states has been a matter of widely varying interpretations. Even though the continuity and change in east German schools must be carefully considered in terms of its particular context – when something was said or done, where and by whom (Döbert, 1997, p. 346) – this is not always what happens from those making judgements. The context at the end of the decade, when most teachers have adjusted to the 'new' system and become well-paid civil servants, looks quite different to the outside observer and is also explained as different by teachers on the inside from what it was at the beginning of the decade when there was much professional uncertainty (Streitwieser, 1999, 2000). That is, while it may appear that teachers were making great changes and adapting to the West German system in 1991/92 but since have fallen back into familiar GDR schooling patterns, it may just be that the superficial, structural adjustments were made when adaptation was the only alternative, but the core pedagogical training remained intact. Observers who were pleased with suddenly great (but superficial) changes in 1991 may now be disappointed to find that teachers in the east have in fact not all completely abandoned their former training and pedagogical belief system, even if they are glad that the political pressure is gone.

In most cases, the discussion of precisely which elements continued from GDR schooling into *Bundesrepublik Deutschland* (BRD [Federal Republic of Germany]) schooling falls into starkly opposing negative and positive categorisations. There does not appear to be enough of a balance of the positive and the negative elements of the GDR and what has been transferred by way of its teachers (unofficially, of course, since officially no aspect of the GDR's educational system was incorporated into West German schooling). Some 'observers' are only too eager to grasp at any proof supporting the claim that all teachers were warped by the ideology of the SED/state and continue unchanged in their rigid ways, much to the harm of today's school-age population. This negative interpretation might argue that teachers continue to strictly enforce an authoritarian classroom atmosphere that includes uncreative, rote learning and the unquestioning absorption of information. Teachers' past reliance on fulfilling the automaton-like function of conveying information from above to below hinders them today, where directives have fallen away, from adapting to the ways of a democratic education process (Klier, 1997). A positive interpretation, on the other hand, might instead see a continuity of GDR teachers' 'ethos of responsibility' that still includes educating students to societal norms and values and caring for their well-being beyond the classroom rather than 'merely' conveying the academic material and then leaving at the sound of the bell. In this interpretation, teachers' experience in the past working socially with students (for example, by way of the required *Pioniernachmittage*) now serves as an extra qualification they bring to the job (Händle, 1998B). The two understandings of continuity differ in every possible way. Under the first definition, the teacher is not believed to be capable of independent thinking and so in the absence of directives from above stands helpless, neither with clear guidelines in hand telling them what to do, nor having the creative capacity to begin anew. In the second interpretation, in contrast, the teacher is believed capable of free thinking, able to interpret and creatively act upon the needs recognised in students, combining the dual experience gained in both educational systems to become an overall better educator today.

In surveying much of the research literature as well as many of the materials in the public domain produced over the decade, it has become clear that while both definitions of continuity exist, the overwhelming tenor is still that there is more continuity than change in the running of eastern German schools and the behaviour of their teachers at this particular time. Those recognising positive continuity have been neither as large in number nor as loud in public as those who charge negative continuity – even if in most cases doing so without factually-based supporting research.

While a reliance on one's training and experience in times of sudden change would seem a natural coping mechanism for most people, teachers perhaps more than any other professional group in Germany have been held critically accountable for this behaviour. This critique has grown louder over the decade as more time passes under the liberal-democratic school system of the west, and east German teachers are judged as still not yet transformed into the 'west teachers' they were supposed to be by now. During the short period following the collapse of the Government of the GDR and before official German unification, the excitement for educational reform and the willingness, especially on the east German side, for change and improvement (but not complete abandonment of their educational ideas and structures) was clearly expressed in the research. The call was loud for critical reflection and a 'readiness to change or to conserve as necessary' (Behrendt et al, 1991, p. 38), and the overture clearly made to the west for an 'exchange of methodological experience' and a search for 'what is common to both' (Hinke, 1991, p. 92). However, when west German school structure and educational philosophy quickly overran what had existed in the east beginning with the school year 1991/92, the opportunity to work with a ready and committed intellectual potential in the east and perhaps reform united German education for the better was abandoned.

Following this development, the earliest predictions at the beginning of the decade were that with the help of re-education courses over the ensuing years, teachers who had so far been 'loyal executors of the hitherto official doctrines' would gradually adjust to west German schooling (Mitter, 1992, p. 51). At the same time, however, this early research on teachers right after the implementation of the new school system also anticipated a difficult transformation and one that would require time (Rust & Rust, 1995, p. 15). Faced with completely new professional responsibilities and rights, the initial coping strategy of relying on practised operating procedures was mostly forgiven in the research, it seemed, out of understanding for teachers' plight.

Furthermore, early comparative achievement tests showed that education in East Germany had also achieved strong academic testing results compared with those in West Germany, particularly in mathematics and the natural sciences (Schabel et al., 1996). However, for many teachers, it was also found that when the hope was dashed of working together on a better school system or being allowed to improve their own, initial excitement gave way to disappointment and resignation (Tillman, 1996, p. 13). Four years later, teachers were still observed as rather closed off to an analysis of their past roles in the East German schooling apparatus and still being seen as reinforcing the old authority patterns (Mintrop, 1996, p. 376). Although trying to work out how to adapt and adjust to new instructions in the West German school system, teachers by and large were still found to 'stress continuity over change with regard to their values and teaching styles' (Weiler et al, 1996, p 110). Two years later, an evaluation again revealed a continuing transfer of 'pedagogical notions and behaviour' from GDR schooling, and the continuing 'recourse to what is familiar and accustomed' (Döbert, 1998, p. 14). Besides these studies, many others – including the most recent – continue to buttress the general view that there remains more continuity than change (for examples of longitudinal, empirically-based studies, see IFS Umfrage, 1992, 1994, 1996; Arbeitsgruppe Bildungsbericht am Max-Planck-Institut für Bildungsforschung, 1994; Döbert & Rudolf, 1995).

Perhaps most importantly, many teachers today readily admit that while they were glad to have the freedom to try out other teaching methods and to experiment, often relying on what worked before still makes the most sense. As one teacher, Wilma W., at a *Realschule* explained it:

> At first after the Wende *I just stood there and thought, 'So, now what are you going to do with the students?' Everything that we had known was now all of a sudden bad and suspected as coming from the GDR. We didn't even dare ask our students to memorise things any more or use other valued teaching methods that had never been all that bad to begin with. No! Now experimentation was all the rage ... and so after the* Wende *we tried to teach differently, with teamwork and arranging students into different learning groups and so on. But to be honest, I shy away from all of that. If you look around you, even if group work with 30 kids in the class is supposed to be the be all and end all and frontal teaching style is seen as the bad old method, you'll see that almost all teachers still teach frontally because it works. (my translation)*

According to Tillman's research in Brandenburg schools (1996), the issue of continuity and change in east German schooling in the end comes down to whom at the school one asks: while teachers have often attested to feeling overburdened with all of the large and small changes they have faced over the decade (new school structure [11], new salary and legal conditions, a suggestive and no longer directive curriculum framework, changed parental rights in involvement in school affairs, new student rights toward the teacher, the lack of ideological controls from above, among other things), students reply that the only changes they notice are in their colourful new textbooks (p. 18). Considering the massive shifts forced on to east German society as a whole – and industry, law, medicine and higher education in particular – secondary schooling, according to Tillmann, has remained a bastion of stability and can rightfully be characterised by continuity (although he is not implying the negative, authoritarian continuity mentioned by some of the other observers).

With the personnel questionnaires [12] examined with the help of the Gauck Commission by now, and cleared for the most part (approximately 10% of East German teachers had been forced into early retirement for their politically burdensome pasts by 1993 – Mintrop & Weiler, 1994, p. 257/footnote; less than 1% in East Berlin), and the rest of the teaching force finally regaining stability and balance in the 'new' system, it is hardly justifiable to condemn teachers for grasping back at what little in terms of the familiar and helpful remains from their experiences – especially with the repressive political structures now gone. However, while most of the education researchers have conducted their work with the intention to understand and explain teachers, other voices have not proceeded with such sensitivity. Newspaper stories, fuelled by two notable firestorms in the second half of the decade, intensified the continuity and change debate, taking it out of the careful hands of researchers and throwing it into the public arena.

Issues in the Public Domain

East German public school teachers must contend with a great deal today: not only does much of the population regard them as overpaid and underworked (*Der Tagesspiegel*, 7 June 1998), but their function as carriers of the political system in the past, and as civil servants today (even while this status renders them unable to go on strike and thus politically powerless as a group) is held against them by many. As Sarafina S., a teacher at a *Hauptschule*, lamented:

> *Many people back then said, 'Teacher! That's a job for reds'. They still say it today and you hear stuff like, 'So, you were a red pig, huh!' You still get labelled that way ... In general you hear people say, 'You're a teacher? Oh, God, you work for the government ... People seem to forget that you are a teacher because you like to work with kids! Many forget that and just think that teaching is a political job today just as much as it was back then. (My translation)*

While the suspicion of teachers on the one hand is tied to the fact that they indeed were critical ideological buttresses of the SED's power structure, on the other hand, how this past function is judged in the public sphere often seems lopsided. A happy balance has not yet been discovered. Those who charge that the necessary confrontation with the past has become reduced to Stasi files call for a dialogue at the same time that they want the files put away and an amnesty declared for GDR injustice. Meanwhile, on the other side, those who claim that former GDR teachers are unable to carry out the functions of a democratic school system *also* call for a dialogue while they simultaneously disqualify teachers' pedagogical worth. The incompatible accusation and defensiveness mechanism on the one hand and the call for dialogue on the other makes any constructive meeting very difficult at this stage. In all of this, teachers are stuck in the middle, somehow having to find the best way to come to terms with their students and parents on those issues generated by the press and then battered around in the public arena.

In the public debate about confronting the GDR's past, perhaps the biggest and most important moral question has been that of how to deal with the Stasi files.

As already mentioned, the political nature of the teachers' job in the GDR deeply involves them in the wider context of this debate and impacts how they are perceived by the public majority. Ironically, it is two religious figures from former East Germany (a state that officially banned religious practice) who today occupy nearly opposite ends of the public storm. Pastor Friedrich Schorlemmer of Wittenberg advocates an end to the Gauck Commission's work, while the other pastor, Joachim Gauck, runs that commission. In 1991, both still spoke out together for the creation of an open tribunal for the GDR's victims and perpetrators to be brought together for a public airing of their respective roles, much in the style of South Africa's Truth and Reconciliation Commission. The tribunal, however, was never established, in the face of political and legal disagreement and lack of public interest. Since then, the tenor of Schorlemmer's public statements, many of which in the past he has retracted only to reformulate after creating a public outcry, supports handling GDR human rights criminals through a soul-searching, cathartic process but one without legal recourse to the incriminating materials the Commission could provide and the power of punishment this would entail. Schorlemmer's comment in 1993 that the Stasi files would do well to end up in a 'bonfire of joy' [13] angered many Germans, particularly those in the east, not only for its literal suggestion but also, even if unintended, for its reminiscence of the Nazi book burnings. Wolf Biermann, a celebrated dissident who fled the GDR in 1976, responded to the comment in *Der Spiegel* (1993):

> *Oh, of course, you didn't mean any of it ... but don't try to eloquently tell me that*
> *books by Brecht or Heinrich Heine are any more important than the 'poetry' of Erich*
> *Mielke. In these files are lives' worth of documents and private photographs belonging*
> *to the victims, as well as verdicts the accused never got to see. Now they will be able to*
> *use these to file reparations claims. (pp. 44–46; my translation)*

More recently, Pastor Schorlemmer has come to publicly support an amnesty for the perpetrators of crimes committed during the GDR (*Frankfurter Rundschau*, 23 August 1999). It is no surprise that his allies in this wish are well represented within the PDS. Even so, with only 21 of those responsible tried in court as of January 1999 – including the president of the GDR, Erich Honecker, and his head of state police, Erich Mielke – but hardly any since, Schorlemmer's call strikes many as disingenuous at best and cynical at worst (Mangelsdorf, in *Berliner Morgenpost*, 1 Janueary 1999). Schorlemmer's comments have made him the spokesman for a rose-coloured memory of the GDR, where brotherly love and honesty prevailed while today's Federal Republic represents everything that is wrong with humanity:

> *The Federal Republic of Germany after unification is a country of deliberate coldness*
> *and the naked rejection of all those who cannot afford to pay. Its most important value*
> *is the value of money. What does a handshake between people mean any more when*
> *every handshake has to be paid for; when by giving a handshake you can never be sure*
> *that it counts for anything? (Schorlemmer, 1998, p. 18; my translation)*

Günther Gaus, a west German former editor-in-chief of the magazine *Der Spiegel* and a one-time representative of the Federal Republic in the GDR, has also become a passionate spokesman for east Germans over the decade and a strong critic of the behaviour of west German politicians and society, including, like Schorlemmer, the work of the Gauck Commission. Gaus blames much of the difficult adjustment since the *Wende* on the arrogance of the west Germans, who he claims have not tried to recognise the positive elements of the GDR and respected the east Germans' right to retain their individuality. His claim is that the death of post-unification illusions in the east, coupled with west German narcissism and frustration at an insufficiently grovelling posture of east Germans for being 'allowed' to become 'Wessies', explains the growing estrangement between both sides. He charges that the feelings against those who politically and/or morally do not conform with the west German view have become not only more base but also more vicious over the decade, and that the pressure to conform is no less of an oppressive feature of west German society than it was of east German society (Gaus, 1998, pp. 155 and 205). In his speeches and his book, *Kein Einig Vaterland* (Not a United Fatherland), he criticises the fact that the memory of East Germany is becoming reduced ever more to a single-minded concentration on the negativity contained in the Stasi files, and that the west German government and the media have not handled their democratic responsibilities sufficiently. Gaus argues that:

> *I would like to publicly and without any suggestion of irony oppose Gauck-ing: what I see as the usual treatment of the Stasi files which Pastor Gauck determinedly administers ... the biggest danger I see in allowing much of the most recent history to become reduced to Stasi files is that our minimally-developed ability to critique our own West German system also gets further atrophied in the process ... What kind of society are we in when we can hardly see for all of the Stasi files and yet cannot courageously discuss how to deal with them? One important privilege and advantage the BRD had over the GDR was that we had a legal system of administrative courts and the hygienic function of the media: to the first we could and can voice our complaints against the state, and through the second we are warned about undesirable developments. But is that still the case? In terms of the examination of teachers and other personnel through the Stasi files there were questionable and unjust legal proceedings carelessly passed over by the media. (Gaus, 1998, pp. 161–165; my translation)*

The absolute dominance of west German institutions, politics and economics over the east, he argues, has become so powerful that in western German schools the image of the GDR is overbearingly negative and out of line with the reality its people experienced. This view of the myopic version western German high school students are taught about the GDR is mirrored by those at the other end of the scale who charge that eastern German high school graduates also learn an equally unbalanced perspective, but this time overly positive, and thus also graduate out of line with reality (*Unser Schwerin*, 12 November 1997).

Daniela Dahn, an east German writer who for many today represents an intellectual 'other voice' and whose works have appeared alongside Schorlemmer and Gaus, has also argued passionately for the rescue of east German individuality in the face of west German dominance. Like Gaus, Dahn charges that east

Germans were no more politically complacent than west Germans. In her book of essays, *Vertreibung ins Paradies* (Expelled to Paradise), Dahn (1998 a) writes:

> *Today a new kind of conformity is demanded. One issue where we particularly appear to offend the majority of west Germans to their core is when we of all people coming from our totalitarian structures determine that they too are conformers. Different maybe, but still definitely so ... The east Germans did not come out of the* Wende *they themselves created without their pride and political self-confidence intact. They successfully prevailed in getting their most important political demands, such as the dismantling of the old party and state apparatuses, the dissolution of the hated state security service, free elections and the opening of the Wall accomplished. And yet most of their new masters from the west who came over and occupied the executive level positions everywhere treat them indiscriminately like corrupt opportunists who served a regime of horror without putting up any resistance. (pp. 60–61; my translation)*

Dahn also adds her criticism of the Gauck Commission. She charges that it has been too easy for the press to access its materials and then distort them to ruin the innocent reputations of prominent east German individuals who then have a very difficult time clearing their names. One of her strongest arguments is that the victims of the Stasi's injustices today continue to be punished through what she charges is uncontrolled misuse of Pastor Gauck's files, while their Stasi offenders had the luxury of stealing or destroying their own incriminating records in 1998. She speculates that the press and public's 'voyeurism' for anything incriminating has led to the unscrupulous probing of at least ten times more people than could ever have realistically worked for the state security to begin with (1998, pp. 173–175). Suspicion, that is, has outrun fact. Charging not only that the work of the Gauck Commission in its present capacity distorts the GDR to a society of terrified and constantly spied upon citizens, Dahn goes beyond Gaus's argument to say that because this black and white view offends the memories of those who experienced a more complicated and not always horrible GDR reality, the result is an unconstructive, nostalgic and rose-coloured memory for many (1998, p. 184).

Another work entitled *Kolonializierung der DDR* (Colonisation of the GDR; Dümcke & Vilmar, 1998) argues that most of what has been written about the events of 1989 characterises the GDR's fall into West German hands as a fully unexpected process of few alternatives, while in fact if only the right questions are asked about responsibility, why the wrong decisions were made, and how undesirable developments were allowed to happen, it will be revealed that there were other alternatives that would have led to a better result (Dümcke & Vilmar, 1998, p. 12). The charge of colonialism – a word not infrequently used throughout the decade but rarely as directly as in this work – is defended by the authors' assertion that:

> *The carrying out of the destruction of a 'domestic' economic structure, the exploitation of the available economic resources, the social disqualification of not only the political elite but also of the intelligence of a nation, and the devastation of a matured – even if problematic – identity of a whole people does factually justify the use of the term in its precise meaning. (p. 13; my translation)*

Echoing the conclusions reached by the other aforementioned serious works on the problematic post-*Wende* decade, the authors argue that the perception among East Germans of an identity loss and resulting resignation and/or resistance to West German colonialism will only be improved when the West Germans begin to recognise the accomplishments of their former East German citizens and respect the difficulties they have faced in the transition (1998, p. 235).

In defence of itself, the Gauck Commission holds to the important service it provides and particularly stresses the importance of this confrontation with the past through an open discussion in schools between teachers, on the one hand, who were in the system, and students, on the other, whose parents at home may be telling them a different story (Hennings, in *Das Magazine*, 1997, p. 9). The current belief held by the commission is that not enough history is being taught in the schools of the east about the GDR and that if the topic is handled at all it is either minimised or depicted in an overly positive way. As the acting director, Dr Peter Busse, explained it:

> *Today we should be more sensible, we should by now have learned from our history, from not properly confronting the Nazi dictatorship. But, in many ways we still have not managed to do this. It is on this very point that teachers are such an important segment of society where this has still not occurred ... It is necessary that teachers themselves make an effort to come to terms with what happened during the GDR and to force themselves to remember. They first have to educate themselves, which they could easily do with our brochures and the lectures we offer, but they aren't doing this: they are blocking this whole period out for the most part ... We have to start pulling the 'Wall in the Mind' down now but if students – and I want to phrase this carefully – are still being taught in the old way, then it will take a lot longer before this barrier is really removed. (Personal communication, 8 April 1999; my translation)*

Firestorms

The image many young people today have of east German schools and what they were like during the GDR, more often than even the innocuous and rose-coloured memory that their parents may be feeding them at home, is often a clichéd one filtered to them through the media. There is no shortage of newspaper articles and other outlets in Germany where those wishing to make the claim that East German schooling was only negative and continues in that vein today can find support. The stereotypes about former East German schools and their teachers abound and, while some are justifiable, many are not. In the past 3 years alone there has been a rash of sensationalised stories about those individuals who have experienced harassment and ostracism (in Germany called *Mobbing*) for trying to open up dialogue about GDR education and its legacy. Two particularly bitter public debates in 1997 and 1999 were sparked by comments openly criticising the GDR's education system.

The first firestorm was brought on by the comments of an east German secondary grammar school teacher, Birgit Siegmann, in the state of Thuringia; the second by a west German criminologist, Christian Pfeifer from Hannover, who came east to discuss his controversial thesis. In both instances, the initiators of the furore were surprised by the immediate vehemence of the public reaction and chagrined that the dialogue they were hoping to open was met with such resistance. Each of the two critics in both cases was flooded with feedback of a particularly vitriolic nature and immediately labelled: Siegmann became a *'Nestbeschmutzer'* (homewrecker), Pfeifer a *'Besserwessie'* (a know- it-all West German). Both firestorms led to a rash of open letters, commentary, and discussion forums, but hardly what could be called constructive developments on the issue of east German educators.

Siegmann might have been the perfect vehicle for breaking open the gates to dialogue: during the GDR she had been a teacher of civics (*Staatsbürgerkunde*), notoriously the most ideologically-controlled subject in the GDR, and her mother, Almuth Beck, had held a high educational post in Thuringia and after the *Wende* had gone on to represent the PDS in that state's parliament. Siegmann's efforts to broach those more controversial aspects of the GDR's educational system at her own school, such as political control, strict discipline and so forth, were met with stiff resistance from other faculty members who refused to attend her seminars and also tried to prevent their students from attending. Soon she was assigned the most inconvenient teaching schedule and bombarded with anonymous threats from her own school and community. Her work at the school became increasingly criticised and eventually she was driven out of full-time employment. Today she only teaches a few classes per week at her old school and seeks part-time work elsewhere (personal communication, 30 April 1999). Siegmann's efforts to open a dialogue and the ensuing harassment she was subjected to led to the creation of a committee calling itself 'Schul-Speisung'.[14] Directly after its establishment, the group received wide media coverage throughout Germany for its manifesto against the continued 'old guard' in eastern German schools. In its opening press statement, Schul-Speisung set out in no uncertain terms that it saw schools and teachers in the east as not yet having accepted the process of democratisation and still holding on to the old structures, with the 'old SED-Guard' still entrenched:

> *We see more continuity than change in schooling in the new federal states. We do not believe that with the transfer of democratic institutions into the east a democratisation process has been accepted or implemented. There are continuing repercussions of the educational dictatorship of the SED-state that, without wanting to blame teachers, we believe they must confront. (Bohse et al, Schul-Speisung, 10 January 1997; my translation)*

In its coverage of the opening of Schul-Speisung, *Der Spiegel* noted:

> *Opening up a past that has been carefully kept under wraps by educators of the SED-State today among teachers remains a dangerous taboo. (July 1997; my translation)*

Another of Germany's leading magazines, *Focus*, noted equally pessimistically:

> *Faculties are again under the control of the strict and rigid cadre of the old SED and*
> *torpedo any attempt at democracy. (1997; my translation)*

Today this non-partisan group of five east and west Germans is affiliated to the Free University of Berlin's research centre on the SED-state, to the Federal Office for Education on Politics [15], and to the Stasi Museum and Research Centre. The group regularly hosts seminars for teachers and conferences throughout the new federal states in an attempt to establish what they regard as a lack of democratic thinking and behaviour in the schools of former East Germany (*Die Welt*, 7 September). Participation at their seminars is growing, they claim, and as soon as enough funding is available, they will also conduct an empirical study to show support for their assertions, which for now remain based more on their assumptions than on supported facts. Their thesis is that the purely functionary role that teachers in the GDR carried out as conveyors of a rigid belief system from above without questioning it on their own is such an ingrained pattern that for many the methodology and strict adherence to lesson plans continues today. As one of their members, Uwe Hillmer, contends, while teachers are not necessarily to blame for not being 'real' pedagogues in a Western democratic sense, it is nevertheless their responsibility to confront their former indoctrinating function (personal communication, 30 September 1998).

Freya Klier, a civil rights champion in East Germany and a member of Schul-Speisung today, is probably the most outspoken critic of GDR teachers. Her fiery condemnation, coupled with her own documented recollections of a difficult GDR childhood, are held up by her critics as proof for what seems like an almost gleeful effort on her part not only to perpetuate the negative image of teachers but to destroy them. Media coverage of her tirade has been, as can be expected, widespread. For those not directly researching the question of teachers' motivation and what the situation in schools in fact is like today, one may indeed be led to believe that *all* schools in the east reject experimentation and change and that all teachers prefer the old authoritarian school atmosphere (*Berliner Zeitung*, 7 October 1997).

The other firestorm set off earlier this year is the work of a west German criminologist, Christian Pfeifer, whose thesis finding a link between the GDR's collective education and today's anti-foreigner violence set off a rash of counter-statements and dismissals. As with Siegmann, Pfeifer claimed that he was only hoping to begin a dialogue on an issue that should not be glossed over by silence (*Sächsische Zeitung*, 25 March 1999). By attacking education in the GDR, he had hit a raw nerve, criticising that very controversial institution that nevertheless remains a point of pride for many in the east:

> *The people in the east are sick of the arrogance of the west German colonial masters*
> *and being treated like second class citizens, and in that very context I dared attack the*
> *holiest of all areas. (Der Tagesspiegel, 31 March 1999; my translation)*

Perhaps more antagonising even than the fact that this critique came from a west German was Pfeifer's quick deduction from a stricter, less individually-centred education system to the warping of young minds into hate-filled aggressors.

Although the accusatory tone of his argument created a public shouting match, the unfortunate results were only more denials and defensiveness (even if understandable), but again, not the successful launching of an objective dialogue. In fact, the most obvious response was that exemplified in the following day's newspaper coverage after Pfeifer's heated public forum in Dresden: in an interview with Saxony's criminal investigations office, youth crime statistics were cited as too minimal to lend Pffeifer's thesis any credibility and with that the debate was dismissed (*Sächsische Zeitung*, 25 March 1999). But the actual issue of East Germany's education system and its aftermath since 1989 that Pfeifer had hoped to raise was for all intents and purposes thereby silenced.

A Sample of East Berlin Teachers: repercussions of research and public debates

In the end it is teachers themselves who are most affected by debates in public; they are the ones who on a daily basis must confront the issues that the media and politicians – usually from the safety of their lofty posts – put into the hands of students and parents to bring to school. One view is that the raising of these issues is precisely what Siegmann, movements like Schul-Speisung, and Pfeifer intend, and that they are courageously pioneering a process of confrontation with the past that is yet in its infancy. The other view, however, is that the broaching of these issues, especially if not done with extreme sensitivity, also has the effect of making schools and teachers feel attacked and recoil into themselves – the opposite of what should be happening. As Aida S., a principal of a *Gymnasium*, expressed it:

> *I think there are mechanisms at work here. I notice it in myself too: If you are constantly criticised and always have to hear again and again how teachers in the GDR didn't learn anything, then you can't help but begin to defend things that in your heart of hearts you never really thought were so good anyway. This is a coping mechanism that just starts to work by itself after a while. (My translation)*

There are many reasons for the firestorms that resulted from comments finding fault with the East German education system, but perhaps among the many (often quite understandable), the two most noticeable would be the following. First, a growing sensitivity on the part of east German teachers who are frustrated at their inability to escape the image of homogeneous, like-minded ideologues and still feel largely disrespected as a professional group for their educational work in the GDR. Veronika V. of the *Realschule* expressed her frustration in the following way:

> *Over the whole decade since the Wende we have lived with professional uncertainty. Would we be able to keep our jobs? Would we be transferred? Do we have to go through another trial period before getting civil servant status? I think that the school senate [in Berlin] did this intentionally. This has caused a lot of discontentment over the past years. This uncertainty is clearly something that the senate purposefully subjected the teachers of the east to just to hit us one more time because they think we were upholders of the system – but you know, there were many ways one could*

'support' the system – and I think that the senate picked special punishment out just for us. (My translation)

Even today, east German teachers in part still wear the scarlet letter of serving the government [16], much as they did in the GDR. Clearly, this issue must be approached cautiously and with sensitivity: the GDR teacher's work as an educator in the best sense of the word deserves to be looked at in an objective and level-headed way. For an accurate picture of the GDR teachers and their legacy, just as their formerly political function should not be ignored, it should also not determine the entire image; those positive elements of their training and experience must also be brought to the surface.

The second consideration is that many teachers feel that while *they* have been open to what has been an overanalysis of their pasts throughout the decade, too often negative conclusions are reached. What also bothers them is that these findings are often determined by observers who never themselves experienced the GDR school and yet claim to know it better. Additionally, as a professional group, teachers feel that they have not been given a voice to tell their own side of the story and thereby balance out a lopsided image. Ulrike U., a principal at a *Realschule*, expressed this well:

> *It bothers me that researchers do studies about the GDR but never experienced it themselves. Discussion forums are set up with people who were never really in the system. Articles are published about us and yet few take the time to really get to know the school from the inside.*

Detlef B., a teacher at a *Realschule*, explained that the barrier most east and west Germans still feel today exists because most people do not bother to leave their 'side' and make the effort to get to know the other more genuinely. Public debates are so inflammatory because suspicion and assumption rules over personal experience. The image of schooling in the east remains negative because it is assumed to be of a certain kind, while in reality it is quite different today:

> *The psychological barrier is in the heads only because we do not know one another yet ... people just don't know us! People who came here were surprised. But then they came out of interest. (My translation)*

Those who feel that teachers remain stuck in those patterns of GDR schooling that are negative will reject whatever teachers say in their defence. Everything will be taken to be an excuse. But the context of the situation as teachers face it must also be understood. One teacher explained that while she is not opposed to a discussion, because all former faculty groupings in Berlin were dispersed to the four different West German school types after 1989, bringing up the past with someone who was not a work colleague during the GDR can hardly be productive. In that sense, it is rather avoided. Heidi E., also at the *Realschule*, rationalised this in the following way:

> *If we had stayed in the same schools after the* Wende *we'd have worked through our past more, but today we are all in separate places so the issue does not come up. None of us knows what the other did, we are all in different groups now. We'd have to*

> *confront one another now but no one does that ... That would be a mistake. (My translation)*

This teacher went on to explain that not only is bringing up the past awkward among a faculty that was newly formed after the *Wende*, but also that since this personal, pre-unification history of friendships is missing among colleagues, a confrontation now would only create further problems. She sees many in the east as having found it easier to forget what they did in the past since it is likely to be negatively interpreted today. Her conviction is that the GDR is not being dealt with openly enough yet, and thus the danger of being misinterpreted is too great. Silence is the safer and easier solution:

> *Most teachers don't even notice today how deeply they were in the system. Me too. Some teachers don't say anything because it gets misinterpreted, not only by 'Wessies' but also by 'Ossies'. (My translation)*

Detlef B., quoted earlier, added that his own confrontation with the past is for him an internal process, but not one which is ready for public discussion yet. The suspicion that remains at this point is neither productively brought up among faculty nor wanted between some teachers and their students. A certain private sphere – as stipulated by the west German teacher's requirements the way the following teacher understands them to be – cannot be overstepped:

> *I mostly try to say what I feel today, but still feel that certain things have to be kept hidden. The state wants the teacher today as a teacher of the lesson content and not to cause a break between school and private life. That's how I see it. (My translation)*

In my own research I have found teachers in the east very open to an exchange about their past roles, in both positive and negative senses, and many of them proud of their contribution to what they feel was very solid education in the GDR. Their disappointment today is not only with what they feel is a less academically challenging west German curriculum, but a generally colder, more self-centred society that no longer has humanistic, child-centred goals at its core. Many teachers today evidence a deep disillusionment with the collapse of the GDR and the beliefs they had invested in the system. Some teachers speak about their work in the GDR as if it had taken place in a haze of sorts and that, for instance, they never realised the extent of the Stasi's deep reach into school matters. Annette K. of the *Hauptschule* represents this well:

> *I have to say that, as a member of the SED, I did not [become a teacher] for career climbing reasons, but really because I believed in the idea of Communism and had gone to work for that cause. For that reason it was bad for me to find out what had gone on in the GDR. There was a lot that I hadn't known or thought existed.*

Their feelings of betrayal and disappointment after 1989 and the revelations of Stasi activity and other abuses of power undertaken in the name of their commitment is clearly expressed. Teachers who admit to having believed in Communism argue that at the same time they still maintained their professional autonomy. For instance, Thea M. of the *Hauptschule*:

I still am convinced today [that the socialist education system had a lot of merit], and I support that opinion openly. In the GDR I also supported that very strongly, but I did not hide away from openly saying in the school that I saw teaching as the primary, main task, and not political education to such an extent that everything is always tied to politics. (My translation)

Overall, the feelings of teachers today, whether seeing more fault or more praise for their old school system in hindsight, are unanimous in their conviction that the opportunities for reform and creative, better schooling were wasted in 1989. Many problems have resulted from putting East Germans into a system they did not have any voice in shaping.

Conclusion

It is understandable that one's own school experience and treatment by the 'other' are clearly contextual factors that have a bearing on the way one remembers and discusses schools and teachers today. Döring's more positively remembered experiences and images gave him a vantage point from which to remember education in the GDR rather differently from, for example, Klier's more negative personal experiences. Although none of the opinion camps as I have sketched them in this chapter (and the collage I have made here certainly does not claim to represent every opinion on the matter) has necessarily won over a representative majority in Germany, my belief is that the middle camp – those who are not yet resolute but still open to considering the questions of continuity and change – offer the best chance for eventually allowing a balanced and constructive judgement in its proper historical context to be made about the successes and failures and rights and wrongs of the GDR. This middle ground might be termed the 'benefit-of-the-doubt' school. For those stretching to either ends of the opinion scale (and this includes research as well as the public domain, even if the former is more subtle than the latter) and either rejecting all teachers as conformist ideologues on the one side or demanding an end to confrontations with the past on the other, it is understandable that if not bound by the conventions of objectivity, most remembering and judging of the GDR today remains too emotionally conflicted and close to the events to be capable yet of finding a suitable balance.

Notes

[1] This research was funded with support from the Bundeskanzler Fellowship of the Alexander-von-Humboldt Foundation, Bonn. I wish to thank Drs Hans Döbert, Gita-Steiner-Khamsi and Christa Händle, respectively, for their contributions.

[2] German: 'neue Bundesländer': East Berlin, Brandenburg, Mecklenburg-Western Pomerania, Saxony, Saxony-Anhalt, and Thuringia.

[3] German: 'The Turning Point' or 'Changing' is the general term used to refer to the unification. The term '*Wende*' (first officially used by Erich Honecker's successor, Egon Krenz), however, remains highly problematic and disputed today, with other designations such as *Zusammenbruch, Anschluß, Kolonializierung, Wiedervereinigung,* and

Vereinigung also in use. *Umbruch* should be used to describe the actual overthrow of the GDR's Government during the 1989/90 'Peaceful Revolution', while the term *Wende* should be used when discussing the adaptation of the GDR's institutions to those of the Federal Republic in the years after 1991 when unification had already been officially established.

[4] German: 'Deutschland, einig Vaterland!'

[5] Willy Brandt, 24 February, 1990: 'vernünftig zusammenwachsen zu lassen, was zusammengehört' (my translation) (as cited in Bahrmann & Links, 1995, II, pp. 7 and 137).

[6] German: '*Ossie*' is an East German; '*Wessie*' a West German. While the second term has been in use since the Berlin Wall was built and referred to those West Germans living in West Berlin, the first term came into use only after 1989. Now the term denotes not only West and East Berliners, but all citizens of former West and East Germany. '*Besserwessie*' is a know-it-all-better West German.

[7] PDS, Party for Democratic Socialism (German: *Partei des demokratischen Sozialismus*); SED, Socialist Unity Party of Germany (German: *Sozialistische Einheitspartei Deutschlands*); SPD, Social Democratic Party of Germany (German: *Sozialdemokratische Partei Deutschlands*).

[8] German: 'Kontinuität und Wandel im Schulwesen der ehemaligen DDR'.

[9] German terms: '*Aufarbeitung der Vergangenheit*' (confronting the past); '*Schlußstrich Mentalität*' (end-the-debate-mentality); '*Nostalgie,*'/'*Ostalgie*' (Nostalgia, or 'East-algia' – the yearning for the old GDR); '*Schwarz-Weißmalerei*' (black/white characterisations), '*rote Socke*' (Communist hanger-on or sympathiser); '*Mauer im Kopf*' (the Wall in the mind); among many other terms.

[10] The 'Gauck Authority' – unofficially so named after its first director, Pastor Joachim Gauck of Rostock, (East) Germany – is officially known as the Federal Authority for the Records of the State Security Service of the former German Democratic Republic and was a federal commission set up in December of 1990 to investigate all files of the secret police (Stasi) (German: *Bundesbeauftragter für die Unterlagen des Staatssicherheitsdienstes der ehemaligen Deutschen Demokratischen Republik*).

[11] In the GDR, schooling was comprehensive and included a unitary 1–10th grade comprehensive 'polytechnical' school (German: POS, '*Polytechnische Oberschule*'), and a highly selective 2-year college preparatory extended secondary school (German: EOS, '*Erweiterte Oberschule*'). The West German school system offers four school 'tracks:' the *Hauptschule* (secondary general school); the *Realschule* (intermediate school); the *Gymnasium* (university-preparatory grammar school) and the *Gesamtschule* (comprehensive school). Each federal state has the autonomy (German: *Länderhoheit*) to structure its own school system with few federally overarching guidelines.

[12] The personnel questionnaire (German: *Personalfragebogen für die Bewerbung um Einstellung als Angestellter oder Arbeiter*) was required after the *Wende* of all former citizens of the GDR seeking governmental employment. The questionnaire was very specific in its probing as to the nature of any kind of work for the State Security Service, including payment received, signatures given and particular assignments carried out, where and for how long.

[13] German: '*Freudenfeuer*'

[14] Literally meaning 'School meal' but symbolic for the everyday 'dishing out' of indoctrination at school.

[15] German: 'Bundeszentrale für politische Bildung'.

[16] German: 'im Staatsdienst ... ein Politikum'.

References

Andert, R. (1993) *Unsere Besten: Die VIP's des Ostens* (Our best: the VIPs of the east). Berlin: Elefanten Press.

Andert, R. (1994) *Rote Wende: Wie die Ossies die Wessies besiegten* (Red turning point: how the Easties conquered the Westies). Berlin: Elefanten Press.

Arbeitsgruppe Bildungsbericht am Max-Planck-Institut für Bildungsforschung (1994) *Das Bildungswesen in der Bundesrepublik Deutschland* (Education in the Federal Republic of Germany). Reinback: Rowohlt.

Bahrmann, H. & Links, C. (1995) *Chronik der Wende I & II* (A chronicle of the turning point I & II). Berlin: Ch. Links Verlag.

Behrendt, W., Knoop, J., Mannschatz, E., Protz, S. & Sladek, H. (1990) Schul- und Bildungsreform in der Diskussion, *Pädagogische Forschung*, 2, pp. 52–62. (Translated and republished in 1991 in *European Education*, 23, pp. 37–50, under the title, 'Discussion of School and Educational Reform'.)

Benner, D., Merkens, H. & Schmidt, F. (1996) *Bildung und Schule im Transformationsprozess von SBZ, DDR und neuen Bundesländern. Untersuchungen zur Kontinuität und Wandel* (Education and schooling undergoing transformation from the Soviet Zone of Occupation, the German Democratic Republic and the New Federal States: studies on continuity and change). Berlin: Zentrale Universitäts Druckerei.

Berliner Zeitung (1997) Krebsgang ins Vertraute (A cancerous path back to the familiar), 7 October.

Berliner Zeitung (1999) Berlin wählt die große Koalition, doch die SPD will noch nicht verhandeln (Berlin chooses the big coalition, but the SPD does not want to deal yet), 11 October.

Biermann, W. (1993) Des Satans Spießgesellen (Satan's Pal), *Der Spiegel*, 49, pp. 42–46.

Billhardt, T. & Hensel, K. (1999) *Alles war so. Alles war anders: Bilder aus der DDR* (Everything was like that. Everything was different: pictures from the GDR). Leipzig: Gustav Kiepenheuer Verlag.

Bohse, C., Klier, F., Siegmann, B., Drieselmann, J., Halt, F. & Hillmer, U. (1997) *Schul-Speisung Press Release*.

Cohen, R. (1999) Nazi and Communist Art Show Angers Germans, *International Herald Tribune*, 19 August.

Dahn, D. (1996) *Westwärts und nicht vergessen: vom Unbehagen in der Einheit* (Head west and don't forget: on the discomfort of unity). Berlin: Rowohlt Verlag.

Dahn, D. (1998) *Vertreibung ins Paradies* (Expelled to paradise). Berlin: Rowohlt Verlag.

Die Welt (1997) In den Klassenzimmern überlebte die Ideologie der SED (The ideology of the SED survived in the classroom, **7** September.

Die Welt (1997) Masse der Lehrer war auf SED-Kurs (Masses of teachers were in line with the SED), 12 September.

Der Spiegel (1997) Krach im Osten (Trouble in the east), 28 July.

Der Tagesspiegel (1998) Und der Lehrer ist immer schuld (And it's always the teacher's fault), 7 June.

Der Tagesspiegel (1999) Angriff auf das Allerheiligste (Attack on the holiest of all), 31 March.

Döbert, H. (1997) Lehrerberuf und Lehrerbildung (The teaching profession and teacher training), *Zeitschrift für Pädagogik*, 37, pp. 333–356.

Döbert, H. (1998) Changes in Schooling: results of research in transformation in Germany. Presentation at the World Congress of Comparative Education Societies, Cape Town, South Africa, June 1998.

Döbert, H. & Rudolf, R. (1995) Lehrerberuf – Schule – Unterricht: Einstellungen, Meinungen und Urteile ostdeutscher Lehrerinnen und Lehrer: Ergebnisse einer empirischen Untersuchung in Berlin-Ost, Brandenburg und Sachsen (The teaching profession, school, classroom teaching: attitudes, opinions and judgements of eastern German teachers: results of an empirical study in eastern Berlin, Brandenburg and Saxony). Frankfurt am Main: Deutsches Institut für Internationale Pädagogische Forschung.

Döring, V. (1996) *Fröhlich sein und singen: Schule vor der Wende.* (Rejoice and sing: school before the turning point). Berlin: Dietz Verlag.

Dümcke, W. & Vilmar, F. (1998) *Kolonialisierung der DDR* (Colonisation of the GDR). Münster: Agenda Verlag.

Engler, W. (1999) *Die Ostdeutschen: Kunde von einem verlorenen Land* (The East Germans: bearing witness to a lost country). Berlin: Aufbau-Verlag.

Ensikat, P. (1998) *Hat es die DDR überhaupt gegeben?* (Was there even a GDR?). Berlin: Eulenspiegel Verlag.

Focus (1997) Tyrranei der Altkader (Tyranny of the old guard), no. 46.

Frankfurter Rundschau (1999) PDS fordert 'Schluβstrich' (PDS wants an end to the debate), 23 August.

Gaus, G. (1998) *Kein einig Vaterland* (Not a united fatherland). Berlin: Edition Ost.

Händle, C. (1998a) Kritik der Ost-West Beziehung als Dominanzbeziehung (A critique of the east–west relationship as a relationship of dominance), in M. von Lutzau (Ed.) *Frauen Kreativität macht Schule.* Weinheim: Deutscher Studien Verlag.

Händle, C. (1998b) Kontinuität und Wandel im Bildungssystem der neuen Bundesländer (NBL) und der Berliner Ostbezirke. Eine Skizze (Continuity and change in the education systems of the new federal states) (unpublished manuscript).

Hartmann, R. (1999) *Mit der DDR ins Jahr 2000* (With the GDR into the year 2000). Berlin: Karl Dietz Verlag.

Hennings, A. (1997) Es war doch nicht alles schlecht (But not everything was so bad), *Das Magazine*, 9.

Hinke, B. (1991) Herausforderung: Konfrontation oder Begegnung der Bildungssysteme zwischen Ost und West? *Katholische Bildung*, 5, pp. 257–271.
(Translated and republished in 1991 in *European Education*, 23, pp. 74–96, under the title, 'A Challenge: confrontation or encounter between the educational systems of east and west?')

ISF-Umfrage (1992, 1994, 1996) Die Schule im Spiegelbild der Öffentlichen Meinung (School as reflected in public opinion), in H.G. Rolf (Ed.) *Jahrbuch der Schulentwicklung*. Weinheim: Juventa.

Klier, F. (1990) *Lüg Vaterland: Erziehung in der DDR (Deceitful Fatherland: Education in the GDR)*. München: Kindler Varlag.

Klier, F. (1997) ASTAK Open Letter, January (no date given).

Luft, C. (1994) *Die nächste Wende kommt bestimmt* (The next turning point will definitely come). Berlin: Aufbau Taschenbuch Verlag.

Maaz, H-J. (1991) *Das gestürtzte Volk: Die unglückliche Einheit* (The fallen people: the unhappy union). Berlin: Argon Verlag.

Mangelsdorf, F. (1999) Sprachlose Opfer und Täter (Speechless victims and persecutors), *Berliner Morgenpost*, 9 January, Internet archive.

Mintrop, H. (1996) Teachers and Changing Authority Patterns in Eastern German Schools, *Comparative Education Review*, 28, pp. 45–52.

Mintrop, H. & Weiler, H. (1994) The Relationship between Educational Policy and Practice: the reconstitution of the college-preparatory *Gymnasium* in East Germany, *Harvard Educational Review*, 64, pp. 247–277.

Mitter, W. (1992) Educational Adjustments and Perspectives in United Germany, *Comparative Education*, 28, pp. 45–52.

Pfeifer, Christian (1999) Anleitung zum Haβ (Instructed to hate), *Der Speigel*, 12, pp. 60–66.

Rathenow, L. & Hauswald, H. (1990). *Berlin-Ost: Die andere Seite einer Stadt* (East Berlin: the other half of a city). Berlin: Basis Druck.

Röhl, E. (1996) *Wenn's mal weider anders kommt* (When it comes round differently next time). Berlin: Eulenspiegel Verlag.

Röhl, E. & Jankofsky, H. (1999) *Zehn Jahre sind zu viel!* (Ten years are too long!) Berlin: Eulenspiegel Verlag.

Rust, V. & Rust, D. (1995) *The Unification of German Education*. New York: Garland Publishing.

Sächsische Zeitung (1999) Provokationen und Emotionen (Provocation and Emotion), 28 March.

Schnabel, K., Baumert, J. & Röder, P. (1996) Zum Wandel des Schulsystems in den neven Bundesländern (On the Changes in the School System in the New Federal States). *Neve Sammlung*, 4, pp. 531-544.

Schönherr, A. (Ed.) (1992) *Ein Volk am Pranger? Die deutschen auf der Suche nach einer neuen politischen Kultur* (A people in the stocks? The Germans in search of a new political culture). Berlin: Aufbau Taschenbuch Verlag.

Schorlemmer, F. (1998) *Eisige Zeiten: Ein Pamphlet* (Ice cold times: a pamphlet). München: Siedler Taschenbuch.

Stadtmuseum Dresden (1999) Brochure from the exhibit, *Die andere Vergangenheit: 40 Jahre Leben in der DDR* (The other past: 40 years of life in the GDR).

Statistisches Bundesamt. Fachserie 1, Heft 3, *Entgültige Ergebnisse nach Wahlkreisen* (Final results per voting district), 1994, 1998.

Streitwieser, B. (1999) Some Thoughts on Post-*Wende* Pedagogical Adjustments, in T. Mebrahtu, M. Crossley & D. Johnson (Eds) *Educational Reconstruction and Transformation in Europe*, Bristol Papers in Education. Oxford: Symposium Books.

Streitwieser, B. (2000) Lehrersein vor und nach dem Fall der Berliner Mauer: Lehrer aus Prenzlauer Berg berichten von ihren Erfahrungen und Eindrücken vor und nach 1989 (Being a teacher before and after the fall of the Berlin Wall: teachers from Prenzlauer Berg share their experiences and impressions before and after 1989), in Bernt Roder & Klaus Grosinski (Eds) *Begleitbuch für die Ausstellung zur Geschichte der Schulen im Bezirk Prenzlauer Berg*. Berlin: Prenzlauer Berg Museum für Heimatgeschichte und Stadtkultur.

Tillmann, K-J. (1996) Von der Kontinuität, die nicht auffällt – Das ostdeutsche Schulsystem im übergang von der DDR zur BRD (On the unnoticeable continuity: the eastern German school system in the transition from the GDR to the FRG), in Wolfgang Melzer & Uwe Sandfuchs (Eds) *Schulreform in der Mitte der 90er Jahre*. Opladen: Leske & Budrich.

Unser Schwerin (1997) Wo doch früher weiss Gott nicht alles schlecht war (God knows! Everything before was not worse), 12 November.

Weiler, H., Mintrop H. & Fuhrmann, H. (1996) *Educational Change and Social Transformation: teachers, schools and universities in eastern Germany*. London: Falmer Press.

Zedler, P. & Weishaupt, H. (1996) *Kontinuität und Wandel: Thüringer Schulen im Urteil von Schülern, Lehrern und Eltern* (Continuity and change: Thuringia schools as judged by students, teachers and parents). Weinheim: Deutscher Studien Verlag.

Retraining Language Teachers in Mecklenburg-West Pomerania, 1992–96: experiences of a British instructor

KAREN GALTRESS-HÖRL

Introduction

The political and economic repercussions of German reunification are well documented. The no less significant consequences of unification on the secondary education system of the former German Democratic Republic (GDR) and, more importantly, their impact on the future of English as a foreign language (EFL) teaching in state schools also deserve such close attention and continuing discussion. This chapter briefly summarises foreign language teaching in the GDR pre-1991 (after which the new school structure and syllabuses were officially introduced), then describes the *Nachqualifizierung* (retraining) programme for teachers initiated by the Ministry of Education in Mecklenburg-West Pomerania (*KM-Erlaß*, 1991, issued on 16 July 1991 Decree from the Minister of Education), highlighting EFL courses, and finally presents a critical appraisal of the programme, pointing to future difficulties which may arise in the teaching of EFL in Mecklenburg-West Pomeranian schools.

Foreign Language Teaching in the GDR

The first year when *Abitur* (18+ examination and university entrance requirement) pupils had been taught English continually from the first year of secondary school (class 5: age 10+) onwards was 1999. Now seems an appropriate point to look back at a time when this notion would have been considered fantastical, to a time before the secondary education system and curricula of the former GDR were remodelled along west German lines. Although both English and French *were* taught in GDR schools, Russian was the first compulsory foreign language for all pupils from class 5 to 12. In addition, Russian was taught in approximately 200 schools in class 3 (primary school). Understandably, therefore, Russian foreign language teaching methodology, applied linguistic research and syllabuses played an important role in the development of EFL pre-unification. Böhme (1985) describes a typical Russian lesson in the 1960s as starting with the introduction of lexis and grammar, then reading (aloud) and translating the textbook passage and finally, a retelling of the content of the passage. Transfer/application phases of lessons, and personalised exercises were rare. Despite significant developments in the late 1960s, which led to greater emphasis being placed on practical and communicative language skills, a perusal of the syllabuses for Russian of that time shows that the teaching of grammar was overt, deductive and carried more weight than functional and communicative activities (cf. 1987 syllabus for Russian: Ministerium für Volksbildung, 1987).

In his 1992 article on the teaching of modern languages and German unification, Klapper states that both English and French foreign language methodologies were modelled on Russian foreign language teaching, and that this 'had serious consequences for the "minority languages"' (1992, p. 240). He goes on to illustrate some of the key problem areas these 'minority languages' faced: a heavily structural syllabus, only three lessons a week and those only in the afternoon, target language (in)authenticity, an absence of stimulating pictures in course books, and the unavailability of realia with which to motivate learners. This contrasts greatly with the approaches in western Europe at the time, which were focusing on functional/notional syllabuses, the development of a communicative orientation in classroom activities, the aim of using (only) authentic target language texts, and on the emphasis on meaning rather than form. Another major difference can be seen in the GDR belief in the usefulness of applying contrastive analysis, and in the employment of translation (both into and from the foreign language) as a suitable learning exercise; both of these were losing/had already lost favour in the west.

Despite revised syllabuses for English which focused more on communicative intent, and the introduction of a television series, *English for You*, EFL teaching immediately pre-*Wende* was still heavily influenced by Russian foreign language methodology. The *Wende* in 1989 threw the education system of the GDR into confusion. It took until 1 August 1991 for this education system to be given a new structure. With effect from this date, the five newly constituted *Neue Länder* (new federal states) were given the right to select some combination of the *Gesamtschule* (comprehensive school) or three-tiered *Haupt- und Realschule, Gymnasium* (selective secondary school) systems. Foreign language teaching was also deeply affected by the *Wende*: 'Foreign languages were among the first to feel the effects of pupils' sense of liberty and their rejection of everything that smacked of the old order' (Klapper 1992, p. 241). Some educationists even argued for the abolition of all foreign language teaching. However, on 1 September 1990, suggestions made by the 'Foreign Language Round Table' were taken up. The group had recommended that the range of foreign languages on offer should be enlarged, that all pupils should learn one compulsory foreign language (English or Russian or French) and that they should have the option of learning a minimum of one further foreign language. From 1990–91, approximately 85% of all class 5 pupils elected to learn English as the first foreign language. One obvious result of this was a superfluity of teachers of Russian, and the logical knock-on effect was a lack of teachers of English.

The *Nachqualifizierung* Programme in Mecklenburg-West Pomerania

After unification and the resultant restructuring of schools and syllabuses, over 3000 teachers in Mecklenburg-West Pomerania found that their professional qualifications were in some way lacking. As in the other four new federal states, a *Nachqualifizierungsmaßnahme* (retraining scheme) was devised to qualify five different categories of teachers whose qualifications were in some way affected by unification. (cf. *KM-Erlaß*, 1991) However, in effect, it is possible to divide the teachers concerned into two main groups. The first were either teachers of subjects specific to the GDR curriculum, for example, *Staatsbürgerkunde* (civics), and which were therefore obsolete post-unification; or, quite simply, teachers who had only ever taught one subject, for example, physical education. These teachers were obliged by the Ministry of Education to retrain (*KM-Erlaß*, 1991). The second group were those whose '*Fach in der Stundentafel rückläufig ist*' (school subject no longer has as many lessons on the timetable) (*KM-Erlaß*, 1991).

Una Dirks describes the situation for this second group in the following way:

> *In view of the great need for teachers of English, no small number of teachers, who were worried about losing their jobs, said they were willing to teach English although they were not qualified to do so, and endeavoured to retrain in this subject. (1996, p. 3; my translation)*

It is estimated that in some areas in the GDR immediately post-*Wende*, up to 70% of teachers of English were non-graduates in the subject (Seifert, 1990). These teachers were given the chance to take part in a 3-year retraining programme which would give them a teaching qualification in a further, i.e. third, subject. It comes as no surprise that 80% of the Mecklenburg-West Pomeranian *Nachqualifizierung* (*NQ*) trainees for English were teachers of Russian. Prior to starting the *NQ* programme, over 50% of the *NQ* trainees were already teaching English.

Both groups of teachers had two things in common. Firstly, they had a basic existential need to obtain a certificate in a second or third subject. Without it, they would either have been unemployable, or would not have been able to teach a full timetable. Secondly, from a political perspective, they were a minefield. Many teachers had already been made redundant because of the restructuring and past political allegiances, and in a state where the unemployment rate was already high, adding over another 3000 would have amounted to political suicide. A total of 3239 teachers in Mecklenburg-West Pomerania participated in retraining programmes in various subjects This figure certainly reflects the natural desire to secure their future, and the effectiveness of extrinsic motivation.

The *LISA* (*Landesinstitut Mecklenberg-Vorpommern für Schule und Ausbildung*) prospectus (1994) describes the *NQ* programme for English thus:

> *On the basis of the Decree regarding the qualification of working teachers, the retraining programme is a one-off exception caused by historical events. For this reason a primarily* pragmatic approach *must be chosen when solving the problem. This approach must satisfy the needs of the schools, the pupils, the parents and the teachers alike. (My translation; italics in original)*

The fact that the *LISA* states that the exceptional situation called for a pragmatic approach is, to my mind, very realistic. The unanswered, and possibly unanswerable, question is to what extent the *NQ* necessarily had to be as public-spirited a programme as it, in my opinion, was. Given the unique nature of the *NQ* programme, that some compromises were necessary is undisputed. What concerns me is whether the compromises made in such an intrinsically expedient programme could be justified, given that the effects on EFL teaching are of a long-term nature. This concern is expressed in the following section.

A plethora of institutes, including the Universities of Rostock and Greifswald, the *LISA*, west German teacher training institutes and distance learning schools, were responsible for the state-wide retraining programmes for the subjects outlined in Table I.

Subjects	Number of trainees
Modern languages	742
Social studies	650
Primary school	406
Special needs	340
Information technology	250
Philosophy	235
Religious education	201
Careers	127
Art	111
Geography	100
Music	47
History	30
Total	3239

Table I. Source: *LISA NQ Handreichung* 1994 (1994 Brochure provided by *LISA* containing global information regarding the *NQ* programme).

The *LISA* was jointly responsible for retraining 492 teachers in English, and solely responsible for retraining 322 of these. As head of English teacher training at the Güstrow Institute for Teacher Training, one of five regional *LISA* outposts, I was directly involved in the two retraining courses (1992–95 and 1993–96). Both 3-year courses comprised 1000 hours – 50% compulsory courses and 50% study at home *'mit dem Ziel der Lehrbefähigung für Haupt- und Realschulen'* (with the aim of qualifying trainees to teach in 11–16 secondary schools).

I came to Güstrow in August 1993, one year after the first (1992–95) *NQ* course had started. Lessons in that first year had focused exclusively on developing general language skills. The *LISA NQ* syllabus describes this course as follows

> *In the first year intensive language courses will be held (eight lessons a week each term). These aim at the trainees attaining a language competence level which corresponds to Cambridge First Certificate (CFC) – minimum (8 SWS). (My translation)*

So, in that first year, the *NQ* trainees had attended a block lesson of 3 hours every week for 35 weeks (which corresponds to two university terms). Although the course is described as comprising *8 SWS* (8 x 45 minutes), in fact, four of these lessons were not class time, but rather time allotted for homework tasks. This means that after the first year, the trainees had actually had a total of 105 contact hours plus the time necessary for homework tasks. Although most students had already been taught English at school, for some, this experience lay a long way back in the past, and it would be justifiable to describe these trainees as false beginners. The courses were often crassly mixed-ability. Whereas some trainees only had a rudimentary knowledge of English, others were already teaching English in school (some in higher level classes, too). At this juncture, it is essential to point out that there had been *no* linguistic selection procedure prior to the *NQ* course starting, and that there were *no* courses run at different ability levels. A lack of native-speaker trainer staff, the sheer size of the state of Mecklenburg-West Pomerania, and the necessity of qualifying the trainees as expediently as possible meant that most of the intensive language courses had been held by *StudienleiterInnen* (non-native-speaker teacher trainers of English) from the *LISA* at the various outposts. This situation changed in the autumn of 1994 when 20 native-speaker trainers of EFL arrived (a project sponsored by the British Council in conjunction with the University of Manchester). However, up until that time, the majority of courses were held by non-native-speakers.

At the end of the first year (in October 1993), there was a centralised examination to test linguistic competence. Shortly before this examination, I took over a group of *NQ* trainees from a colleague. This was my first contact with *NQ* students. Despite 5 years' previous experience in adult education and teacher training, I had never before met such nervous and frustrated students. These emotions were understandable; I would have felt the same had I been at their level of English and had the examination been truly of a Cambridge First Certificate standard. It was not; and consequently most students passed. To my mind, this low standard, and there having been no entrance examination, was where many of the problems experienced in later courses originated.

The examination at the end of the first year comprised listening and reading comprehension, and a free writing component. There was no oral examination. In my opinion, the focus of the test was at odds with one of the most important aims of the *LISA NQ* programme described in its own syllabus as:

> *The most important aim (of the retraining programme) is to ensure that the students attain good* oral *and written linguistic abilities. (My translation and emphasis)*

In fact, there were no compulsory state-wide oral examinations in the *NQ* course until the final at the end of the 3 years. And yet, surely oral competence (especially adequate pronunciation) and confidence in one's ability to apply the foreign language are the very basic tools necessary when standing in front of a class teaching a foreign language? A colleague in Chemnitz-Zwickau, training on a similar *NQ* programme there, described fossilised pronunciation problems he had to deal with as *irreparabel* (irreparable). Certainly, trainees' spoken English skills often left something to be desired. Such problems could, however, have been rectified in many cases had there been greater emphasis on productive language skills in the syllabus and had trainees been required to spend a period of time in an English-speaking country. This was not a compulsory element of the *NQ*. A minimum of 3 weeks abroad was only mentioned in the *LISA* syllabus as *vorgesehen* (planned). A large percentage of the *NQ* trainees were working mothers. Their family obligations meant that for many an extended period away was impossible to organise and language school courses were prohibitively expensive. However, some trainees did manage to travel to the United Kingdom, most doing so immediately before their final examination.

In terms 3 and 4 of the *NQ* 1992–95 course, the trainees had to deal with the following:

1. *Literature:* one twentieth-century play (for example, *Death of a Salesman*), two novels (for example, *Lord of the Flies, Animal Farm*), and a selection of modern poetry. In addition to these texts, which were dealt with explicitly in class, the trainees were expected to have read a minimum of 10 complete texts (novels and/or plays) by the end of the sixth term. The *LISA* syllabus describes the aims of the literature course as:

> *Various theories of literary criticism are to be shown and genre-specific methods of interpretation to be elaborated using selected works of literature (novels, plays, lyric poetry and short epic texts). The following aspects are of particular importance.*
>
> *i. Comparison: immanent interpretation/sociocultural interpretation*
>
> *ii. Genre-specific characteristics of structure and style*
>
> *iii. Adaptations (e.g. film versions)*
>
> *iv. Comparison with literary works on similar topics. (My translation)*

2. *Landeskunde* (cultural studies): current affairs and historical background in the USA (a course referred to by insiders as: 'Columbus to Clinton') and the United Kingdom – in fact, the whole of the English-speaking world.
3. *Linguistics:* varieties of English, 'modern English' and word formation.
4. *General Language Development:* only two 45-minute lessons a term, aimed at improving receptive skills.
5. *Methodology:* a discussion of problems which occur(red) in EFL classes.

All these courses were held in English and were essentially of a workshop character. The trainees were required to write extended essays and projects in English about literature and cultural studies; there were regular end of term examinations (2–5 hours in duration), and otherwise, testing was done by continuous assessment. On the whole, examinations were not centralised and were usually of a teach–test nature. It was also possible for students to retake an examination if they failed. In one case, it was even possible for students to fail a second time, but to pass overall.

The fifth and sixth terms were similarly structured and concluded with a final written paper and an oral examination. A debate about the suitability of the syllabus here would go beyond the parameters of this chapter. The compulsory elements of the course, listed earlier, merely demonstrate the dramatic linguistic leap required of the trainees after having passed a language examination which was lower than Cambridge First Certificate. As is so often the case, classroom reality was far more pragmatic than the eloquent aims stated in the syllabus. However, with the *NQ* course, this clash of stated aims and training/learning reality was saddening. Many trainees, especially those who had had problems passing the linguistic competence examination after term 2, struggled to understand the literature and the cultural studies texts. Consequently, a lot of classroom time was spent working on the level of basic primary text comprehension rather than on interpretation and critical analysis, the latter being what was expected.

Critical Appraisal of the *NQ* Programme

The following are just a few instances of the chalk-face realities of the *Nachqualifizierung*; it was a programme which involved far more than just the teaching and learning of a new language. Perhaps a portrait of an average *NQ* trainee will be illuminating: female, over 40, married, a mother, a qualified teacher of Russian and one other subject. She had spent some time in the Soviet Union, was an experienced teacher and had enjoyed a relative amount of status and security in GDR society. In addition to the natural frustrations which arise when people are faced by a challenge they have difficulties meeting, the *NQ* trainees often verbalised resentment that they had to retrain at all. Indeed, it must have been strange for them. Whilst retraining, all the trainees were still teaching (albeit a reduced timetable), and, as mentioned earlier, 50% were actually already teaching English. So, on the one hand, they had a certain amount of status and standing in the changing and changed world, and had already been considered able to teach English by the headteacher of their respective schools. However, on the other hand, compared to their colleagues who taught, for example, German, mathematics, or natural sciences, the *NQ* trainees were disempowered, back at school, having to spend a lot of time at home reading and doing homework. They had to give up weekends and even some school holidays for block seminars. This they resented.

Additionally, the status of EFL in schools became greatly enhanced after the fall of the Berlin Wall; and, for some teachers of Russian it was difficult to see their once high-status subject being so relegated and rejected. Klapper reports that in 1989:

> *initially large numbers [of students] stayed away from Russian classes and there were*
> *even isolated cases of pupils attacking their Russian teachers, then in the following*
> *year, when Russian became optional alongside English and French in classes 5 and*
> *7, the vast majority of pupils who had the choice abandoned the subject altogether.*
> *(1992, p. 241)*

For me, the *NQ* trainees can be seen as educational soldiers 'doing battle' with a new subject. The political changes had made them sign up. Although they had already been through a university programme, they were now, many years later, in the position of 'freshers' again. They fought on many fronts simultaneously and were confronted by their own limitations as learners. One trainee described her *NQ* group in the following way: '*Wir bestehen zu 90% aus Angst*' (90% of what makes us up is fear). Their battlefield was anything but uncomplicated. Generally speaking, all of the *NQ* trainees were fighting for an existence which they had already once enjoyed. Even those who were still teaching a reduced timetable (with, or without English) were frightened about west German English teachers who might take their jobs away from them before they had finished the *NQ* course. One trainee described his perception of the situation (1993) in this way (the language used is a true transcription):

> *I think it is better for me to finish this language course. ... I thought my knowledge*
> *were better, but I have been recognised that the level is to differnd in our group ... My*
> *decision has got varied reasons. One of them is political too. I won't that my minister*
> *say in 5 years to me, 'Mr X, we have many new English teacher from West Germany*
> *or from the university. They are more better than you, you can go'. Then I have got a*
> *half professional and a half salary. Moreover we are discriminate against about the*
> *west German teacher for the next years. In the language subjects is this may be okay,*
> *but in the other subjects, I don't know?*

The trainees also 'fought' the appropriateness of such a literature-based syllabus, arguing that in *Haupt- und Realschulen* (secondary schools, years 5–10) no literature is taught. Moreover, many trainees realised their own language skills were lacking and pleaded for more practical language work. Unfortunately, due to the constraints put on the *NQ* syllabus, it was not possible to alter the weighting of the programme. One trainee wrote me a lengthy, very personal letter describing the emotional problems she was having with the topics contained in *Animal Farm* – indeed, a very insensitive choice of book (which had been censored in the GDR). I also received angry letters, threats of legal action (after having failed a candidate), and letters and cards written by classes apologising for their behaviour. For instance:

> *By unloading our fears on you I think that we created an unpleasant working*
> *atmosphere in the seminar on Saturday. This set me thinking, and I would like to*
> *apologise. (My translation)*

Some trainees who were history teachers found the cultural studies courses disturbing as they were receiving information that was diametrically opposed to what they had been taught and had been teaching for years. As Klapper states, 'the countries where the target languages (English and French) were spoken belonged to the camp of the ideological enemy' (1992, p. 240). Many trainees also articulated their fears of not having a 'right' answer to be learnt off by heart and then regurgitated in an examination – they had had to learn a lot off by heart in their Russian lessons, and still applied this method in their own lessons (*Gedächtnis-Training* – memory training). Here I would like to quote a section from a letter I received from a *NQ* student shortly before a *Landeskunde* (cultural studies) examination in 1994. She wrote:

> *Contradiction promotes development! K. Marx once said. But what will most of the students in our group do? They will learn the cultural studies and essay-writing information off by heart. I will do so, too. But that's wrong! You can only really remember things that you use constantly and learn, can't you?*

In addition, and again for historical reasons, trainees reacted strongly to a grade lower than a *drei* (three: satisfactory). In short, they were confronted (bombarded?) with completely new ways of learning and evaluation.

Whilst training three *NQ* groups, I also trained on a parallel programme: the *Referendariat* (2-year teaching practice to qualify as a state school teacher). The groups of *ReferendarInnen* (student teachers) had studied English at (east or west German) universities for a minimum of 4 years, and during their 2-year postgraduate teaching practice concentrated on language teaching methodology. These 20+-year-olds were required to attend regular methodology seminars in the target language, there were also regular observations – both non-graded and graded (continuous assessment), and the student teachers had to write an extended essay on EFL teaching methodology which included critical reflections on an experimental teaching unit. Their final examination involved a 'one-off' graded lesson in both subjects, and an oral examination concerning subject methodology, pedagogics and the legal aspects of teaching. This training programme was both rigorous and practical. Most of the student teachers enjoyed experimenting with new methodologies, were innovative, developed their own materials, showed an ability to select appropriate procedures, and were highly reflective; and their teaching skills developed considerably over the 2 years.

Let us now return to the *NQ* programme. There were methodology courses here, too. Unfortunately, they had nothing of the rigour, nor the practical nature, of those during the *Referendariat*. There were *no* observed lessons, *no* graded lessons; just input seminars (and some peer group teaching). Admittedly, from a logistical point of view, it would have been difficult to organise observations, and perhaps for some trainees such observations might have evoked unhappy memories, but it certainly would not have been impossible (video-recordings, for example).

There were three major problem areas in the methodology classes, which were often emotional battlefields. Firstly, even if the trainees accepted that they needed assistance with the 'what' of a new language, trying to teach the teachers of Russian the 'how' was often viewed as an impertinence. It was as though the last section of historical carpet was being pulled from beneath them. The second issue was the trainees' own level of English competence. Often, in a peer group teaching session – all ungraded – the language input they presented to the class was inaccurate. Once this was discovered, some trainees resorted to writing a script based on instructions from the teacher's handbook and learning the peer group lesson off by heart. This links in with the third problem, namely, that it was very difficult to wean them off the teacher's book. Apart from the fact that using a teacher's book is the safe option when a novice teacher lacks methodological expertise, possibly this habit was also a historical legacy as both the GDR syllabuses and the accompanying *Erläuterungen der Lehrpläne* (explanatory notes) were very prescriptive and meticulously detailed. Perhaps they had left the GDR teacher of Russian with little room for innovation or personal interpretation. Unfortunately, as the following extract from a trainee's extended essay on methodology painfully demonstrates, my endeavours to encourage innovation failed:

> *The first English lesson – year 5 (the pupils are 11–12 years old)*

> *The teacher organises things so that he enters the classroom at the beginning of the lesson. Perhaps he has already been standing close to the classroom door, telling pupils how to behave. When he comes into the classroom, all the pupils will be standing at their desks. He enters the room and greets the pupils with the word 'Hi', if possible he accompanies this greeting with an appropriate gesture. By repeating the greeting, he is certain to obtain a choral answer from the class. Then he greets the class with the word 'Hello', to which they answer. By moving both arms downwards and by sitting down himself, the teacher assists the pupils' understanding of the instruction 'Sit down'. (My translation)*

Conclusions and Future Considerations

To my mind, sadly, the two potentially most significant (and ultimately most practical) aspects of the retraining programme, English language competence and modern language methodology, were both woefully underemphasised. Although by the end of the 3-year programme many trainees had attained an (upper?) intermediate level of English, I remain unconvinced that they had internalised new teaching methodologies, although perhaps some were prepared to do so. How is it possible to gather merely from an extended essay on methodology whether a trainee is able to teach English? Other, classroom-oriented criteria were used for the *ReferendarInnen*; surely it would only have been fair to apply similar norms to the *Nachqualifizierung* trainees –more especially so, as most of the *NQ* graduates are in work, teaching English in *Haupt- and Realschulen*, whereas many of the *ReferendarInnen* are unemployed.

In my opinion, many of the problems both trainers and trainees had with the *NQ* programme were the result of an inappropriate syllabus. This is a fact for which the *LISA* cannot be held responsible. I can only hope that it was possible for the *Landesinstitut* to optimise the syllabus and remove at least some of the glaringly irrelevant components of it for the two subsequent retraining courses for English it ran, one for primary school teachers, and a 1-year introductory course for *Englisch-Lehrer an Berufsschulen* (teachers of English at vocational schools).

I also hope that the *LISA* has been able to establish a support network for its *NQ* graduates to assist them in improving both their linguistic and methodological skills. The *NQ* trainees were most definitely a special (exceptional?) group; they remain such as graduates. Consequently, their teacher training needs are of a different nature from those of other teachers of English in Mecklenburg-West Pomerania. Despite the pragmatic approach taken, I believe we did not design a course that truly catered for the chalk-face needs of the *NQ* trainees, and, by failing to do so, we have done a disservice to many school pupils in the state. On the other hand, the *LISA*, as a relatively autonomous postgraduate teacher training institute, would be in a position to design a special *Nach-Nachqualifizierungmaßnahme* (post-retraining scheme*)* which would be tailor-made to the needs of its *NQ* graduates.

References

Böhme, Günter (1985) Vierzig Jahre Russischunterricht an den Schulen unsweres Landes (1), *Fremdsprachenunterricht*, 29, pp. 465–471.

Dirks, Una (1996) Lehrerinnenbiographien im Umbruch, *Fakultät für Geistes-, Sozial- und Erzeihungswissenschaften, Magdeburg. Preprint No. 2.*

Klapper, John (1992) German Unification and the Teaching of Modern Languages, *Comparative Education,* 28, pp. 235–247.

Kultusministerium des Landes Mecklenburg-Vorpommern (1991) Erster Erlaß zur Qualifikation tätiger Lehrer an öffentlichen Schulen des Landes Mecklenburg-Vorpommern, VII, 205–330.30.3.

Kultusministerium des Landes Mecklenburg-Vorpommern (1991) Richtline zur Ausgestaltung der Ergänzungs- und Erweiterungsstudiengänge, VII, 205–330.30.31.

Kultusministerium des Landes Mecklenburg-Vorpommern (1993) Vorläufige Ordnung der Staatsprüfung für Lehrämter auf der Grundlage des Ersten Erlasses zur Qualifikation tätiger Lehrer an öffentlichen Schulen des Landes Mecklenburg-Vorpommern, VII, 202–321–7.42.

Landesinstitut Mecklenburg-Vorpommern für Schule und Ausbildung (1994) Nachqualifizierung für tätige Lehrer im Fach Englisch mit dem Ziel der Lehrbefähigung für Haupt- und Realschulen – eine Handreichung.

Landesinstitut Mecklenburg-Vorpommern für Schule und Ausbildung (1994) Studienpläne für die Nachqualifizierung Englisch 1992–1995 and 1993–1996.

Ministerium für Volksbildung (1987) Lehrplan des zehnklassigen allgemeinbildenden polytechnischen Oberschule – Russisch, *Fremdsprachenunterricht*, 31, pp. 545–576.

Seifert, J. (1990) Beitrag zum Forum *Fremdsprachenunterricht und Lehrerausbildung in Bayern, Sachsen und Thüringen anläßlich des FMF-Landesverbandstages.*

The Transformation of Higher Education and Research in Eastern Germany: a review 10 years after the *Wende* [1]

NINA ARNHOLD

Introduction

This chapter aims to develop some aspects of the transformation of higher education and research in eastern Germany from the perspective of 10 years after the *Wende*. The events of 1989/90 continue to be a point of reference in the political discussions of today. Newspapers still report the transfer of substantial amounts of public money to the eastern part of the unified Federal Republic, the wages in many professions continue to be lower in the east, and the discussion on how to deal with protagonists of the old regime continues. Most observers view the process of German unification as a success story with minor flaws. However, can the transformation of higher education and research in eastern Germany be seen in the same light? This chapter sets out to describe some aspects of the transition process in order to answer this question. It devotes some attention to the Science Council, an advisory body which can be seen as one of the key players in this context.

The terms 'transition' and 'transformation' are sometimes used synonymously. However, what transition means in the context of this chapter is a special form of transformation, namely a 'set of interdependent economic, political and social reforms' (Bîrzea, 1994, p. 12) which were applied in some countries of eastern and central Europe in the late 1980s and continued in the 1990s.[2] It is difficult to say when exactly this reform process comes to an end, i.e. when the transition is complete. Overoptimistically, some expected the change of mentalities to keep pace with the changes of institutions. Ten years after the turning point of 1989, most observers are more realistic. Bîrzea suggests making a distinction between institutional transition and cultural transition. Whereas a thorough reform of institutions can be realised within a rather limited period, cultural transition is a more complex process which needs significantly more time.

> *In general, analyses ... have focused exclusively on institutional transitions, that is on setting up the three pillars of the new social order: political pluralism, the rule of law and a market economy. These transformations, while significant, cannot stand alone.* Cultural transition – *the changing of mentalities, attitudes, values and social relations* – *is a more delicate matter. The institutional transition may last five to six years, whereas the cultural transition could take at least a generation. (Bîrzea, 1996, p. 674)*

Despite obvious similarities, especially as far as the point of departure – that is the authoritarian socialist state – is concerned, the process of transition in east Germany differs greatly from that of other states of the former socialist bloc. The main reason can be seen in the role of the 'external actor', the Federal Republic (FRG), which began to determine the future political structure of eastern Germany soon after the German Democratic Republic (GDR) started to corrode. That this course, towards unification of the two parts of Germany, was backed by the majority of the people in the east became evident in the first free elections in eastern Germany in March 1990. Whereas the other former socialist countries had to find their way, in respect to a democratic state and market economy, within Germany, structures just had to be transferred with slight adjustments to the new environment. This was still difficult enough in terms of economic and human resources. However, in many respects East Germany's way to democracy was much 'smoother' than the path its former allies had to follow. From what has been said so far, it is clear that this applies only to the institutional level. The change of mentalities and attitudes will take at least as long as in other countries.

Advisers from the West played an important role in shaping institutions in the 'nascent' democracies of central and eastern Europe. For East Germany, not only the structures were provided but, to a large extent, the personnel. For example, just one third of senior civil servants in Brandenburg – one of the five eastern *Länder* – come from the east nearly a decade after unification.

As far as the education system and its subsystems are concerned, most authors picture the process of unification as one of mere adjustment of institutions in the east to the western system and modalities (e.g. Kocka, 1994; Weiler et al, 1996), as a 'departure and reform from above' (Mayntz, 1994). This applies, to a large extent, to the school system [3] and to an even greater extent to higher education and teacher education. The reform of the education system of the former GDR turned out to be a 'conservative reform' as it was not used as an opportunity to reconsider some of the weaknesses of the western model. This will become obvious when some aspects of the transformation of higher education and teacher education are discussed in more detail.

Higher Education and Research in East Germany before 1989

The fact that the educational subsystems were organised in very different ways in the two German states made the process of unification difficult, and sometimes painful, for some of the East German actors. As far as higher education is concerned, there are significant differences regarding the aims and structures of the courses of study, as well as the institutions themselves.

Some Characteristics of Higher Education in the GDR

Whereas primary and secondary education as well as teacher education fell under the administrative power of the Ministry for People's Education [4], the higher education institutions were administered by the Ministry for Higher Education Institutions and Training Institutes.[5] The administration of the higher education institutions was highly hierarchical. Subgroups of the SED, the Communist Party, existed in each institution and had a strong say regarding all aspects of academic life. In this context, they played the same dominant role as in nearly all other areas of public life in the GDR. The task of the academic teachers was – according to the Decree on the Appointment and Status of Academic Teachers on Scientific Higher Education Institutions of 1968 – to educate and form 'highly qualified socialist personalities'. Compared to the West, there were relatively few posts for professors. Many qualified scientists had to remain in subordinate posts. Raiser (1998, p. 27) considers the related appointment procedure as one of the instruments to ensure loyalty to state and party.

After World War II, there were six universities, a technical college and colleges for art and music on the territory of what would later become the German Democratic Republic. Bieber (1994) points to the fact that, in contrast to the FRG, the GDR did not found any universities, but numerous specialised higher education institutions, for example, for civil engineering, for technical chemistry, and for diplomats and senior administrators. Most of these institutions had university status. There were no *Fachhochschulen* [6] as in the FRG. As well as this different development, Bieber points to some of the main differences between higher education in East and West Germany before 1990. These include the following.

- Most higher education institutions in the east were substantially smaller. The average number of students per institution was about 2500 in 1990 compared to 6400 in the west.
- There were proportionally fewer students. In 1990 about 13% of the age cohort studied compared to 25% in the west.
- There were strict regulations concerning the choice of the courses of study (and for the upper secondary school, of which the leaving examination [7] qualified for university entrance [8]). Students were allocated to courses of study in accordance with the demands of the economy, i.e. especially to subjects such as engineering sciences and teacher education. There were comparatively few students in the humanities and social sciences.
- Higher education institutions had on average twice as many employees in the academic sector as comparable institutions in the west. The proportion of academic teachers to students was 1:6 in the east compared to 1:15.5 in the west. There were relatively few professorships. Nearly all employees working in the so-called *Mittelbau*, i.e. the medium-level academic teaching force, had, in contrast to the FRG, non-fixed term contracts.

- Courses were organised in a similar way to secondary school classes. Marxism-Leninism was compulsory for all students and accounted, with physical education and Russian language for about 20% of the timetable.

The general conditions were in some respects more favourable for students in the GDR. Nearly all students received a scholarship and had the option to live in student accommodation. Students were expected to complete their course of study in the time allocated without changing their subject. Because of these conditions, the number of graduates was relatively high, and in this context 'higher education in the GDR seems much more efficient than in Western Germany where 30–40 percent of the students do not graduate' (Bieber, 1994, p. 63).

One of the most important differences from West Germany is the division of academic teaching and research which largely prevailed. The unity of education and research had been one of the demands of the Prussian university reform initiated by Wilhelm von Humboldt in the nineteenth century. According to the education law of the GDR of 1965, the principles of the unity of academic teaching and education, the unity of theory and practice and the unity of academic teaching and research applied to the East German universities. Whilst in some respects the first two principles were overemphasised, the third principle was only partially fulfilled. One could find excellent examples of research at some departments of higher education institutions. Other departments and some academic employees focused entirely on academic teaching. One of the reasons for this situation was the existence of separate research institutions: the academies.

Research at the Academies

The task of the higher education institutions in the GDR was – as the Decree on Higher Education of 1970 states – to educate and train 'highly qualified specialists with a profound socialist class consciousness'.[9] Students were in general trained for specific professions and in this respect higher education institutions can be seen as training institutions. Research was to a large extent conducted at four major academies (Academy of Sciences, Academy of Agricultural Sciences, Academy of Civil Engineering and Architecture, and the Academy of Pedagogical Sciences) which were organised according to the Soviet model. The academies were highly centralised and housed different institutes. They had the right to confer qualifications at the same level as the universities, such as doctorates and post-doctoral qualifications. The conditions for research were in some respects better than at the universities and other higher education institutions. The rather isolated and independent position of the two 'tracks' of research in eastern Germany and the lack of cooperation between these two 'tracks' was seen by some academics as an advantage, but was also criticised (e.g. Kuczynski, 1994, p. 76ff).[10] One gains the impression that the academies and their personnel were rather privileged as far as the availability of literature, and international contacts was concerned. This led to tensions between higher education institutions and the academies, which became obvious in 1989/90.

The academies housed not only different institutes but also the so-called *Gelehrtengesellschaft*, the society of scholars which elected its members. The last president of the Academy of Sciences, Horst Klinkmann, stresses the importance of the third higher education reform, with its changes of tasks and ideologisation which proved nearly fatal for the universities of the GDR (Klinkmann, 1993, p. 27) and for the orientation of the academies in the 1980s. The Academy of Sciences was supported:

> *as the center for the development of science but also as an instrument for the realization of science policy ... and was in accordance with its statute of 1984 firmly integrated into the political power structure. It was – as it was often said with an envious and mocking undertone – the 'research factory of the people' [11] of the GDR, in which the real core of the academic idea, namely the scholar society had increasingly lost influence and was just used more as ... decoration and allowed to be used in this way.' (Klinkmann, 1993, p. 27)*

The structure and function of the academies mirror priorities and procedures of a highly centralised state. In the 'old' Federal Republic, institutions comparable to these academies did not exist.

The Role of the Science Council in the Transition Period

The Science Council is an independent West German advisory body, which was founded in 1957. Its main task is to give recommendations to the federal government and to the governments of the *Länder* on the development of higher education and research institutions. In the context of shared responsibilities in a federal state, the Science Council has to be seen as a navigation instrument (Schlingmann, 1975). We will discuss the role of this advisory body in the transition period in some depth as it has to be seen as one of the key actors as far as higher education and research is concerned.

The Working Group Education Report at the Max Planck Institute for Educational Research has summarised some major aspects of the structure and procedures of the Science Council (Arbeitsgruppe Bildungsbericht, 1994; also Arnhold, 1998). The Science Council consists of the Science Commission and the Administrative Commission.[12] Both commissions have to decide on issues prepared by working groups. For a yes vote in the plenary assembly (which consists of the two commissions), a two-thirds majority is necessary. The fact that in the working groups members of both commissions have to work together leads to an early 'dovetailing of advice and decision-making' (Arbeitsgruppe Bildungsbericht, 1994, p. 91):

> *The Science Council is often accused of making conservative science policy. In general, this is true, but it is the direct consequence of a consulting conception, aimed at the broader agreement of all persons concerned. This is both the strength and the weakness of the Science Council. (Arbeitsgruppe Bildungsbericht, 1994, p. 91)*

When in spring 1990, the Science Council was asked by the governments of the FRG and the GDR to examine higher education and research institutions in east

Germany and to make suggestions on their future development, this task required a new level of analysis. Until 1990, the Council had given recommendations concerning single institutions, subjects or selected aspects of higher education and research in the FRG. This time the Council was expected to analyse an entire system. After the East German elections of March 1990, both German states moved towards unification. But at first, the specific modalities of the unification process were not yet clear.

In the second half of the 1980s, major science and research organisations in the FRG expected a decline in the number of students and the 1988 recommendations of the Science Council were based on this prognosis. Already at the time of publication it was clear that this prognosis had been wrong and that there would be an even stronger trend towards the 'mass university'. The Science Council started to consider this development in the context of cooperation between higher education and research institutions. The recommendations concerning the *Fachhochschulen* (1990) and concerning cooperation between National Research Centres (*Großforschungseinrichtungen*) and higher education institutions (1991) are results of these considerations. It was obvious at this time that the West German model was in desperate need of reform. This insight affected the initial intentions of the Science Council when it was asked to give recommendations on the future of higher education and research in East Germany. In July 1990, the Science Council published a paper on 'Perspectives for Science and Research on the Way towards German Unification'. The key passage, which was later frequently quoted, was the following:

> *In general it cannot be the aim to simply impose the ... system of the Federal Republic on the GDR. In contrast the process of unification offers the chance to proof self-critically how far parts of its education and research systems need reforming themselves. (Science Council, 1990, p. 6)*

What is described here was exactly what happened in the process of unification, although the Science Council wished to avoid it. As the unification treaty lays down the modus of unification as *Beitritt* (the entry of the eastern German territory into the Federal Republic of Germany), 'the fastest and least risky solution ... was to take over the programmes and structures of [academic, A.] production from the Western German system of higher education' (Neidhardt, 1994, p. 37). After that decision, institutions in the east were no longer seen as part of the education system of the GDR and the question of how far they would fit into the western German model became decisive for their future existence.

Procedures of the Science Council in Connection with the
Transformation of East German Higher Education

The modus of the unification of the two German states determined the modus of the unification of the two science and research systems. Concepts like 'dovetailing' of the two science and research systems – a term used by the Federal Minister for Education and Science in May 1990 – were replaced by the idea that steps had to be undertaken in order to 'incorporate' [13] the East German institutions, to make them fit into the West German system. It was declared the task of the Science Council to give recommendations on which institutions should continue to exist and in which form. This task led to a key role for the advisory body in the transition process and gave it a 'power it did not have before' (Bieber, 1994, p. 64). In accordance with the division of the East German higher education and research system, the Science Council created two major committees: the Evaluation Committee, which dealt with the academies, and the Structural Committee, which dealt with the higher education institutions. It was the task of the Commission for Coordination to link the work of the two committees.[14] Within the two there were 25 subject-related working groups. Apart from members of the Science Council, about 500 experts were involved, among them experts from abroad and also experts from eastern Germany.[15]

In 1990, the Science Council had already evaluated about 40 research institutes and had given recommendations on many aspects of higher education in the 'old' Federal Republic. International standards and peer review had played an important role in these evaluations. But it was questionable how far the same criteria which worked in the west could be applied in the east German context as there were severe problems concerning publications and international cooperation. In general, the Council followed the pattern of evaluation which had proved useful in the west. At the beginning, members of the working groups received material (articles, statistics etc.) in order to get a better understanding of the institution(s) concerned.[16] The Science Council employees had developed and sent out questionnaires to the respective institutions which contained questions, for example, on the past development of the institution, number and qualifications of its employees and plans for its future structure and profile. Findings from the questionnaires were also passed on to the experts. The next step was visits to the institutions, which were used to get a clear picture of buildings and equipment, and for conversations with the staff and – at the higher education institutions – with the students. In a letter to the higher education institution that announced the details of the visits, it was explained that there had to be separate conversations with the different groups. This was done in order to avoid a situation in which the presence of superiors could have caused difficulties.

Often there was not enough time to discuss all the important issues. That was seen as a shortcoming by those under evaluation (see, for example, Krüger & Rauschenbach, 1993) and by the working groups themselves. The employees of the institutions and the students were sometimes rather reserved and shy at the beginning (Führ, 1993). As experts have noted, the conversation often had to come to an end because of pressures of time when people had just started to warm up. Apart from conversations in the institutions themselves, those commissions which dealt with higher education institutions also had conversations with senior civil servants and sometimes the ministers of the education ministries of the *Länder* concerned. Employees of the Science Council's offices produced minutes of the visits and conversations. These minutes were taken into account when the members of the working groups had meetings in order to prepare recommendations, which finally had to be approved in a voting procedure by the general assembly of the Science Council. The recommendations went through various stages. On more than one occasion it was almost certainly difficult to find a compromise between the different opinions of the experts, who were likely to represent not only diverging points of view in their subjects but also different political opinions. The Science Council published its 'Recommendations for the Future Structure on Higher Education in the New *Länder* and in the Eastern Part of Berlin' in 1992. This was only possible because of intense personal effort on the part of the experts, the members of the Science Council, and the employees of the offices of the Council. Some of the people involved in this task remember this time with some sort of 'surprise', such as the then Head of the Science Council, Dieter Simon:

> *Most of the [advisers] are elderly gentlemen. There are also some ladies amongst them. In their subjects they are [considered to be real experts]. They do not have to make an effort any more ... Now they travel rather uncomfortably. They live in rooms with two or three beds. The air is yellow and smells of sulphur. They are just moderately welcome. Occasionally they are told that they perfectly correspond to the picture of the bourgeois imperialist that was drafted of them.*

> *Why do they not stay at home? It has to be their age. In their youth convictions were drummed into them the pulverised residues of which now [develop] into sentimental patriotism. Their children know nothing about this. In case of the attempt of unification 10 years later they would have sent THE PEOPLE back at the Wall. (Simon, 1991, p. 403)*

Taking into consideration the extent of the Science Council's task, one has to be surprised at how quickly a comprehensive text was published. But in many respects, publication was too late as some of the recommendations were already meaningless. We will come back to this point later.

The Evaluation of the Academies

It has already been mentioned that two different commissions of the Science Council were dealing with higher education and the academies in east Germany in the transition process. This was partly due to the fact that both institutional forms fell under different responsibilities in the aftermath of the *Wende*. In the highly centralised state of the GDR, which had abolished the *Länder* structure in the 1950s [17], higher education and research at the academies both fell under the responsibility of the central government. In west Germany, higher education, whilst partly financed by the Federal Government [18], is – due to the principle of cultural autonomy – mainly the responsibility of the *Länder*. The situation is different for the majority of the research centres. Krull (1992) gives an overview of how research is institutionalised and financed in west Germany. There are four major groups of research institutes in west Germany: the Max Planck Institutes, the National Research Centres, the Fraunhofer Institutes and the so-called 'Blue List' Institutes.[19] The Max Planck Institutes are mainly devoted to basic research whereas the Fraunhofer Institutes carry out a broad range of applied research. In the National Research Centres, one can find a concentration of personnel and equipment for expensive tasks which are unlikely to be carried out at the universities. The 'Blue List' institutes are either mission-oriented or service institutions. The Federal Government often plays an important role in the financing of these institutions. Krull (1992) stresses the fact that west Germany does not have a centralised research system.

> *Due to the federal structure of the German state and the division of powers anchored in the constitution ..., a marked emphasis on the freedom and autonomy of science, and a market-economy which fosters the initiatives of industry and private foundations, there is only limited room for centralised decision-making. However, the Federal Ministry of Education and Science (BMBW) and the Federal Ministry of Research and Technology (BMFT) do take responsibility for the general principles governing the publicly financed areas of R & D. (Krull, 1992, p. 6)*

This 'responsibility for the general principles' led to the evaluation of the academies in order to make them fit into the research structure of the FRG coming from the Federal Governments of the two German states and the major responsibility remaining with the (later unified) Federal Government. We will see later why this is of some importance for the transition process. Another major difference was the principle of subsidiarity, which existed in the west. Research carried out at the research institutions referred to earlier is rather the kind of research one does not find at universities and other higher education institutions. In contrast, one could find the same subjects as at the universities at the east German academies.

As stated earlier, an Evaluation Committee of the Science Council dealt with the east German academies. The major science organisations of the FRG were represented in this Evaluation Committee.

> *Its primary task was to co-ordinate the results of the various evaluation[s] and to ensure that recommendations addressed to the autonomous scientific organisations would, later on, be implemented by them (therefore, the participation of representatives of the Max-Planck-Society, the Fraunhofer-Society, etc. was an important factor for the overall success of the evaluation and restructuring process). (Krull, 1992, p. 15)*

Within the evaluation committee, nine working groups existed. In general, their procedures were the same as outlined earlier for the groups dealing with higher education institutions. That means that the institutes had to fill in questionnaires, which were analysed by the Science Council, the members of the working groups had conversations with scientists and staff, and further insights were gained from site talks. One of the major problems was the compatibility of the eastern institutions, which – as stated earlier– were organised in a different way from institutions in the west.

Results of the Transformation

The recommendations of the Science Council for higher education and research in eastern Germany were presented in two different forms. The Science Council gave general recommendations on future development, which can be seen as a result of its extensive involvement in higher education policy in the FRG and its numerous analyses of problems which occurred in the west. These ideas were partly laid down in the 'Twelve Recommendations' which were published in July 1990 and which provided a 'conceptual frame' (Krull, 1994, p, 205) for the transformation process. The major aims were:

- to strengthen research at the universities, to reintroduce the principle of subsidiarity in non-university research, and to improve cooperation between higher education and research institutions;
- the integration of the specialised higher education institutions (mentioned earlier) into larger units (universities, *Fachhochschulen*) and the establishing of *Fachhochschule*';
- the consolidation of existing universities should have priority over the foundation of new universities;
- the despecialisation of the courses of study in order to enhance the flexibility of the graduates; and
- the promotion of young scientists and transparent appointment procedures for the professorships.

All in all, these principles were realised in the transformation process. Further, the Science Council gave concrete advice in respect to certain subjects [20] and institutions. The transformation rate of the Science Councils recommendations was different for the two types of institutions. For the former academies, which were integrated into the research system of the FRG, the transformation rate was close to 1:1. As the *Länder* had a strong say in respect to higher education, not all ideas promoted by the Council became reality.

The Transformation of the Higher Education Institutions

Originally, the Science Council supported the existence of 10 universities in the area of the former GDR; there are now 15. In some cases, the *Länder* decided against the advice of the Council, which often adjusted its recommendations to the decisions already made. Some of the projects of the *Länder* were rather overambitious and financing them will continue to be a problem over the next decades. This applies, for example, to the three universities in Brandenburg, which are struggling to find convincing profiles. Plans for the limitation of costs provided by the Council were in some cases ignored, for example, when it suggested a law faculty either in Rostock or in Greifswald, and also not to introduce computer sciences and economics at the university in Potsdam, as the two other universities in Brandenburg already offer the same subjects. The *Fachhochschulen*, which were newly established in the east as a – in East Germany – new type of higher education institution have been well accepted. This affinity might also have historical reasons as the *Fachhochschulen* are perceived as training institutions. In the centre of the restructuring process at the universities was the aim of overcoming the shortcomings of the East German higher education and research system, which had to do with the ideological instrumentalisation of these institutions and issues such as the problem of the partial division of academic teaching and research.

Arnhold (1998 [1996]) describes the impact and limitations of the Science Council's recommendation in respect to teacher education. In contrast to the 'old' Federal Republic, teacher education outside the universities played an important role. Primary teachers were trained at teacher training institutes. These institutions were closed down by the *Länder* in the summer of 1990 because such institutions did not exist in the west and they were not considered to be appropriate. Secondary teachers were trained at the universities and at teacher training colleges. The Science Council recommended the continuation of some of the teacher training colleges at least for a limited period. The practical orientation of these institutions, as well as the favourable teacher–student ratio, were seen as advantages. The working group dealing with teacher education pointed to the fact that some of the western *Länder* host teacher training colleges themselves. However, the east German *Länder* decided to close down these institutions as well (to integrate them into the universities). The working group praised some good aspects of the East German one-phase model [21] of teacher education. But the respective passages of the recommendation have been too general to have any binding force.

As stated earlier, the Science Council just gave advice – the structural commissions and the appointment commissions at the universities themselves [22] were responsible for the concrete realisation of its ideas. The work of these commissions corresponded to the suggestions made by the Council to a different extent. Berlin is one of the examples where the concrete realisations conform to the recommendations to a large extent. There are other *Länder* which had political and regional priorities which led them to ignore some of the experts' advice. In general, the notion of 'structural adjustment' of the institutions in the east is correct. However, in some subjects, eastern experiences were taken into account. Medicine is one of them. The inclusion of the (natural) sciences into medical research at the clinics was considered to be worth promoting in the western part of the new Federal Republic as well.

Outcomes of the Restructuring of Non-university Research in East Germany

The East German academies were replaced by a variety of research institutions, most of which belong to the big research organisations. As many institutes of the academies carried out applied research, the Science Council suggested the foundation of nine *Fraunhofer* Institutes on the former GDR territory. Apart from eight Max Planck Institutes, various National Research Centres were founded; the centre for molecular medicine in Berlin-Buch is one of them. The number of 'Blue List' institutes nearly doubled in the course of German unification. This led to repercussions for non-university research in the 'old' *Länder*. After having finished its tasks in connection with the unification process, the Science Council began to carry out a thorough evaluation of the 'Blue List' institutes in the west. This was not always welcomed by the respective institutions, which sometimes perceived the newly-established institutions primarily as competitors.

Without doubt, a lively and vital research landscape emerged in the east, and many scientists (especially those at the universities) viewed the disappearance of the GDR academies with relief. However, there were also critical voices, especially on behalf of certain subjects and projects linked to the academies. Some highly developed subjects in the GDR like, for example, epidemiology, went into decline. One of the major problems of the transformation of higher education and research has been the situation of the scientists who originally worked at the academies and of the majority of academic employees at the universities. At first, jobs were cut by half; later, partly because of the newly-established institutions, nearly as many new jobs were created. But many scientists of the academies it proved difficult, or very nearly impossible, to find further employment. The Scientists Integration Program [23], initiated in order to help these scientists, ended without any success worth mentioning. For the majority of the newly-established posts at the universities, especially in the humanities and subjects such as pedagogics, academics from the west were appointed. They were neither ideologically 'burdened' nor exposed to substantial restrictions concerning publications and attendance at conferences. The strong academic *Mittelbau* – the medium-level academic teaching force at the universities – was drastically reduced.[24] For many of the *Mittelbau* employees it was too late in their careers to qualify for one of the posts offered by the new system. Whereas the institutional reform of the East German higher education and research system might be rated as a success, this reform turned out to be a crisis in respect to their careers and personal lives for many of the East German actors.

From the perspective of the Science Council, two structural problems continue to exist in eastern Germany. Compared to the GDR, the unequal distribution of research institutes has declined to some extent. Still, there are relatively few institutions in less developed areas. Another problem continues to be the humanities, which are still underrepresented in the east.

Conclusions: a success story?

In his article on the liquidation of the Academy of Sciences, Laitko (1997, p. 59) claims that the academies as an institutional form which did not exist in the west were 'neither inferior nor superior, but simply different'.

> *The ideology which prevailed in the unification process, saw the development in the ['old'] federal republic as ... normal, and in the GDR [by definition] different and hence as something which had to be completely corrected with no other possibility than the total liquidation of the Academy. (ibid.)*

In this respect, he considers the adjustment of the East German higher education and research system to structures in the west as a sort of 'natural necessity'. Laitko, who worked at the Academy of Science, attested the Science Council not only a high personal commitment but also sensitivity for the situation of those under evaluation. However, from his point of view, mainly political reasons determined the evaluation of the research institutions.

This leads to the question whether there could have been alternative courses for the transformation of East German higher education and research. The answer is yes and no: no, as the overwhelming majority of institutions did not have the power, the know-how and the courage for a thorough self-reform (see Klinkmann, 1993); yes, as there were in concrete situations different possibilities and often the technically easiest solutions were chosen, which were not always the most democratic (see Pasternack, 1993) or the most future-oriented. Often the question has been asked, why was the process of unification not used for the necessary reform of the West German system of higher education. Kocka (1994) summarises the aspects which were decisive in this context.

- It was necessary to act quickly. This is correct in so far as there were just slight changes in the numbers of students at the eastern institutions.
- The crisis of 1989 was just a crisis for the eastern part of Germany. For the political system of the FRG, the collapse of the GDR was seen as a confirmation, even as a moral victory. Science organisations in the west blocked a comprehensive reform.
- It is difficult to transfer isolated aspects of one system without taking over other aspects which one does not wish to transfer.

Ironically, the last point was already anticipated in a propaganda leaflet published in the GDR in 1968:

> *Today in Germany – and this is no secret – two pedagogical conceptions are standing opposite each other, which correspond to two educational realities and the reputable pedagogists in East and West make no secrets of which educational conception belongs to the future. But educational conceptions, education systems, educational realities are not floating in the air, they are realities linked firmly to the power relations which produced them, and their future prospects or backwardness, their worth or unworth let one draw conclusions on the societies and state systems they belong to: capitalism and socialism ... Our modern education system is inseparably linked to our socialist society. (Bildung, 1968, p. 79)*

One of the former presidents of the Science Council, Gerhard Neuweiler, compared the task of using the unification process for a higher education reform in both parts of Germany with the task of transforming a giant tanker into a luxury liner in a heavy sea. He stresses the fact that already minor deviations from the West German path (e.g. the establishment of the humanities centres) led to a storm of indignation in the west. Recent years have seen some attempts to put the evaluation process into a different light. The president of the Science Council at the beginning of the 1990s, Dieter Simon, has stated that the Council has made 'striking misjudgements'. Too often, the Council had taken over prejudices concerning the East German model.

Can the transformation of East German higher education and research be seen as a success story? Certainly, the sometimes gloomy predictions from the beginning of the 1990s (e.g. Ellwein, 1997 [1992]) did not come true. A network of research institutions was installed in the east, which is well prepared for international competition. As far as higher education is concerned, a comprehensive reform which will tackle the obvious problems of the western German model still has to be carried out.

Notes

[1] This term is frequently used in Germany to describe the political changes of the year 1989. Literally: Turning point.

[2] Bîrzea states that the term 'transition' rather refers to former communist countries (Bîrzea, 1994, p. 7). Some authors, for example, Merkel (1994), include parts of the world as different as Latin America, Africa, and southern and eastern Europe in their investigations.

[3] Most of the eastern *Länder* were reluctant to accept the tripartite system of secondary education and modified it to some extent. Brandenburg, as the only eastern *Land*, introduced comprehensive schools and children remain in elementary schools for 6 years (as opposed to 4 years elsewhere).

[4] *Volksbildungsministerium*. The minister was Margot Honecker, wife of the state and party leader Erich Honecker.

[5] *Ministerium für Hoch- und Fachschulen*.

[6] These institutions are in some respects comparable to the polytechnics.

[7] The *Abitur*.

[8] For some subjects an additional entrance examination was required.

[9] In the original: 'hochqualifizierte Fachkräfte mit festem sozialistischen Klassenstandpunkt'.

[10] Kuczynski mentions that researchers at the academies are in danger of becoming specialists in a narrow field. He suggests that these researchers should give lectures at universities to counteract this self-limitation. On the other hand, he suggests a sort of sabbatical leave for academic teachers at the university which they should use for research. Kuczynski was unable to publish the manuscript which contains these suggestions before 1989.

[11] 'Volkseigener Betrieb Forschung'.

[12] The members of the administrative commission come from the Federal Government and the governments of *Länder* whereas the members of the Science Commission are appointed by the Federal President – partly through the common suggestions of the most important scientific organizations, partly because of common appointments of the Federal Government and the *Länder* governments. This appointment procedure 'already contains the structural necessity of a compromise, that pays off in the long run in the acceptance of the Science Council' (Arbeitsgruppe Bildungsbericht, 1994, p. 90).

[13] Artikel 38 of the Unification Treaty uses the German term 'Einpassung'.

[14] But this coordination did not happen. The two committees were working separately. The originally envisaged coordination might have helped to find better solutions for the future employment of the scientists of the academies.

[15] The involvement of experts from East Germany created in some cases severe problems, which would be worth discussing in more detail.

[16] I follow here the procedure of the working group dealing with teacher education, which I was able to investigate in some detail. Apart from minor differences, the basic line of procedure is very likely to be the same for all working groups.

[17] Instead, East Germany was divided into 13 administrative areas. As the *Länder* structure existed before, the often used term 'new *Länder*' is somehow confusing.

[18] The allocation of funds provided by the Federal Government especially for buildings was the first and continued to be one of the major tasks of the Science Council.

[19] Financed commonly by the Federal Government and *Länder*. A list of these institutions was issued in 1977. The name derives from the fact that it was printed on blue paper.

[20] In many cases, GDR-typical subjects and institutions ceased to exist soon after unification. The *Länder* had to make up their minds regarding their future existence or liquidation in just 3 months.

[21] In contrast to West Germany, teachers in the GDR were trained in one phase. Practical exercises and periods of teaching were an important part of this training from the beginning onwards. In the FRG, teachers are trained in two phases: after studying at a university (or in some cases at teacher training colleges) the prospective teachers have to do the so-called *Referendariat*, a period in which they start teaching under the supervision of teacher trainers and practitioners.

[22] Some case studies give a clear picture of the actual process of transformation at different institutions (e.g. in Mayntz, 1994). Neidhardt (1994) and Raiser (1998) describe the restructuring of the Humboldt University, Berlin.

[23] *WIP – Wissenschaftler-Integrationsprogramm.*

[24] Women especially found in this employment modus the possibility to combine some sort of academic career with their plans regarding family and children. The percentage of woman in academic teaching in eastern Germany has declined significantly.

References

Arbeitsgruppe Bildungsbericht am Max-Planck-Institut für Bildungsforschung (1994) *Das Bildungswesen in der Bundesrepublik Deutschland. Strukturen und Entwicklungen im Überblick.* Reinbek bei Hamburg: Rowohlt.

Arnhold, N. (1998) The Science Council in the 1990s: continuity in a period of change, paper given at the Comparative and International Education Society Conference in Buffalo, USA, March 1998.

Arnhold, N. (1998 [1996]) The Transformation of East German Teacher Education, in D. Phillips et al (Ed.) *Processes of Transition in Education Systems*. Oxford: Symposium Books.

Bieber, H-J. (1994) Die Empfehlungen des Wissenschaftsrates für die Hochschulen in den neuen Ländern, *Das Hochschulwesen*, 42(2), pp. 62-71.

Bildung für heute und morgen. Eine Information über das einheitliche sozialistische Bildungssystem der DDR (1968). Berlin: Staatssekretariat für westdeutsche Fragen.

Bîrzea, C. (1994) *Educational Policies of the Countries in Transition.* Strasbourg: Council of Europe.

Bîrzea, C. (1996) Education in a World in Transition: between post-communism and post-modernism, *Prospects*, XXVI(4), pp. 673-681.

Ellwein, T. (1997 [1992]) *Die deutsche Universität. Vom Mittelalter bis zur Gegenwart.* Wiesbaden: Fourier.

Führ, C. (1993) Die Empfehlungen des Wissenschaftsrates zur Lehrerbildung in den neuen Ländern. Ihre Entstehung und ihre Ziehlsetzung, *Transformationen der deutschen Bildungslandschaft. Lernprozeß mit ungewissen Ausgang, Zeitschrift für Pädagogik*, Supplement, No. 30.

Klinkmann, H. (1993) Absturz in die Zukunft. Die Akademie der Wissenschaften der DDR in der Wendezeit 1989/90, in P. Pasternack (Ed.) *IV. Hochschulreform. Wissenschaft und Hochschulen in Ostdeutschland 1989/90. Eine Retrospektive.* Leipzig: Leipziger Universitätsverlag.

Kocka, J. (1994) Reformen von oben und außen, *Das Hochschulwesen*, 42(2), pp. 93-96.

Krüger, H-H. & Rauschenbach, T. (1993) Über die Schwierigkeiten deutsch-deutscher Annäherung. Notizen zum 'Neuaufbau' der Erziehungswissenschaft am Beispiel Halle, *Transformationen der deutschen Bildungslandschaft. Lernprozeß mit ungewissen Ausgang, Zeitschrift für Pädagogik*, Supplement No. 30.

Krull, W. (1992) The Evaluation and Restructuring of Non-university Research Institutions in East Germany by the Science Council – an overview, paper given at the Conference on 'Methodologies for Evaluating the Future Potential of Research Institutions' in Prague, Czechoslovakia, March 1992.

Krull, W. (1994) Im Osten wie im Westen – nichts Neues? Zu den Empfehlungen des Wissenschaftsrates für die Neuordnung der Hochschulen auf dem Gebiet der ehemaligen DDR, in R. Mayntz (Ed.) *Aufbruch und Reform von oben. Ostdeutsche Universitäten im Transformationsprozeß.* Frankfurt a. M.: Campus Verlag.

Kuczynski, J. (1994) *Ein Leben in der Wissenschaft der DDR.* Münster: Westfälisches Dampfboot.

Laitko, H. (1997) Abwicklungsreminiszenzen. Nach-Denken über das Ende einer Akademie, *Hochschule Ost* ,6(1), pp. 55-81.

Mayntz, R. (Ed.) (1994) *Aufbruch und Reform von oben. Ostdeutsche Universitäten im Transformationsprozeß.* Frankfurt a. M.: Campus Verlag.

Merkel, W. (Ed.) (1994) *Systemwechsel 1. Theorien, Ansätze und Konzeptionen.* Opladen: Leske und Budrich.

Neidhardt, W. (1994) Konflikte und Balancen. Die Umwandlung der Humboldt-Universität zu Berlin 1990–1993, in R. Mayntz (Ed.) *Aufbruch und Reform von oben. Ostdeutsche Universitäten im Transformationsprozeß.* Frankfurt a. M.: Campus Verlag.

Pasternack, P. (1993) Studentisches Bewegtsein in der DDR/in Ostdeutschland 1989/90, in P. Pasternack (Ed.) *IV. Hochschulreform. Wissenschaft und Hochschulen in Ostdeutschland 1989/90. Eine Retrospektive.* Leipzig: Leipziger Universitätsverlag.

Raiser, T. (1998) *Schicksalsjahre einer Universität. Die strukturelle und personelle Neuordnung der Humboldt-Universität zu Berlin 1989–1994.* Berlin: Verlag Arno Spitz.

Schlingmann, I. (1975) *Zur Funktion des Wissenschaftsrates als wissenschafts- und bildungspolitisches Steuerungsinstrument*, Thesis, Technische Universität, Berlin.

Simon, D. (1991) Evaluationssplitter, *Rechtshistorisches Journal*, 10, pp. 399-425.

Weiler, H.N. et al (1996) *Educational Change and Social Transformation. Teachers, Schools and Universities in Eastern Germany* London: Falmer Press.

The *Wissenschaftsrat* and the Investigation of Teacher Education in the Former German Democratic Republic, 1991: a personal account

DAVID PHILLIPS

In anticipation of and following the unification of East and West Germany, there was an urgent need for advice on a wide range of subjects regarding the future provision of higher education in what were to constitute the five new *Länder* of the new Germany. The German Science Council, the *Wissenschaftsrat*, was the obvious body to undertake the kind of investigations that would be necessary for the formulation of such advice. Established in 1958, the *Wissenschaftsrat* is an organisation consisting of two 'commissions'; its 'science' commission comprises academics appointed by the Federal President on the recommendation of various appropriate bodies [1]; the 'administrative' commission is a group of delegates of the federal and *Länder* governments. The *Wissenschaftsrat* is a highly regarded body, producing each year an impressive array of reports and recommendations. Its utterances are taken seriously – 'Der Wissenschaftsrat hat gesagt ...' (The *Wissenschaftsrat* has said ...) is a formula often heard to support a view on how to proceed with a policy issue in higher education.

In the autumn of 1990, I was invited to be a member of a working group (*Arbeitsgruppe*) on teacher education set up by the *Wissenschaftsrat* in the context of a request by the BRD (*Bundesrepublik Deutschland* [Federal Republic of Germany]) and former GDR governments and the parliaments of the *Länder* for advice on plans for the development of higher education institutions in the five new *Länder*. The letter of invitation indicated that the outcome of the group's work would be recommendations from the *Wissenschaftsrat* on the future structure and location of teacher education in the five new *Länder*.[2] I was to be the only non-German member of the working group.

I had no illusions about the reasons for my involvement. In exercises of this kind it is often regarded as a sort of guarantee of the independence of the group to have a member from outside – preferably a foreigner – whose credentials are such that no accusation of prejudgement of the issues to be considered might be made. In my case there was the combination too of knowledge of Germany and of the higher

111

education system in particular and ability in the German language, as well as long involvement in teacher education. Being an academic at the University of Oxford was not a disadvantage.

When I received the invitation, I was conscious of a remarkable set of parallels. I had many years previously made a study of the so-called 'Blue Report' (*Blaues Gutachten*) of 1948. This was a set of recommendations on higher education in Germany made by a German commission appointed by General Sir Brian Robertson, the Military Governor of the British Zone of Occupation in Germany after the Second World War. The Commission had a broad brief, and it acted entirely independently of any influence of the Military Government. As a 'guarantee of its freedom', Robertson appointed two foreign members, the Swiss academic and man of letters Jean Rudolf von Salis, and Lord Lindsay, Master of Balliol College, Oxford. I had had access to all the papers of the Commission and was able to interview or correspond with some of its surviving members. Its work formed the basis of my Oxford DPhil thesis and of several publications on related subjects.[3]

It was therefore especially intriguing for me to be able to observe and participate in the work of a commission set up to investigate higher education issues following another period of upheaval in Germany. The parallels between the post-war and post-unification periods are enticing, if highly problematic, and I have discussed them in some detail elsewhere (Phillips, 2000), but for me the inexactitude of the comparison was in itself of interest, and I was attracted too by the opportunity to experience at first hand how a German expert commission would go about its work.

In what follows, I shall draw upon a detailed record of the meetings of the working group, which I kept in diary form (hereafter 'Diary'), and on the voluminous papers which supported the group's work. I shall make use of direct quotations from the diary interspersed with observations from the perspective of some 10 years after the events. And so this will be a highly personal account of the working group on teacher education (*Arbeitsgruppe Lehrerbildung*) and its visits to universities and colleges in eastern Germany at an early stage of the post-unification reform discussions, concentrating on a few of the most striking themes that emerged. An evaluation of the evolution and effects of the group's recommendations will have to await the outcome of further analysis and research.[4] Reference to individuals has for the most part been anonymised.

*****

At our first meeting in Berlin at the end of January 1991, we were informed that our task was to collect information and specifically not to 'evaluate'. This was something that had to be reiterated many times, since while so much evaluation was happening in the new *Länder*, it was difficult for our various interlocutors not to assume that we were in some sense reporting on their individual qualifications and abilities. Another point that emerged at this early stage, and about which I was to feel strongly in the discussions and experiences that were to come, was the role of many West German academics in proffering help and advice to their colleagues in the east. They were not helping the situation at all, it was said, and some proper coordination of their efforts was necessary – close cooperation between paired individuals was suggested. One of our members speculated about the people we would meet and how they would have been selected, suggesting that one of our tasks would be to consider what information had *not* come our way. In the event, we were confronted with an embarrassment of informative material, and our discussions – in my perception – were always remarkably open and frank.

> *Berlin, 31 January*

> *We visit the* Landesregierung *of Brandenburg, where we meet the Minister ... (who was not expecting us) and three of his staff (one of whom is on loan from or has moved from Nordrhein-Westfalen). It is clear from our discussions that everything is in a most almighty muddle, despite the frenzied activity to get a new* Schulgesetz *[school law] formulated and to arrange* Sofortprogramme *[emergency measures] to cope with immediate needs ... The ministry is accommodated in a building with makeshift signs everywhere, and its administration seems very precarious. I begin, in these run-down surroundings so typical of East Berlin, to be reminded of the post-war years, and the improvisation that informed everything then. (Diary, pp. 2–3)*

The situation in Brandenburg was not untypical, since uncertainty and improvisation were characteristics of the education ministries at this early stage. Buildings had had to be quickly converted and equipped, and a very steep learning curve had to be negotiated by the ministry officials. Important questions could not be answered because of lack of information and experience.

> *In Potsdam we are welcomed by a nervous-looking* Rektor, *who immediately and to our dismay talks of being open to the kind of evaluation we are undertaking ... The* Rektor *is very open with us, and does not attempt to conceal the improvisation of much that is happening; the professors who respond to our questions are much more defensive, even though they now have the imprimatur of their colleagues, having been voted in as heads of departments. (Diary, p. 3)*

The visits to teacher training institutions consisted usually of three groups of meetings: discussions with the *Rektor*, deans and professors; with the *Mittelbau* (the non-professorial staff); and with representatives of the student body.

> *We have a discussion with a group of sad-looking and somewhat reserved students. They are worried about what the transformation of the* PH [Pädagogische Hochschule] *into a university will mean for the length of time they will have to study. [One of our colleagues] does not help by pointing out to them – what is the truth – that someone who has studied, say,* Wirtschaftswissenschaft *[business studies] under the old GDR system will have no chance of employment ... We learn that the tendency of students to leave the East to study in W. German universities is quite small; it seems to me that it is indeed much better for the students to stay put and to help develop their institutions in an uncertain future. (Diary, p. 4)*

Discussions with students were generally of the most open character; like the *Mittelbau* representatives, however, they tended to look to the *Arbeitsgruppe* to solve their problems, imagining we had powers to intervene in administrative processes and local policy decisions.

Cottbus, 1 February

> *We have a good discussion with the* Mittelbau. *I am struck by the wide age range of the people we see ... There is an impassioned plea from a woman of 48 to be allowed to do her* Habilitation *[post-doctoral qualification by thesis, the prerequisite for appointment as professor]. They are all worried about the uncertainties − will they be allowed to continue as educationists under future conditions, and if so will they be able to stay in Cottbus? ... I note during the meeting: 'Moving to see how these people are struggling to put together an academic life which will be appropriate for the future, which will enable them to catch up on so much lost time, and simply to learn about all that has been happening in the BRD and to be able to make contributions to conferences, etc. − which some have begun to do.'*

> *We keep hearing people say to us, 'I've made contact with Prof. X in Frankfurt, or Prof. Y in Bremen or Hamburg', etc. − there seems to be enormous faith in the simple process of contact, but I wonder about the quality of much of the advice they might be getting.*

> *Time is the recurrent problem: the 48 year old says to us: 'Man kann nicht in einem Jahr nachlesen, was man in 30 Jahren nicht lesen konnte' [You can't catch up in one year on the reading you have not been allowed to do for 30 years]. (Diary, p. 6)*

The *Mittelbau* in the GDR was rather different from the non-professorial teaching body in the Federal Republic, who constituted − and still do − a kind of professoriate-in-waiting. Only the 'call' (*Ruf*) to a professorship would normally create security of tenure. In the GDR, the *Mittelbau* was in itself a profession. It was possible to spend a whole career as a university *teacher* (usually with the doctorate, but normally without *Habilitation*), and so after unification this substantial group of academics was left high and dry, with no proper corresponding professional group in the larger Federal Republic and with a pressing need to make a name for themselves in research and publication if they were to compete for posts (not least in due course their own) with colleagues from the western *Länder*.

Later, at the *Technische Hochschule* in Halle, there was much talk of the difficulties the *Mittelbau* faced:

> *They have a real problem − the professors have passed on a lot of work to them, so that they are severely overloaded, the state has connived at the arrangement since it is cheaper for a member of the* Mittelbau *to give eight lectures a week than for a professor to do so, because of the overwork they haven't been able to get further qualifications or to do their own work, they have therefore grown old in their posts and have no chances − not even the chance now to catch up. Their position is quite tragic. (Diary, p. 16)*

The following day, at the Martin-Luther-Universität in Halle, we were reminded by a group of *Mittelbau* representatives that the whole question of limited tenure must be seen as a political and social matter:

> *One of those present says with strong feeling that they are angered by the suggestion that they are sitting around and growing old and costing a lot of money – is it to be assumed that the professors are young and fresh? (Diary, pp. 21–22)*

*****

Magdeburg, 4 February

> *The offices [of the Education Ministry] are furnished with the latest West German-style tables and chairs and general equipment – including the fanciest computers. A stark contrast with Potsdam. Here we wait and wait for the Staatssekretär, who is with the Minister. 'Er kriegt noch Instruktionen, was er hier sagen soll' [He's still receiving instructions as to what he should say to us], says [Colleague A].*

> *All the plans here are provisional, we learn. The school system will consist of the* Gymnasium *plus the* Realschule, *though how the* Realschule *will have a proper identity is unclear (without the* Hauptschule ...)

> *West German* Gastprofessoren *[visiting professors] and* Gastdozenten *[visiting lecturers] appear to be playing a large role here in Sachsen-Anhalt – we are told that in Halle some 70% of the law faculty come from the West. [Colleague B] asks the good question as to how many of [the visiting academics] could be described as first class. The* Staatssekretär *declines to answer, but he does say that he doesn't think it right for West German academics to be dashing to and from E. German universities and cramming everything into one whole day's teaching. (Diary, pp. 11–12)*

The impression here was that important decisions had already been made at a political level about the future shape of education, and that our recommendations (about training for teaching at particular levels and in particular types of school) would have to accommodate changes which were not up for discussion. I found this very surprising.

Magdeburg, 4 February

> *There are over 30 'Gastlehrkräfte' [visiting teachers] here, and contacts have been built up with the* Gesamthochschule *[comprehensive university] in Essen, with Hannover and with Braunschweig. We are told that they are being used not just to teach the students but also to help with the further training of the academic staff, as well as providing stimulus for research projects, some of them co-operative ...*

> *[A member of the* Mittelbau*] lets loose about his experiences with the newly established* Strukturkommission *here. He speaks with very strong feeling about the behaviour of West German members on it who asked about the openings in Magdeburg – would they be offered C3 or C4 professorships? Would financial*

*support be available so that their existing living standards could be maintained? ...
Our interlocutor says it is for them [the* Mittlebau*] not a question of C3 or C4
professorships but one of whether they will have a job at all; they are happy to be
'evaluated', but against the processes of* Abwicklung *[the 'winding-up' of
institutions]. The group as a whole looks depressed and bitter – and angry. They
appeal to us for greater clarity about their situation, and the answer 'Ein solcher
Umbruch muß mit sich Zeiten der Unsicherheit bringen' [An upheaval of this kind
inevitably brings with it a time of uncertainty] does not satisfy their fears, though I
think they understand that this must be the reality.*

*There is a very bitter complaint from one woman present that nothing is being decided,
as she sees it, at* Stadt, Kreis, *or* Land *level. (Diary, pp. 12–13)*

The *Pädagogische Hochschule* (*PH*) was facing particular staffing problems as a result of
the collapse of Russian teaching; by this stage half the staff in this subject had been
lost. Russian looked set to become a subject limited to upper secondary level (as
second or third foreign language), but the *PH* was limited to training for the *lower*
secondary level. Many teachers of Russian in the eastern *Länder*, of course, were
eventually to be retrained as teachers of English.

The process of *Abwicklung* formed the subject of a discussion with students;
they felt that:

*the processes have been unjust, particularly in so far as only a few subjects were
affected (psychology,* Erziehungswissenschaft, Pädagogik*) – but why was not history
included, they ask – or maths, or chemistry? The people in these subjects are equally
'belastet' ['burdened' (with their past activity)].*

*We ask them about the spectrum of involvement with the SED [Socialist Unity
Party], etc., and the students say they could always 'place' their teachers. There were
those they met at demos (which surprised them) and those who said – even in their
lectures – don't go to the Dom, there's a demo there today and there will be trouble,
etc. They were able to reach their own conclusions. It is quite clear that they feel the
wrong people have suffered in many cases, and that others have – unjustly – escaped.
(Diary, p. 14)*

This is reminiscent of much that happened in higher education after the War, when
the 'purging' or denazification of the academic staff resulted in many bad decisions.

Halle, 6 February

The Rektor *[of the Martin-Luther-Universität] says that there were four basic
principles which controlled their thinking about the way the University should now
develop. It must*

– regain freedom of 'academic thinking' (Freiheit des wissenschaftlichen
Denkens)*;*

– open itself up to international contact;

– *ensure its own academic development;*

– *undertake an 'innere Demokratisierung'. (Diary, p. 20)*

This too reminds us of some of the tasks higher education institutions in Germany faced after the War. All eighty *Studiengänge* (courses of study) at the University had been examined to ascertain whether they matched the standards of equivalent courses in West Germany; there had been a review of the teaching personnel, and needs had been identified. 'Wir wissen wo wir was berufen müssen' (we know where and what professorial appointments are needed), the *Rektor* told us. Much of the early efforts from within higher education to adjust the teaching and research staff was overtaken by events, as people (including those who had 'survived' the selection procedures) had to apply for their own and new positions in competition with applicants from the west.

> *The professors ... are all – or mostly all – grey-haired and conservative-looking. I would not imagine that they are going to be the most progressive group in the university, and I am reminded of how little faith was placed in similar groups after the War. (Diary, p. 21)*

A 1947 report by the British AUT (Association of University Teachers) on the German universities and their situation after the War had concluded:

> *The German universities are at present controlled, as far as internal affairs are concerned, by groups of senior professors whose average age is high, whose academic ideals were formed under conditions very different from today's, and whose capacity for responding to new circumstances is therefore likely to be in general small.[5]*

The direct parallel is probably unfair, but the power of the German professoriate should not be underestimated; its conservative features had for so long in Germany's past militated against change and reform that in the context of the immediate post-unification period, when a dynamic new beginning was needed, it was inevitable that thoughts should return to a similar need – for too long unmet – in the post-war years.

Halle, 6 February

> *At our meeting with the professors [at the* PH, *Abteilung Halle] there is a man from the Ministry present, as well as the* Gründungsdekan *[founding dean] of the new* Fachbereich Erziehungs- und Sozialwissenschaften *[faculty of education and social studies], a* Privatdozent *from Marburg. His* Prodekan *is also from the West. Everything looks very provisional – the old* Erziehungswissenschaft *faculty was subjected to the* Abwicklung *process and the former* Mitarbeiter *[colleagues] there put into the* 'Wartestand' *[the term used for a period of abeyance, pending decisions about the future]. They want the new* Fachbereich *to be fully operational by the* Sommersemester *and regard the teaching here as of fundamental importance, providing as it does a kind of* Allgemeinbildung *[general education] for all students. They know they need to carry out* 'Evaluierungen' *and to get the new* 'Berufungen' *[appointments to the post of professor] instituted as soon as*

possible – in our documents we are given copies of an advertisement which has already appeared in Die Zeit.

A Strukturbeirat *[structural committee] has been set up to look at the new conditions which will operate in the* Fachbereich, *but this has not yet been 'confirmed' by the Ministry, and the* Rektor *expresses astonishment when the man from the Ministry reports this to us. Is the status of the* Gründungsdekan *then in question? he asks. This seems typical of the poor communication and uncertainty evident in these struggling institutions.*

This PH *seems to have particular problems in so far as it wishes desperately to retain its high status ... It is made clear to us that the* Pädagogische Hochschulen *in the GDR were regarded as having equal status with the universities (and it has been said generally that they could be regarded as being more successful as far as producing teachers is concerned than the universities, and that their* Absolventen *[graduates] were often preferred) ...*

A great advantage they have, so they say, is a 'strikte Orientierung auf den Lehrerberuf unserer Studenten' [strict orientation towards the teaching vocation of our students] compared with the university, where teacher education is seen, as one person puts it, as an 'Anhang zum Diplomstudium' [appendage to students' (academic) degree work]. One of the Deans says that here they can manage 'Einheit von Lehre und Forschung – und Schule' [unity of teaching and research – and the school]. (Diary, pp. 18–19)

A considerable part of our discussions at every institution we visited naturally centred on the form which teacher education might take in the future. In the Federal Republic the pattern of teacher education has traditionally – there have been exceptions – been two-phased: the first stage takes place in a university, where students study the 'didactics' (*Didaktik*) of their teaching subjects, together with courses in education as an academic field of inquiry; the second (2-year) phase (*Referendarzeit*) is more practically oriented and takes place in *Lehrerseminare*, where the trainee teachers are taught by experienced practitioners, study the methods appropriate to their subjects (*Methodik*), and are attached to schools where they teach a substantial timetable. In the GDR, a one-phase model was used, and this was seen as a considerable strength. In particular, so it was argued, the one-phase model ensured a close relationship with the training institution and the world of practice, as has been the general case in England.

The BRD model is predicated on a division between the academic (in the sense of *Wissenschaft*) and the practical. The university teachers concerned with *Didaktik* would not wish what they do to be confused with *Methodik*, which is not *wissenschaftlich* in nature and therefore does not belong in a university context.

Halle, 5 February

[Technische Hochschule] *The question of 'Zweiphasigkeit' comes up again, and [colleague B] warns that the people here will not be able to continue with their ambitious plans to keep a high profile of* Praktika *and* Übungen *in the schools during the first phase; these school-based matters will be the responsibility of the people responsible for the* Referendarzeit. *(Diary, p. 15)*

[PH Halle-Köthen] ... we talk to the Mittelbau, *and again the questions of the close relationship of theory and practice, and of content (in connection with* Zweiphasigkeit*) crop up. The first speaker on these subjects, a man in his late 50s or early 60s, speaks to us from the heart. [Colleague B] reassures everyone that nobody is going to* force *their* Land *to do the same as the West German* Bundesländer. *He points out that a clear strength of an institution like this is that a kind of person is being trained who sees himself primarily as a* teacher, *rather than as a* subject specialist. *(Diary, p. 17)*

Though of course the parliaments of the *Länder* could not be forced by the *Wissenschaftsrat* or any other comparable body to move in a particular direction, there was by this stage little hope of the decision to embrace the two-phase model being reversed.

Halle, 6 February

[Martin-Luther-Universität] In developing, they want to take West German examples into account, but they don't want 'Gleichheit' at all costs. Their students are asking why they will have to do a Referendarzeit *if they have already had teaching experience during the 'first part' of their studies. (Diary, p. 21)*

*****

Berlin, 6 February

[I have] time to reflect on some of the impressions of the last week. [Colleague A] says that she couldn't sleep [through] worrying so much about the fate of the good people we have been meeting with. It is tragic *to see the position they are in and not to be able to do much − if anything − to help them. Most of them − I would have to except most of the professors − are forward-looking, positive people, who feel very strongly about their professional skills and the good experience they have of training teachers to* teach. *They are now in a state of shock and clearly feel very bitter and, in many cases, angry, about their situation. They are not happy with the* Abwicklung *processes, and they are worried − while not being at all anxious about* Evaluierung *− about their jobs, for a number of reasons.*

First there is the question of a future structure for teacher education generally − they simply do not know whether their institutions will survive ... Then there is the threatening Zweiphasigkeit, *which will probably remove from them that close contact with school practice which they consider to be the great strength − rightly so − of their contribution to teacher education.*

Then there is the question of whether their institutions are to offer only Sekundarstufe *I (in the case of the* Pädagogische Hochschulen*). On top of all this is the whole problem of whether they will be able to progress up the academic*

119

ladder. Many have been so overworked that they have not been able to do a Habilitation, *let alone keep up their academic work. In competition with West German academics, they will have no chance at all – and in any case they feel that the recommendation (in itself sound) that there should be no* Hausberufungen, *will cut off all their hopes of being able to stay.*

The age range of these people is astonishing. Many of them are in their sixties – and this is explained by what I have noted above, namely that the Mittelbau *has always regarded itself as a* profession, *perhaps as in England. There have been relatively few professors, compared with the old Federal Republic, and so the* Mittelbau *has remained fairly large and has had security of tenure (for the most part), which has not been the case in West Germany.*

[Colleague A] keeps saying that they should feel themselves to be in a relatively good position compared with their West German counterparts, but this is not something they take to very kindly, and in any case they understand very little about the education system of West Germany. This latter point is quite striking – they either know nothing at all about education there, or they only know enough to be in danger of getting things wrong. We have often heard them refer to West German experience, and not always accurately. Of all the problems we have seen, I suppose it is the position of the Mittelbau *which has most moved us. (Diary, pp. 23–25)*

The checklist of problems here reflected the tenor of much of our discussion and formed the basis of the long deliberations from March to June 1991 which preceded the publication of the group's recommendations (*Wissenschaftsrat*, 1992).

Jena, 24 February

[Colleague C] talks of developments leading to 'eine Perpetuierung des status quo aus den alten Bundesländern' [a perpetuation of the status quo in the old Federal Länder*] as the probable outcome of all the current discussions about change in the five new* Länder. *If something quite different from that which exists in the old FRG can be properly defended, however, there seems no reason why it could not be included in our recommendations. (Diary, p. 29)*

In retrospect, this was an optimistic view to take. I had argued at several meetings that the apparent strengths of the GDR's *Einphasigkeit* in teacher education should be retained, at least in an adapted form, but the ministries had decided on a two-phase approach, in emulation of the West German norm, and so such a proposal was academic.

Erfurt, 25 February

In our discussion with the Mittelbau *they again talk of the close relationship they have with practice – they would wish to retain such a relationship under the conditions of* Zweiphasigkeit. *There is a long discussion about 'Didaktik' and 'Methodik', and people won't admit that 'Methodik' in the East German sense ... is really a low-level activity; all the responses dress it up as the more respectable (West German) 'Didaktik'. (Diary, p. 21)*

Erfurt, 25 February

The Minister speaks a lot about the Mittelbau. *Many people have never had the chance to be* berufen *[appointed to professorships], and they must be helped. He thinks that* Hausberufungen *should be allowed for the time being, especially to give those in areas which have been* 'abgewickelt' *a chance. Advertisements should mention that applications from such people will be welcome. As an interim measure, qualified people whose achievements have been properly recognised might be chosen without the full* 'Dreier-Liste' *convention. At the same time it is clear, he says, that the size of the* Mittelbau *must be reduced.*

The Minister uses the term 'Krisenmanagement' *several times to indicate the provisional and improvised nature of much of the decision-making at present. He says that quite amazing things happened after November 1989 – new subjects were introduced and students were matriculated illegally. All of this has made the present political situation very complicated and difficult. (Diary, p. 20)*

Mühlhausen, 26 February

We arrive in Mühlhausen to be met by anxious-looking people, who fall over themselves in an attempt to do what we want ... We go on a quick tour of some of the labs and the library. The place looks generally run-down to me, and the people look sad and oppressed. We are proudly shown a lot of new equipment, mainly computers from the West, which sits uneasily alongside the old GDR stuff in rooms with old fittings and wallpaper. *In the library I flick through a doctoral thesis which has on its first page of text a reference to what Margot HONECKER (avec majuscules) said about* Allgemeinbildung *at such and such an educational congress.*

From the Mittelbau *we learn that they had little chance to do the* Habilitation, *that they had to subject themselves to a* Forschungsplan; *their research possibilities, moreover, were limited to what they could do with existing equipment. We are told that biology here is better equipped than at the University of Halle.*

... We meet with the students. 'Wir sind an der letzten Station hier' [We're at the last outpost here] says [Colleague B], and there is a titter of recognition from the students, because this does look something like the end of the world in Hochschule *terms. But they are positive about the kind of education they have had, feel themselves well prepared in terms of their subject discipline. Again, the point is made to us that the* PHs *and the universities had equal status in the GDR – why should a student travel away from home to a university, if there is a* PH *in his home town? Indeed, they say, since teacher education was a peripheral business at the universities, those wanting to become teachers were better off at the* PHs. *(Diary, p. 36)*

28 February, en route to London

The universities and Hochschulen *are in a poor way, planning for the future while battling with a host of current problems, and all in an atmosphere of uncertainty and great improvisation. The ... image which most depresses me is that of [a West German academic we had met on one of our visits] [6], 'rescuing' the* Erziehungswissenschaftler *– quite dreadful, and certainly something all could do without. (Diary, pp. 37–38)*

In retrospect, the work of the group was an example of a well-meaning exercise to attempt to understand the difficult problems facing teacher education in the eastern *Länder*, to provide such moral support and help as was possible in the circumstances, and to make recommendations based on a careful analysis of the situation on the ground (*vorort*, in German) and on the expertise and experience of the group members, who came from a wide variety of backgrounds. The remaining impression is that everything in the early post-unification months was so very rushed that there was not sufficient time for the slow and careful deliberation that might be considered desirable when dealing with such important issues as those affecting the future of education.

There was indeed a need for quick and emergency measures to ensure that the new citizens of the enlarged Federal Republic were being fairly treated and provided with adequate materials and facilities, and to rid the system of its undesirable features. But I still feel 10 years or so later that much could have been done at a political level to ensure a smoother process of movement away from the structural arrangements inherited from the GDR towards such 'western' structures as might prove realistic and workable in the east. One of the recurring themes of our discussions in the working group – what might be retained of the old system, and built upon – was not, it seems, given much attention (if any) by those in power as they planned the future structure of educational provision in the eastern *Länder*. This remains a matter of regret, and we are left with the general feeling (deriving also from the situation in education generally in the eastern *Länder*) that many problems might have been avoided had the political imperative for rapid change and reform along western lines not been so irresistible.

Notes

[1] The science commission's members are nominated partly by the German Research Association (*Deutsche Forschungsgemeinschaft*), the Max Planck Society, the University Rectors' Conference (*Deutsche Rektorenkonferenz*), and the Association of National Research Centres, and partly by the federal and *Länder* governments (Führ, 1997, p. 64).

[2] Letter to me from the Chairman of the *Wissenschaftsrat*, 31 October 1990.

[3] David Phillips (1983) The British and University Reform Policy in Germany 1945–49. A Study with Particular Reference to the *Gutachten zur Hochschulreform* of 1948, unpublished DPhil thesis, University of Oxford; (1984) *Zur Universitätsreform in der Britischen Besatzungszone 1945–1948*. Cologne: Böhlau; (1995) *Pragmatismus und*

Idealismus: Das 'Blaue Gutachten' und die Britische Hochschulpolitik in Deutschland 1948. Cologne: Böhlau; (1981) Britische Initiative zur Hochschulreform in Deutschland. Zur Vorgeschichte und Entstehung des 'Gutachtens zur Hochschulreform' von 1948, in: Manfred Heinemann (Ed.) *Umerziehung und Wiederaufbau – Die Bildungspolitik der Besatzungsmächte in Deutschland und Österreich.* Stuttgart: Klett-Cotta; (1980) Lindsay and the German Universities: an Oxford contribution to the post-war reform debate, *Oxford Review of Education*, 6; (1982) British Influences on University Reform Proposals in Germany after the War, *Compare*, 12; (1983) Die Wiedereröffnung der Universitäten in der Britischen Zone: Das Problem Nationalismus und Zulassung zum Studium, *Bildung und Erziehung*, 36 Jg., Heft 1; (1984) British University Officers in Germany after the War, *International Journal of Educational Development*, 4.

[4] Nina Arnhold is currently researching the genesis and effects of the group's recommendations in the context of the development of teacher education in the new *Länder* (see Arnhold, 1998).

[5] The Universities in the British Zone of Germany, *The Universities Review*, 19 (1947), p. 205.

[6] The person in question had said to me when I came across him during one of our visits – unaware of the colonialist image he was helping to perpetuate – 'Ich wollte hier was retten' [I wanted to rescue something here]!

References

Arnhold, Nina (1998) The Transformation of East German Teacher Education, in Elizabeth A. McLeish & David Phillips (Eds) *Processes of Transition in Education Systems.* Oxford: Symposium Books.

Führ, Christoph (1997) *The German Education System since 1945.* Bonn: Inter Nationes.

Phillips, David (2000) Reconstructing Education in Germany: some similarities and contrasts in the post-war and post-unification rethinking in educational provision, in Leslie Limage (Ed.) *Democratizing Education and Educating Democratic Citizens. International and Historical Perspectives.* London: Routledge Falmer.

Wissenschaftsrat (1992) *Empfehlungen zur künftigen Struktur der Hochschullandschaft in den neuen Ländern und im Ostteil von Berlin*, Teil I, 'Empfehlungen zur Lehrerbildung in den neuen Ländern', pp. 81–159. Cologne: Wissenschaftsrat.

Vocational Education and Training in Eastern Germany: some reasons and explanations for current problems

HUBERT ERTL

Introduction

International comparisons of youth unemployment rates have shown Germany to be in a favourable situation. For instance, in 1997, 10.3% of Germans under the age of 25 were out of work, whereas the corresponding figure for the average of European Union (EU) countries was 21% (Bundesinstitut für Berufsbildung [BIBB], 1999, p. 3; cf. Bundesministerium für Bildung, Wissenschaft, Forschung und Technologie [BMBF], 1998, p. 117ff.) One of the frequently mentioned factors for the relatively effective transition of young people from school to work is the so-called 'Dual System' of vocational education and training (VET). The appeal of the Dual System to other countries [1] is primarily due to its socio-economic potentials. Finegold & Soskice (1988) characterised this system as a 'high-skill equilibrium' in which the majority of the workforce attain certifiable intermediate skills through a combination of in-company and supplementary school-based training. In this Dual System, around two-thirds of all young people between 16 and 18 years of age are trained. The system is based on a contract between the training enterprise (the firm where the practical training takes place) and the trainee. Trainees spend 3–4 days a week at their training enterprise and for the rest of the week attend a state-run part-time vocational school (*Berufsschule*). Blocks of training at external training centres often supplement on-the-job training. The systematic interplay of the system of education and the world of work in the Dual System is regarded as 'best practice' in the area of initial training (BMBF, 1998, p. 1).

However, the Dual System of VET in Germany is called into question by many educationists for a variety of reasons. The future prospects of the system are the subject of great controversy.[2] Arguments in favour of a sceptical position are provided by the symptoms of crisis in the training sector: decreasing appeal of the Dual System to potential trainees, declining willingness of employers to provide training places [3] and drastically dwindling state resources for training (Münk,

125

1997, p. 8). The challenges that the Dual System is facing seem to be enormous: rising educational standards, increasing heterogeneity of trainees, higher demands on training, higher average age of trainees and changing training conditions in companies (Keune & Zielke, 1992, p. 32; Georg, 1997, p. 314). Culpepper (1999) has shown a list of factors threatening the high-skill equilibrium as defined by Finegold & Soskice. Undoubtedly, these challenges do not only concern the Dual System but are rooted in changing social conditions affecting the main structures of the whole educational system.[4] The changing relationship between general and vocational education may represent the most prominent example for this transitional phase in education.

From a quantitative point of view, there are considerable regional differences: whereas there was a surplus of training places in the western *Länder* of Germany for most of the 1990s, the figures for the eastern *Länder* show a constantly severe shortage of training places (cf. BMBF, 1999, p. 2, and Table I). Some observers even conclude that the Dual System has not found its feet in the former East Germany and, therefore, qualified and motivated young people are forced to move to the western *Länder*. Culpepper (1999, p. 51) has termed the situation on the east German training market a 'subsidized disequlibrium'.

Year*	Supply		Demand		Excess/ Shortage	Newly concluded training contracts	
	in total	change in %	in total	change in %	in total	in total	change in %
1992	98,462		96,449		+2,013	95,230	
1993	101,033	+2.6	101,869	+5.6	−836	98,951	+3.9
1994	119,257	+18	119,386	+17.2	−129	117,872	+19.1
1995	123,629	+3.7	128,212	+7.4	−4,583	122,646	+4.1
1996	126,109	+2.0	138,849	+8.3	−12,740	125,028	+1.9
1997	126,336	+0.2	140,920	+1.5	−14,584	125,689	+0.5
1998	129,726	+2.7	141,511	+0.4	−11,785	129,195	+2.8

Note: * for 1991 there are no reliable figures available.

Table I. Supply and demand of training places in the eastern *Länder*, 1992–97 (source: BMBF, 1999, p. 2).

This negative situation of the Dual System in eastern Germany was not foreseen by most politicians and educationists. With the imminent collapse of the entire social structure at the end of the lifespan of the former GDR (including the economic and the educational system), the Dual System was regarded as an important element for a new overall framework that had been successful and well tested in the Federal Republic. It was expected that the system could be easily adopted as legal, financial, political and administrative support was offered by the western Federal States (*Länder*) (Wordelmann, 1992, p. 13). It was also believed that the tradition of duality in the training sector of both parts of Germany could facilitate the transfer of the Dual System from west to east.

The common tradition in VET represents the starting point for this chapter. It aims to shed light on the shared experiences before Word War II. It then portrays how two different systems in VET developed as a consequence of different economic systems and ideological foundations in post-war East and West Germany. On this basis, the legal transition process in eastern Germany caused by unification is reconstructed. Against these backgrounds the continuing difficulties of the transition process and some explanations for them are given.

The research for this chapter was conducted within the thematic and conceptual framework of the European research and training network PRESTiGE (Problems of Educational Standardisation and Transitions in a Global Environment). The network is funded by the European Commission's TMR (Training and Mobility of Researchers) Programme and consists of institutes concerned with comparative education at the universities in Stockholm, Berlin, Dijon, Lisbon, Madrid and Oxford. Each of these institutes has specified a particular research focus within the overall thematic framework.[5]

The Centre for Comparative Studies in Education at the University of Oxford is conducting an investigation into the processes of interpretation and implementation of EC policies in education and training in four EC member states (the United Kingdom, France, Germany and Sweden). The conceptual and theoretical framework of this project in Oxford and the overall PRESTiGE network has been described in some detail elsewhere (Phillips & Economou, 1999; Ertl, 1999a).

2. The Heritage of Vocational Training in Germany

Both former parts of Germany share the underlying principle of dual (i.e. in-firm and vocational school-based) training of young people. Undoubtedly, this principle represents a common heritage, and these common roots – in turn – substantially influenced the developments in East and West Germany during the 40 years of separation. The system can be traced back to the Middle Ages, when the master craftsman trained his apprentice.[6] As in most other European countries, this form of apprenticeship training was widespread in Germany and subject to strict control of the guilds. By the eighteenth century, however, the guilds and the apprenticeship system had degenerated into a deplorable state. The training of apprentices declined into mere exploitation of young people due to the disappearance of the guilds' regulating powers.

Legislative initiatives throughout the nineteenth century (the Prussian Trade and Industry Code [*Allgemeine Preußische Gewerbeordnung*] of 1845 [amended in 1897] and, more importantly, the Trade and Industry Code of the North German Federation [*Gewerbeordnung des Norddeutschen Bundes*] of 1869) can be regarded as attempts to fill the vacuum left by the loss of the guilds' powers (Deissinger, 1996, p. 318ff.) Nevertheless, it was not until 1908 that the 'limited certificate of competence' (*Kleiner Befähigungsnachweis*) [7] was introduced and stabilised the provisions satisfactorily: under this amendment of the Trade Code an employer wishing to provide training had to furnish proof of his qualifications as a master craftsman.

From the last third of the nineteenth century onwards, industry and commerce increasingly based their vocational training on the model of the craftsman apprenticeship.[8] Consequently, the industry-led 'German Committee of Technical Education' (*DATSCH – Deutscher Ausschuß für das Technische Schulwesen*) established industry-specific training structures incorporating the 'concept of the vocation', which also underpins the apprenticeship system as developed within the crafts (Benner, 1997, p. 56ff.).

Within the crafts and industry, the rise of natural sciences and modern technologies made it increasingly necessary to have a theoretical foundation upon which to base practical work. As theory could no longer be learned solely through experience, classes had to be held to remedy any deficits in basic education and to supplement practical training. From the beginning of the nineteenth century onwards, this role was assumed by further training schools (*Fortbildungsschulen*), which often originated in religious Sunday schools which were mostly founded in the eighteenth century. Alongside the industrial Sunday schools, whose ethos drew on the ideas of the Enlightenment and mercantilism, religious Sunday schools gradually assumed the role of teaching the theoretical foundations relating to apprentices' occupations.[9] The Trade and Industry Code of 1869 underlined the generally recognised importance of these further training schools; the dual structure of training began to emerge and was sanctioned by the state for the first time.

From the first half of the twentieth century onwards, this new structure survived the upheavals caused by the Great Depression and the two World Wars. Furthermore, it was not substantially altered by the emerging models of industrial apprenticeship training, but integrated these new models into the framework that was established by craft and industry at around the turn of the century. Also, from 1900 onwards, the further training schools lost their original role of remedying the lack of basic education, as the elementary school sector was substantially expanded (Groothoff, 1964, p. 20). Consequently, they shifted their pedagogic emphasis to that of supplementing vocational training in enterprises and as a result, the development of vocational schools (*Berufsschulen*) in the contemporary sense had begun.[10] The term *Berufsschule* was applied to those institutions in 1920 and by 1938 attendance had become compulsory (Her Majesty's Inspectorate [HMI], 1995, p. 17).

It is important to note that the stabilisation of the craft apprenticeship system, the development of training provisions in the industrial sector, and the expansion of further training schools all took place fairly independently of each other, despite happening at approximately the same time (Greinert, 1994, p. 22). It was not until the turn of the century that attempts were made to amalgamate these different sectors into a special form of qualification, a form which became known as the Dual System of vocational education in the Federal Republic. The former GDR certainly shared this heritage of vocational education in state-recognised training occupations (*anerkannte Ausbildungsberufe*) which combined work at a vocational school and a training company. The way in which this 'central and common starting point of vocational education' (Lemke, 1992, p. 81) was developed further in East and West Germany was, however, distinctly different, as will be shown in the next section.

From an international perspective, the model of vocational training in both parts of Germany represents a special case; in most other European countries school-based training is predominant.[11] In both the Federal Republic and the former GDR, the training of apprentices in a dual mode has been central to the overall system of vocational qualification. In the late 1980s, 80% of those in work in the GDR had concluded an apprenticeship, compared to about 60% in the then 11 *Länder* of West Germany (Max-Planck, 1994, p. 550). Thus, in both East and West Germany, apprenticeship training in quantitative terms represented the largest sector of all initial vocational education and training for young people (Uthmann, 1991, p. 5). Moreover, in combination with schemes of further vocational and/or academic education, the apprenticeship was and still is the centrepiece and foundation of the vocational route within the system of education. In stark contrast to most European countries outside the German cultural area, this form of initial vocational training is no educational dead end, but offers a wide range of possibilities for developing people's occupational prospects. It can therefore be argued that the apprenticeship model in a dual structure in both parts of Germany has not only been a safeguard for relatively high educational standards of the population in the vocational but also in the general/academic sphere of education (Max-Planck, 1994, p. 576ff.).

The concept of 'education by and in work' is closely bound to the German 'concept of the vocation' (*deutsches Berufskonzept*), which has been central to the apprenticeship models in both East and West Germany. This concept underpins the multitude of leitmotivs and acts of legislation regulating the differentiated system of initial and further qualification in Germany (Benner, 1996, p. 3ff.)[12] Most importantly, the concept sets the individual's capability to work and act competently in a vocational environment (*berufliche Handlungsfähigkeit*) as the overarching aim of vocational education and training. This capability is regarded as a necessary precondition for any employment, and goes beyond the mere earning of the individual's living by emphasising the notion of personal development. Education as part of this personal development has been a constant feature of vocational education in Germany. In the east it was linked with the Marxist philosophy, whereas in the west it has always been associated with market ideologies (Max-Planck, 1994, p. 576; Pritchard, 1999, p. 122).

3. The Structural Differences in the Training and Employment Systems of East and West Germany

Due to these different ideological associations, the development of training systems took different directions in the two parts of Germany after the Second World War. The differences were also the consequence of the existence of two diametrically opposed economic systems, both firmly locked into one of the world's two large economic blocs.

Centrally-planned vs. Market-regulated Training Systems

According to the constitution of the former GDR, young people who did not go on to work for the university entrance certificate after school year 10 had the 'right and the obligation to train for a vocation' (Constitution of the German Democratic Republic, Art. 25, para. 4). Furthermore, upbringing, education and vocational training were state-organised, planned and unified (Autsch, 1995, p. 16). These principles were implemented by educational and labour legislation and resulted in the centrally-planned distribution of school leavers to training companies and into training occupations (Burkhardt, 1992, p. 32ff.) There was never any free choice regarding occupation or company as in the Dual System of the Federal Republic, where this allocation process is largely left to market forces. The Vocational Training Act (*Berufsbildungsgesetz* – *BBIG*), adopted in West Germany in 1969, determines a system that may be best described as a 'state-controlled market model' [13], in which the state sets the guidelines for the cooperation of employers and trade unions.[14] This model is regarded as an efficient way of limiting the risks of 'market failure' on the one hand and 'state failure' on the other (Kutscha, 1995, p. 10).

Training Occupations and Scope of Training

To a certain extent, training occupations in the GDR resembled those in the former Federal Republic: there was a similar number of such occupations (in the west: approximately 370 *anerkannte Ausbildungsberufe*, in the east: approximately 316 *anerkannte Facharbeiterberufe*) (Burkhardt, 1992, pp. 31, 34; Horn, 1992, p. 55ff.), and the requirements in both parts of Germany consisted of two basic parts – practical vocational content taught at a training company; and theoretical vocational and general content [15] taught in vocational schools. However, the content of training in East Germany was never of the same breadth or depth. The prescribed training period amounted (normally) only to 2 years, whereas the average period in West Germany is approximately 1 year longer. The comparatively short duration of training in the former GDR was justified with the vocational preparation of all young people in the *Polytechnische Oberschule (POS)*.[16]

Contrary to the Dual System in the west, the system in the former GDR incorporated the double qualification of a substantial part of trainees. After 10 years of schooling at the *POS* and 3 (instead of normally 2) years of training, a vocational qualification (*Facharbeiter*) and the university entrance qualification (*Abitur*) could be achieved.[17] There were also recognised qualifications covering only parts of a standard qualification. Although employers in West Germany have often advocated the recognition of parts of occupational profiles as a means of enabling disadvantaged young people to achieve a vocational qualification, the trade unions have always opposed the introduction of such 'substandard' qualifications. In contrast, in 1989, 7% of all trainees in East Germany were qualified in partial-training schemes which were designed for young people who left school without a leaving certificate (Werner, 1992, p. 221).[18] This expansion of the mainstream training system has not happened in West Germany and came to an end when the former GDR adopted the provisions of the Federal Republic.

Training Sectors and Size of Training Companies

Whereas small- and medium-sized companies in the handicrafts and trade sector (in which most trainees in the Federal Republic work after their training) were comparatively less important in the GDR, the economy was dominated by the large nationalised industrial and agricultural companies and combines. The skilled industrial worker represented the leitmotiv of the entire training sector (Sloane, 1997b, p. 366). Companies in these sectors trained substantially more young people and employed many more trained workers than their counterparts in the west (see Figure 1 and the detailed analysis of Werner, 1992). On the other hand, training in the commercial sector was chronically underdeveloped as market-oriented commercial companies played no part in the centrally-planned economy.

This structural difference between East and West Germany is also reflected in the size of the training companies: in the GDR, 37% of all people in work were trained in companies with more than 500 employees; prior to unification the corresponding figure in the Federal Republic was only 11%. In the west, two-thirds of trainees were trained in companies with fewer than 50 employees, and in the GDR this group of companies was only accountable for the training of one-quarter of all trainees. As a consequence, trainees in the east were much more likely to be trained in groups than in the west: Statistically, each training company in the west employed three trainees, and many of them trained only one. In the east, each training company employed 70 trainees on average at a time (Max-Planck, 1994, p. 581ff.).

Figure 1. Training qualifications gained in the different economic sectors by percentage.[19]

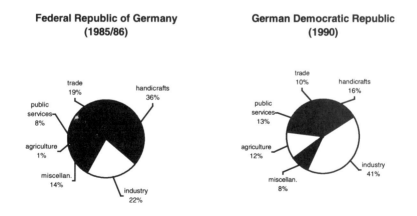

Federal Republic of Germany (1985/86)   **German Democratic Republic (1990)**

Furthermore, the substantially different sizes of the average training company in the east as compared to the west also affected the allocation of roles for the training personnel. In the west, trainers in small- and medium-sized companies would often only have a few hours per day or even per week to supervise their trainees as training was only one of a number of work tasks. Although there were also many of these part-time trainers (*Lehrfacharbeiter/Lehrbeauftragte*) in the former GDR, they always had a superior, full-time trainer (*Lehrmeister*) for whom training issues represented the only responsibility. These full-time trainers created the framework for the training process and assisted the part-time trainers in all questions arising (Neubert, 1999).

As we will see later, these differences have created major problems in the training sector in the new *Länder* after German unification.

In-company vs. Municipal Vocational Schools

More pronounced than in the west, the official training policy in the eastern part of Germany followed the aim of an ever-closer connection between theoretical knowledge and practice as it was manifested in the world of work. Both areas of the training process were developed in close interrelation, with most of the training being based in the 'work collective' (*Arbeitskollektiv*).[20]

On an institutional level, this close connection meant that most vocational schools – in contrast to the Dual System in West Germany – were part of the individual training company (*Betriebsberufsschulen*). These schools formed a department of the large nationalised companies and combines, with the head of the school being directly responsible to the company leadership (Horn, 1992, p. 53ff.) After its introduction in 1948, this type of vocational school was soon the dominant kind of institution for the theoretical and general instruction of trainees (Waterkamp, 1987, p. 193). The institutional duality of training sites was in these cases largely not existent any more. Trainees from smaller companies that did not have the capacity for their own *Betriebsberufsschule* were taught in municipal vocational schools (*Kommunale Berufsschulen*). These trainees came predominately from smaller socialist craft and retailing companies.[21] The trend towards in-company vocational schools did not change the basic principle of joint financing of training, with the state assuming the costs for the theoretical instruction, and the training company assuming the costs of job-related training (Ernst, 1991, p. 244; Horn, 1992, p. 53). Only for trainees who attended municipal vocational schools in the former GDR were the provisions – at an institutional level – similar to the regulations in the Dual System in the Federal Republic.[22]

Dual vs. Unitary System

The introduction and promotion of in-company vocational schools in the former GDR can be regarded as the central element of a drive towards a 'unitary system' of training, with the training company as the central venue of instruction and learning. For this drive to overcome the duality of training by creating a 'dialectical unity' of provisions there were ideological (differentiating the own GDR training system from the one in the Federal Republic) as well as theoretical (creating a more integrated training structure) reasons. The devaluation of municipal vocational schools as 'second rate' compared to in-company schools from the 1970s onwards indicates an increasingly ideologically-driven development of training provisions (Ernst, 1991, p. 242ff.) Corresponding to the institutional development there were changes in the regulative and administrative powers in the training system of the GDR.

After 1970 the State Office for Vocational Education (*Staatssekretariat für Berufsbildung*) was responsible for all aspects of initial and further training.[23] In a very centralist and directive structure, the *Staatssekretariat* administered and monitored the training companies and combines as well as the two types of vocational schools. It also developed and updated all important regulations for the training process (systematics of training occupations – *Systematik der Ausbildungsberufe*, training materials – *Ausbildungsunterlagen*). This is a marked difference from the system in the west where the term 'Dual' [24] refers to the division of training into two separate training environments, each regulated by its own distinct legislators. Federal law (e.g. training regulations – *Ausbildungsordnungen*) regulates in-company training; vocational schools fall under the legislation of the *Länder* (e.g. skeleton curricula – *Rahmenlehrpläne*). Legally speaking, training at vocational schools is regulated under public law, whereas the in-company training is regulated by the training contract between the training company and the trainee, i.e. under civil law.

The often criticised lack of coherence and cooperation of the learning sites in the Dual System of West Germany could be mitigated by the more centralised approach in the former East Germany. Also, the connection between theoretical and practical training content seems to benefit from the workplace orientation of initial training in the east, an approach which is not always dominant in the western Dual System (Sloane, 1994, p. 205ff.) Vocational schools as part of the training company seemed to be better equipped to prepare trainees for the demands of work in the company, particularly as the company had the obligation to offer every trainee a permanent job after training (Siemon, 1991, p. 269).

However, compared to the requirements of the provisions in West Germany, it seems doubtful that this structure could fulfil the demands of the concept of *berufliche Handlungsfähigkeit* as the major aim of training (cf. section 2). In the west, this concept is interpreted as the need to prepare young people not only for a small number of specific tasks at one company, but to provide a qualification applicable in many employment contexts and responsive to the changing economic and social environments of a whole occupational field (BBIG, para. 25[1]). Although well-conducted attempts were made, the fundamental problem of vocational education and training, namely, the imparting of theoretical-systematic knowledge and occupational practice in an integrated way, was not solved by the approach in the former GDR. A number of reforms in this area over the years, often reversing the innovations of former reforms [25], could be interpreted as attempts to search for a practicable solution to this problem (Max-Planck, 1994, p. 584).[26]

Central Planning vs. Self-governance

With the training sector closely bound to the needs of the centrally-planned economy, the responsibility for training, examinations and contents rested with the East German state. In the west, in contrast, local, self-governing Chambers of Industry and Commerce, the Crafts Chambers, the Chambers of Agriculture and the Associations of Professions have the status of 'competent bodies' (*zuständige Stellen*) and play a crucial role in the organisation, administration and examination of vocational training. As intermediate organisations between state and companies, they put training laws and regulations into practice. Following the principle of corporative structures, supervising and examining bodies set up by the Chambers consist of equal numbers of employers' representatives, employees' representatives and vocational school teachers. The former GDR had no such mechanisms for social partnerships.

Considering these far-reaching differences in the training systems, it becomes clear that the Dual System as developed in the west could not simply be transferred to the east. A whole new infrastructure had to be set up, based on social partnership, including trade unions, work councils and new, small- and medium-sized training companies. In a time of unprecedented change immediately after the fall of the Berlin Wall, this was obviously a daunting task.

4. The Transformation Process of Vocational Education and Training in the East

Even as far back as in the Treaty for the Creation of a Monetary, Economic and Social Union (*Vertrag zur Schaffung der Währungs-, Wirtschafts- und Sozialunion*), signed by East and West Germany in May 1990, the legal basis of the system for vocational education and training in the Federal Republic was identified as one the GDR was aiming to adopt in the near future (Wordelmann, 1992, p. 15). As early as August 1990, some weeks before official unification, the People's Chamber (parliament) of the former GDR adopted the laws most relevant to the Dual System of the Federal Republic – the Vocational Training Act (*Berufsbildungsgesetz*), the Vocational Training Development Act (*Berufsbildungsförderungsgesetz*), and the Crafts Code (*Handwerksordnung*) (Anweiler, 1991, p. 101). From 3 October 1990, newly concluded training contracts were based exclusively on the new legal system. Transitional measures existed in order to facilitate the process of assimilation for already existing training contracts (Weissflog, 1992, pp. 110–114). At the same time, the in-company vocational schools (*Betriebsberufsschulen*) came under the auspices of the newly formed *Länder* and municipalities. By autumn 1990, all eastern *Länder* had introduced the necessary legislation to regulate the sector of vocational schools (Lüth, 1991, p. 300ff.) Thus, the Dual System of the Federal Republic was in place a few weeks before the GDR was dissolved and the training year was about to start. Thousands of institutions concerned with vocational education, tens of thousands of full- and part-time teachers and trainers, and hundreds of thousands of trainees and apprentices had to deal with radically changed legal and organisational conditions.

Most of the vocational qualifications within the system of training occupations of the former GDR were equated with the corresponding qualifications in the old Federal Republic as soon as the Treaty of Unification came into effect. Only a few specific qualifications from GDR times temporarily kept their status as state-recognised qualifications (Walter & Höpfner, 1994, p. 135; BMBF, 1995, p. 46). The Trainer Aptitude Regulation (*Ausbildereignungsverordnung*) of the Federal Republic came into effect in the eastern *Länder* at the beginning of 1992.

As the newly established *Länder* became automatically part of the European Community (EC), their citizens were entitled to free movement within the Community and were eligible to use their vocational qualifications to find work in the different member states. From 1990 onwards, the eastern part of unified Germany was classified as a top priority region for structural help from the EU; the region particularly qualified for supportive measures in the training and education sector (Holldack et al, 1996, p. 5ff.) High quality vocational education and training is seen as a measure to prepare EC citizens for the opportunities of free movement. Therefore, the development of human resources is a central aim of EC policy. In order to achieve this aim, the EC established a special fund for the eastern German *Länder* in 1991. The fund facilitated the extension of the ECs education and training programmes to the eastern part of unified Germany. These included a number of programmes which aimed to promote the European dimension of training, like PETRA, EUROTECHNET, FORCE and ARION. By establishing these programmes, the fund addressed the need to make up for the shortage of cooperation, mobility, competence in western European languages and in educational management. At the same time, it was intended to provide assistance and backing for the restructuring of the training system and its connection to a transformed economy. It was regarded as a precondition that the mechanisms of EC programmes in education and training as they had been developed in the western German *Länder* had to be transferred quickly to the east (Manning, 1994, p. 149). From the training year 1992 onwards, it was expected that the eastern *Länder* would participate fully in the aforementioned EC programmes.[27]

It can be argued that the legal transition in the field of vocational education and training took place extremely swiftly and was well ahead of other areas of the transition process. Despite all the uncertainties created by the rapid adoption of the legal foundation of the western training system at an individual and institutional level, the new framework has created relatively clearly defined conditions for the restructuring of the training sector, following the well-established model in the west. It has been argued, on the one hand, that this new framework and the support from the Federal Republic was a major advantage for the eastern *Länder* in the immediate transition process in comparison to other countries of the former Soviet bloc. On the other hand, it has been argued that the potential of 40 years of development and research in the field in the former GDR was neglected and sacrificed for a system of training that was only seemingly [28] best equipped to minimise the problems of the first and second threshold in a modern market economy, i.e. the transfer of young people from school to training and from training to work (Degen et al, 1990).

It has also been argued that the legal transition process could only take place so swiftly because the systems of vocational education and training in both parts of Germany have not developed as differently as, for example, the system of general education. Therefore, it was not surprising that the new legal framework could be introduced comparatively easily in the newly founded *Länder* (Max-Planck-Institut, 1994, p. 128). Undoubtedly, however, the legal transition process had been formally completed on the surface before most of the underlying problems even became visible.

Because of the common heritage of dual structures in the training provisions, there was an expectation that the training sector of eastern Germany could be easily integrated into a unified employment and training market.[29] However, it soon became clear that the hope of a swift transformation of the economy and the training sector in eastern Germany had not been fulfilled.

5. The Continuing Problems of the Training Sector in Eastern Germany

Most notably, the training sector in eastern Germany has had quantitative problems since unification. From 1993 onwards, there has been a growing shortage of training places, which has primarily been a result of the steadily and substantially increasing number of young people looking for a training place (see Table I). The somewhat better figures in 1998 (a shortage of nearly 12,000 training places in the eastern *Länder* compared to a shortage of 14,500 in 1997) cannot be regarded as a reversal of the general trend, but show the limited success of a new, state-subsidised programme for the creation of training places in the east.[30]

The general trend of an increasingly severe shortage of training places in the east has been due not only to the demographic increase in the number of school leavers, but also to the changing choices of educational pathways; compared to their counterparts in the western *Länder*, a substantially bigger proportion of school leavers from the eastern *Länder* aim for training in the Dual System.[31] The increase in the number of training places has not been able to keep up with the growth rate on the demand side.

With the unification of Germany, the transition of the centrally-planned economy in the east to the market-oriented economic system of the west took place. *Inter alia*, this meant the break-up and privatisation of the large nationalised companies and combines of the former GDR from 1991 onwards (Burkhardt & Kielwein, 1992, p. 15). As we have seen, these companies and combines trained most of the trainees during GDR times. Faced with the severe competition of western German and international companies and with the resulting economic difficulties, many large companies decreased the number of training places drastically from the training year 1990/91 onwards. The strong emphasis of the GDR economy on industry and agriculture contributed to this trend, as these sectors were hit particularly hard by the need for reconstruction. With the discontinuation of training capacities in industry and agriculture, the infrastructure of the whole training system was damaged. Small businesses in the craft and service sector, which traditionally train the majority of young people in the Federal Republic, have only emerged gradually [32] and made up for some of the losses in other sectors (Schwengler, 1998, p. 16).[33] For many of these smaller companies training was an entirely new task, and the necessary experience has still to be accumulated, not the least experiences in the different ways training is financed and resources are tapped (Siemon, 1991, p. 270ff.; Jordan, 1992, p. 506). As there is an expectation that small- and medium-sized companies will train a higher share of eastern German trainees in the coming years [34], assistance for the trainers in these companies seems to be of tremendous importance for the future of the Dual System in Germany.

Due to these structural problems in the training market, even many highly motivated young people (Gericke, 1994, p. 265ff.) do not manage to get a place for their training occupation of choice; instead they have to continue at school, or decide to take on a training contract in the western *Länder* (BMBF, 1998, p. 12ff.; 1999, p. 4). Moreover, the numbers of concluded training contracts include a substantial and increasing share either wholly or partly subsidised by federal or state government sources. In 1997, these places accounted for no less than 79% of all training places (BMBF, 1998, p. 35). Despite the explicit aim to create regular, i.e. in-company training places, many of the subsidised schemes fund school-based training opportunities. In 1994, their share accounted for 22% of all training contracts in the eastern *Länder* (Walden, 1996, p. 173).

Recent research shows that 1 year after they finish training, only 16% of young people with a school-based training qualification work in the occupation they were trained for. The corresponding figure for young people with a work-based training qualification is 42% (Ulrich & Westhoff, 1994). School-based training schemes seem to postpone the employment problem for young people from the first to the second threshold in eastern Germany (Damm-Rüger, 1994; Schöngen & Tuschke, 1999). Within the company- and workplace-oriented Dual System, these kinds of training places must be regarded as adverse to the overall structure because the market forces which ought to balance supply and demand in the medium term are weakened by prolonged state intervention. Culpepper (1999, p. 51) has described this situation as the 'subsidized disequilibrium' on the eastern German apprenticeship market. The subsidies which are most successful in encouraging eastern German firms to invest in apprenticeship training within the Dual System are those that facilitate training alliances among a number of firms (often anchored around a large firm). These schemes seem best equipped to create new training places without endangering the market orientation of the system.

Besides these problems in the training sector caused by the reconstruction of the overall economic system, there are also some difficulties closely related to the transition of the training system in the former GDR. Despite the underlying duality of the training model and the strong role of the nationalised companies, the state assumed the role of the central player in the training sector. As we have seen, centralised state authorities assumed and directed all important regulative powers in the system (Mitter, 1990, p. 337ff.). These regulating authorities suddenly lost their power. It took some time before a new regulative framework was established and the institutions formerly only responsible for the 11 *Länder* in the west covered the new *Länder* effectively. A whole new network of self-governing Chambers which assume the role of intermediate organisations between the state and the training companies had to be set up. The vocational schools had to be disentangled from the strong influence of the training companies. Hence, the duality of the system had to be re-established.

The fact that the new market-oriented structures made new economic thinking necessary also applied in the training sector. Instead of the centrally-planned allocation of school leavers to training places and training occupations, the allocation has to be made by supply and demand on the training market. As there have been more young people looking for training opportunities than there have been places on offer, potential trainees had to develop their skills in application-writing and in going to interviews. A new structure of vocational guidance at schools and job centres had to be established to help to balance supply and demand.

Furthermore, the trainers at companies and the teachers at vocational schools [35] have to come to terms with the new training regulations and curricula. This refers to new contents of regulations and curricula caused by different production processes and methods, organisational structures and institutional hierarchies compared to those during GDR times. For the vocational schools, this meant the introduction of new subjects, for in-company training the development of new training foci and a new allocation of roles for trainers.[36] However, trainers and teachers have not only to cope with new contents but also with new methods to teach or demonstrate the new contents.[37] New micro-didactic orientations have to be developed (Siemon, 1991, p. 277). These new orientations imply distinctly different roles for trainers, teachers and trainees to those predominant during GDR times (Walter & Höpfner, 1994, p. 136). The necessary reorientation of teachers and trainers seems to be particularly difficult as it took place in a phase of personal and professional uncertainty, not experienced by them hitherto. Sloane (1994, p. 202ff.) describes this process as a double change in which they have to detach themselves from the relative stability of the crumbling system and look constantly for new security, both on a personal and on a professional level. Professional knowledge which had been appropriate for the conditions during GDR times suddenly lost its validity; intra-personal tensions are inevitable (Sloane, 1997b, pp. 353–356). For most of the in-company trainers, the transition process also means that instructing trainees is no longer their main occupation and they are increasingly performing other tasks in the company (Walden, 1996, p. 172). Many full-time trainers (*Lehrmeister*) in the large companies and former combines lost their positions (Neubert, 1999).

A further group facing particularly severe problems are female school leavers. During GDR times, many young women were trained in technical training occupations in the industrial sector and other occupations which are regarded as traditional masculine domains. After unification, a reverse trend has taken place. Most female school leavers take up training places in administration, retailing and services, i.e. in sectors in which the female share of trainees has traditionally been high in the Dual System of the Federal Republic (Werner, 1992, p. 225ff.; Voigt,

1995, p. 83ff.). This is primarily due to economic difficulties and restructuring of the companies in this sector. Secondly, there seems to be decreasing acceptance of female trainees on the part of the employers (Walden, 1996, p. 174). The GDR's equal opportunity policy [38] seems to have little prolonged influence in the dramatically changing circumstances of the transition period. It has been argued that the introduction of the social constitution of the Federal Republic no longer guarantees full legal and economic independence (e.g. unmarried mothers no longer enjoy official guardianship on behalf of their children). In connection with the severe competition for training places in which females more often than not lose to their male counterparts (Parmentier, et al, 1994, pp. 37, 42), young women are facing 'growing, escalating discrimination' (Braun, et al, 1995, p. 147).

6. Concluding Remarks

As far as the overall situation on the training market is concerned, it can be concluded that the specific model of dual training structures transferred from the west to the east of Germany in the process of unification has not been consolidated up to now. The growing shortage of training places, the dependence on state-subsidised school-based training capacities, and the increasing discrimination against certain groups of young people all give proof that the supply side of the training market has not yet recovered from the shocks of the transition process. The growing demand for training places emphasises that the Dual System has proven to be attractive to young people, not only in the immediate restructuring process but also almost a decade later.

The crisis on the supply side can be explained by the inevitable problems caused by the enormous task of transforming a whole economy from a centrally-planned to a market-oriented system. Considering the close relationship between a work-based training structure like the Dual System and the overall economic system, the supply-side crisis of the training sector is not surprising. It can be argued that the training system transferred from the west to the east was implemented despite the fact that the economic conditions for which it was developed had not yet been created (Hörner, 1996, p. 52). Due to the prolonged economic depression in the eastern *Länder*, the early hopes that the market forces would soon ease the tensions on the training market and that the relative stable conditions of the western *Länder* would be soon achieved (Werner, 1992, p. 231ff.) were not fulfilled.

On the other hand, there are also problematic areas caused by the transfer of the western model of duality to the east. Sloane (1994, p. 205) argues that this transfer was oriented towards yesterday's solutions. The uncritical transfer of the western system to the east has neglected different social experiences and different background knowledge, and has created strong resentment against everything imported from the west. This is not only true for the training sector (Gieseke, 1994, p. 8). The mere restoration of a training system highly criticised and subject to reform attempts in the west could not solve the problems caused by the unique situation in the east. The negligence of 40 years of development in the training sector – irrespective of whether or not one approves of these developments – seems like a lost chance to create solutions responsive to the circumstances in the eastern *Länder*. Instead, the problems of the training sector in the west were exported to the east (Wordelmann, 1992, p. 27). The lack of coherence of in-company and in-school training and the lack of double-qualifying training modes within the Dual System seem to be the most prominent examples. A critical and constructive discussion of the approaches developed in these areas in the former GDR could have created valuable starting points for solutions not only in the eastern *Länder* but also in the western *Länder*.[39] A further development of the Dual System into a 'Plural System' (Kutscha, 1993, p. 49) with closer cooperation of the training sites involved, and the integration of academic and vocational education could have benefited from such a discussion.

Despite the common heritage of duality in the system of initial training, the reunification of the training sector is far from being completed − even 10 years after its legal reunion. The expectation that all problems will be solved as soon as the economy in the eastern *Länder* gathers pace seems to be dangerous as it neglects the need for the modernisation of the training system. Giving in to economic pressures poses the danger that training degenerates to a mere preparation for a company-specific, short-term job (Sloane, 1993, p. 115). The idea of initial training as a phase in the education and development of young people's personalities must remain central to the Dual System. In the west and in the east of Germany, time and again people have predicted the imminent end of the system and its underlying principles. Nevertheless, it has turned out that the new challenges in both parts of Germany were met by changes within the system rather than by developing an entirely new system. Bearing the long and common tradition of dual training structures in mind, it seems reasonably safe to argue that current challenges in the German training sector will be met by a cautious process of modernisation within the system rather than by replacing it.

Notes

[1] For the influence of the German system on educational policy and practice in other countries, see Wilson (1997, p. 437).

[2] Some observers regard it as a model which has had its day and should be phased out; others regard it as a highly successful export commodity which will be the model for VET not only in the EC but also in the countries of the former Communist bloc (cf. Arnold, 1993, p. 20ff.; Heimerer, 1995, p. 166).

[3] Sloane (1997a, p. 233) speaks of a double-sided crisis within the system: On the one hand, large training companies are reducing their training places because of the high costs, and on the other hand, small- and medium-sized firms have difficulties finding suitable trainees as their training provisions appear not to be attractive enough to gifted young people in contrast to higher education. Kloas (1994, p. 136ff.) questions the statistical bases of many studies concerned with the figures for supply and demand of training places.

For empirical studies on current and future training supply and demand, see

Parmentier et al (1994), Tessaring (1996), and for the relevant statistics in the last two years, see BMBF (1998, 1999).

[4] Cf. Müller & Schaarschuch (1996, p. 9) and Deissinger (1996, p. 324). It has even been argued that the Dual System is not in crisis but its institutions are (Schmidt, 1996, p. 2); in particular the *Berufsschule* seems to have been in need of reform for over a decade now, as the didactic shortcomings and the 'identity crises' caused by improving in-company training in the larger training enterprises were already identified 15 years ago by Kloss (1985).

[5] For further information on the PRESTiGE partners and their work, visit the Internet site http://www.interped.su.se/prestige/ or see the project's biannual publication, *Newsletter* (PRESTiGE, 1998). The areas of interest and the theoretical and methodological concepts of the six part projects are described in Ertl (1999a).

[6] The earliest known document referring to guild-regulated apprenticeship training is the ordinance of the Cologne wood turners dated 1182.

[7] Contrary to this legislation, the 'general certificate of competence' (*Großer Befähigungsnachweis*) of 1936 made the status of 'master craftsman' not only necessary for training apprentices but also for running a business. The status of 'master craftsman', in turn, was regulated by the Chambers of Crafts, constituted in 1900 (Rothe, 1995, p. 79ff.).

[8] Deissinger (1992, pp. 404–412) identifies the reason for the decline of the English apprenticeship system during the twentieth century in the lack of coherence between the development of the educational system and the process of industrialisation from the end of the nineteenth century onwards. Whereas German industry regarded learning exclusively at industrial workplaces as insufficient to ensure comprehensive occupational qualifications, and therefore initiated training workshops for employees and developed industry-specific training, the English education and training system did not react to the new demands of industrial work structures. With the growth of industry, the decline of the crafts-based apprenticeship system was inevitable. For a comparison of the developments of training provisions in England and Germany from the Industrial Revolution to the 1920s, see Deissinger (1994).

[9] Due to differing levels of industrialisation within German states and municipalities, industrial Sunday schools were structured in a variety of ways, and had differing spheres of influence (Neugebauer, 1992, p. 108ff.) In general, it can be said that the typical German particularism (*Kleinstaaterei*) led to a vast diversity of legislative and institutional provisions at this time.

[10] Georg Kerschensteiner's prize essay on the 'Civic Education of German Youth' of 1901 *(Staatsbürgerliche Erziehung der deutschen Jugend*, Preisschrift der Erfurter Akademie der Wissenschaft, in Simons, 1966) represented probably the most important step on the way from the '*Fortbildungsschule* to the *Berufsschule*' (Thyssen, 1954).

[11] Despite the widespread orientation on Soviet models, the GDR established a special position within the Soviet bloc by maintaining the principle of work-oriented training (Burkhardt, 1992, p. 34).

[12] In the Federal Republic, Kutscha regards the 'concept of the vocation', which represents also the basis of the vocational structured employment system in

Germany, as the centrepiece of the Dual System (1995, p. 11), rather than the 'imaginary' duality of training places (1992, p. 539).

[13] This model must be seen in contrast to the *bureaucratic model* (the state alone plans, organises and controls vocational training, e.g. as in the former GDR) and the *market model* (the state plays no role, the provision of training is regulated solely by supply and demand). For other attempts to classify vocational training systems, see Greinert (1994, p. 11ff.).

[14] This *corporative* structure in vocational training can be traced back to the amendments to the Trade Code in 1897 and 1908 (Kutscha, 1998, p. 270). The theory of *corporatism* proposes the organisation of the whole of society into industrial and professional *corporations* serving as organs of political representation and exercising some control over persons and activities within their jurisdiction while still being subordinated to the state (cf. 'corporatism' in *Encyclopaedia Britannica* [1997]; Emile Durkheim's ideas on corporatism in Aron [1967, p. 85ff.] and Wagner [1991, p. 230ff.]).

[15] The continuation of general education in vocational training can be seen as a vital contribution to the 'overall and harmonious development of the personality' (Max-Planck, 1994, p. 577, cf. also Autsch, 1995, p. 16), a characteristic aim of training in East as well as in West Germany.

For a comparison of the shares of theoretical and practical training contents in eastern and western Germany prior to 1990, see Pritchard (1999, p. 122).

[16] From 1963, the 10 -year *POS* was compulsory for all pupils from age 6 onwards. It represented a 'pure' type of comprehensive school, i.e. there were no competing, selective school types or private schools (Phillips, 1999, p. 54). The polytechnic and vocational instructions at these schools were divided into the subjects 'introduction to socialist production', 'technical drawing' and 'productive work' (Lemke, 1992, p. 64ff.)

As this chapter concentrates on the structural and institutional aspects of the training provisions, 'ideological features' of these provisions in the former GDR, such as the involvement of the FDJ (*Freie Deutsche Jugend*), and the influence of military preparation at school are not considered. For a brief overview of these elements, see, for example, Horn (1992, pp. 52, 57–63).

[17] This form of double qualification was seen as a means of creating parity of esteem between academic and vocational education and to establish a more unified structure of educational provisions (cf. Law of the Unity of the Socialist Education System of 1965).

[18] There were varying preconditions concerning the required number of school years and school qualifications in the former GDR, which depended on the specific training occupation (Burkhardt, 1992, p. 37ff.) This represents a contrast to the Dual System in the Federal Republic, where there are no formal requirements concerning general schooling for taking up training.

[19] Source: BMBF (1992).

[20] One of the consequences of this development was that trainees were required to fulfil the equivalents of work output of skilled workers in the last 2 months of their training. This aim was certainly also caused by the pressures of the centrally

prescribed Five- and One-Year-Plans in which the ministries set the target of production for the nationalised companies and combines. For discussion of the pedagogical consequences of this approach, cf. Waterkamp (1985, pp 293–298).

[21] In 1989, two-thirds of trainees received their theoretical and general training at the 951 *Betriebsberufsschulen*, one-third at the 238 *Kommunalen Berufsschulen* (Max-Planck, 1994, p. 583).

[22] In the Federal Republic's Dual System, companies provide vocational training at their own expense, and trainees have to be paid an appropriate training wage. The *Land* authorities bear the costs of in-school training. Thus, the total costs of training are shared in the ratio of approximately 40% (*Länder*) and 60% (employers) (Noah & Eckstein, 1988, p. 61).

[23] For an account of the changes in the power relations between the State Office and the Ministry of Education after 1970, cf. Waterkamp (1987, pp. 170–181).

[24] For a description of other elements of the system demonstrating its duality, see Wilson (1997, p. 439). As in-company training is often supplemented by training at external training centres (Greinert, 1994, pp. 94–97) run by the Chambers or private providers, it has been argued that the term 'Dual' is too ambiguous to describe the relationship between training in enterprises and vocational schools accurately (Kutscha, 1996, p. 10ff.).

[25] For a discussion of the numerous reforms and changes in the institutional framework of vocational education and training in the former GDR, see Waterkamp (1987, ch. IV) and Siemon (1991, p. 271ff.). In particular, the discussions and different approaches tried out in the introduction of basic occupations (for the first year of training) and specialised occupations (for the following years) seems to indicate a problem in the integration of general, more theoretical contents and specialised, more practical training contents (Lemke, 1992, p. 63; Max-Planck, 1994, p. 548).

[26] Ernst (1991) holds a very different view. He argues that the general problem of different training venues was only repressed in the former GDR. The developments towards a 'unitary training system' did not change the underlying duality (i.e. the division of theoretical and practical contents and modes of instruction) of the training provisions. Due to the conscious discussion of the problem, the western system has created possible solutions (e.g. institutionalised cooperation schemes of training companies and vocational schools), whereas the suppression worsened the issue in the eastern system. Waterkamp (1985, ch. IV) even regards the centralised structure in the training sector of the former GDR and its domination by work-based learning as a failure.

[27] From 1993 onwards, a research project by WIFO (*Wissenschaftsforum Bildung und Gesellschaft* – Research Forum on Education and Society) examined the role played by EC programmes in support of education and training. One of its major findings was that the establishment of appropriate and responsive implementation structures prevented a substantial impact on the training structures in eastern Germany for years. For the results of the project, see Manning (1992, 1993, 1994) and Jordan (1992, 1996).

[28] Interestingly, the recurrent discussion about the crisis of the Dual System of vocational training reached a peak in West Germany in the late 1980s as a

consequence of the shortage of training places in the mid-1980s. Owing to the demographic decline of young people at school-leaving age, this discussion slowed down to a certain extent at the beginning of the 1990s, only to gather pace again a few years later when the shortage of training places (see Table I) recurred in both parts of Germany.

[29] For a documentation of the common heritage of apprenticeship training in East and West Germany and the expectations of an easy extension of the western Dual System towards eastern Germany immediately after unification, see, for example, Uthmann (1991) and Ertl (1999b).

[30] Most important in this context is the Initiative for Training Places in the East (*Lehrstelleninitiative Ost*), which created 17,500 new places in 1998. For 1999, the new coalition government of Social Democrats and the Green Party introduced the Ad Hoc Programme for the Reduction of Youth Unemployment (*Sofortprogramm zum Abbau der Jugendarbeitslosigkeit*), to create 100,000 work or training places for young people. It is financed by two billion Marks, including 600 million Marks out of EU structural funds.

For the training policy of the new government and the role of the Ad Hoc Programme, see an interview with the new Minister for Education, Edelgard Bulmahn (1999). For the impact of other programmes on the training market in the eastern *Länder*, see BMBF (1999, pp. 3–10, 36–41).

[31] The proportion of school leavers to the number of applicants for training places is about 20% higher in the east compared to the west (Walden, 1996, p. 172).

[32] Support for training in these smaller companies (250 million Marks in 1991) and for the setting-up of new businesses (172.5 million Marks between 1990 and 1994) was a focus in the government support programme in the eastern *Länder*, 'Development East' (*Aufbau Ost*) (BMBF, 1995, pp. 26–29, 49).

[33] Statistical evidence for these tendencies abounds. Whereas in 1990 three-quarters of all training places were based in big companies (over 500 employees), well over one half of trainees in 1995 found their places in small- and medium-sized companies – a trend that follows the conditions in the western *Länder* (Walden, 1996, p. 172; cf. also Parmentier et al, 1994, p. 43).

[34] In a study conducted by Degen (1995), significantly more large companies plan to decrease training capacities than small- and medium-sized companies in the near future.

[35] For details on the qualifications, responsibilities and the social and professional status of teachers and trainers in the former GDR, see, for instance, Burkhardt (1992, p. 47ff.), Max-Planck (1994, section 13.4), and Dietrich, et al (1996).

[36] Wilde (1991) shows that at a first glance the similarities of subjects and training foci in old and new training regulations and curricula seem to be dominant. Only a closer comparison shows how differently the instruction processes in the two training systems were interpreted and how different the contents were. Wilde argues that an entirely new orientation and further training for teachers and trainers is necessary.

For a comparison of the allocation of roles for trainers in companies in the former GDR as compared to the west, see Neubert (1999).

[37] On the basis of a series of interviews, Sloane (1994, p. 203ff.) argues that the methodological transition of the training process is widely neglected as the trainers and teachers primarily see the need for catching up with the new contents of training but do not regard the reorientation of their teaching and/or training models.

[38] For the foundations, stages, achievements and shortcomings of this policy, cf. Braun et al (1995).

[39] Hörner (1996, p. 53ff.) argues that the introduction of qualifications with a dual orientation could reduce the costly and time-consuming consecutive double (first *Abitur*, then vocational training) and triple (and eventually higher education) qualification of young people in Germany.

References

Anweiler, Oskar (1991) Die Herstellung der Einheit Deutschlands und das Bildungswesen in den neuen Bundesländern. Dokumentation, *Bildung und Erziehung*, 1, pp. 101–120.

Arnold, Rolf (1993) Das duale System, *Berufsbildung in Wissenschaft und Praxis*, 22(1), pp. 20–27.

Aron, Raymond (1967) *Main Currents in Sociological Thought. Durkheim, Pareto, Weber*. New York: Basic Books.

Autsch, Bernhard (1995) Ausgangsbedingungen bei der Umstellung des DDR-Berufsbildungssystems aus der Sicht rechtlicher und organisatorischer Rahmenbedingungen, in Ulrich Degen, Günter Walden& Klaus Berger (Eds) *Berufsausbildung in den neuen Bundesländern: Daten Analysen, Perspektiven*, Series: Berichte zur beruflichen Bildung, vol. 180, pp. 15–28. Berlin: Bundesinstitut für Berufsbildung.

Benner Hermann (1996) BIBB-Positionen zu aktuellen Herausforderungen in der beruflichen Bildung: I. Beruf und Berufskonzept, *Berufsbildung it Wissenschaft und Praxis*, 25(3), p. 3ff.

Benner, Hermann (1997) Entwicklung anerkannter Ausbildungsberufe – Fortschreibung überkommener Regelungen oder Definition zukunftsbezogener Ausbildungsgänge? in Dieter Euler& Peter F.E. Sloane(Eds) *Duales System im Umbruch. Eine Bestandsaufnahme der Modernisierungsdebatte*, pp. 53–69. Pfaffenweiler: Centaurus-Verl.-Ges.

Bundesinstitut für Berufsbildung (BIBB) (Ed.) (1999) *BIBB aktuell. Ausgabe 2/*1999. Berlin: BIBB.

Bundesministerium für Bildung, Wissenschaft, Forschung und Technologie (BMBF) (Ed.) (1992) *Berufsbildungsbericht* 1992. Bonn: BMBF.

Bundesministerium für Bildung, Wissenschaft, Forschung und Technologie (BMBF) (1995) *Die neuen Länder: dynamische Wissenschaftsregion und Werkstatt der Innovation. Erfolge beim Aufbau Ost – eine Zwischenbilanz des BMBF*. Bonn: BMBF.

Bundesministerium für Bildung, Wissenschaft, Forschung und Technologie (BMBF) (Ed.) (1998) *Berufsbildungsbericht 1998*. Bonn: BMBF.

Bundesministerium für Bildung, Wissenschaft, Forschung und Technologie (BMBF) (Ed.) (1999) *Berufsbildungsbericht 1999*. Bonn: BMBF.

Braun, Anneliese, Jasper, Gerda & Schröter, Ursula (1995) Rolling Back the Gender Status of East German Women, in Hanna Behrend (Ed.) *German Unification. The Deconstruction of an Economy*, pp. 139–166. East Haven, Pluto Press.

Bulmahn, Edelgard (1999) Interview, in *Berufsbildung in Wissenschaft und Praxis*, 28(1), pp. 3–6.

Burkhardt, Dieter (1992) Strukturen der Berufsausbildung in der DDR, in Bundesinstitut für Berufsbildung (BIBB) (Ed.) *Neue Länder – neue Berufsausbildung? Prozess, Probleme und Perspektiven des Übergangs der Berufsausbildung in den neuen Bundesländern; ein Reader mit Beiträgen aus Forschung, Wissenschaft und Praxis*, pp. 31–49. Berlin: BIBB.

Burkhardt, Dieter & Kielwein, Kurt (1992) Entwicklung überbetrieblicher Berufsbildungsstätten in den neuen Bundesländern, *Berufsbildung in Wissenschaft und Praxis*, 21(2), pp. 15–22.

Culpepper, Pepper D. (1999) The Future of the High-Skill Equilibrium in Germany, *Oxford Review of Economic Policy*, 15, pp. 43–59.

Damm-Rüger, Sigrid (1994) *Ausbildung und Berufssituation von Frauen und Männern in Ost und West: Ergebnisse aus der BIBB/IAB-Erhebung 1991/92*, ed. BIBB. Bielefeld: Bertelsmann.

Degen, Ulrich (1995) Ausbildungsbeteiligung und –probleme der Betriebe und Praxen sowie Maßnahmen zur Förderung der betrieblichen Berufsausbildung in den neuen Bundesländern, in Friedrich-Ebert-Stiftung (Ed.) *Berufsausbildung in den neuen Bundesländern.* Gesprächskreis Arbeit und Soziales Nr.42. Eine Tagung der Friedrich-Ebert-Stiftung am 27. Oktober in Halle/Saale, pp. 7–27. Bonn: Forschungsinstitut der Friedrich-Ebert-Stiftung.

Degen, Ulrich, Neubert, R. & Wordelmann, P. (1990) *Betriebliche Ausbildungsgestaltung in der Deutschen Demokratischen Republik und der Bundesrepublik Deutschland – ausgewählte Aspekte zum Vergleich der Ausbildungsqualität*, Wiss. Diskussionspapier Nr.2. Berlin: BIBB.

Deissinger, Thomas (1992) *Die englische Berufserziehung im Zeitalter der industriellen Revolution.* Würzburg: Königshausen und Neumann.

Deissinger, Thomas (1994) The Evolution of the Modern Vocational Training Systems in England and Germany: a comparative view, *Compare*, 24, pp. 17–36.

Deissinger, Thomas (1996) Germany's Vocational Training Act: its functions as an instrument of quality control within a tradition-based vocational training system, *Oxford Review of Education*, 22, pp. 317–336.

Dietrich, Rainer, Schwarz, Gabriele & Wricke, Günter (1996) Qualifizierung von Personal der beruflichen Bildung, in QUEM (Arbeitsgemeinschaft Qualifikations-Entwicklungs-Management) (Ed.) *Aspekte der beruflichen Bildung in der ehemaligen DDR: Anregungen, Chancen und Widersprüche einer gesamtdeutschen Weiterbildungsdiskussion.* Edition QUEM, Bd.9. Münster: Waxmann.

Encyclopaedia Britannica (1997) CD-ROM Version 1.1.

Ernst, Helmut (1991) Dualismus in der Berufsausbildung der DDR? in Martin Twardy (Ed.) *Duales System zwischen Tradition und Innovation*, pp. 239–250. Köln: Botermann Verlag.

Ertl, Hubert (1999a) PRESTiGE – Ein internationales Forschungsnetzwerk, gefördert vom TMR (Training and Mobility of Researches) Programm der Europäischen Kommission, *Kölner Zeitschrift für Wirtschaft und Pädagogik*, 27, Dec. 1999, pp. 79–91.

Ertl, Hubert (1999b) *The Transition of Vocational Education and Training in the Eastern Part of Germany: some notes on the structural duality of training provisions*, Series: Münchner Texte zur Wirtschaftspädagogik, vol. 14. München: Institut für Wirtschafts- und Sozialpädagogik.

Finegold, David & Soskice, David (1988) The Failure of Training in Britain: analysis and prescription, *Oxford Review of Economic Policy*, 4, pp. 21–53.

Georg, Walter (1997) Berufliche Bildung zwischen Internationalisierung und nationaler Identität, in Christoph Kodron, Botho von Kopp, Uwe Lauterbauch, Ulrich Schäfer &

Gerlind Schmidt (Eds) *Vergleichende Erziehungswissenschaft: Herausforderung, Vermittlung, Praxis. Festschrift für Wolfgang Mitter zum 70*, pp. 312–329. Geburtstag. Köln: Böhlau Verlag.

Gericke, Thomas (1994) Gelungener Start – Unsichere Zukunft? Jugendliche im Osten Deutschlands auf dem Weg in den Beruf, in Sabine Liesering, Karen Schober& Manfred Tessaring (Eds) *Die Zukunft der dualen Berufsausbildung. Eine Fachtagung der Bundesanstalt für Arbeit*. Series: Beiträge zur Arbeitsmarkt- und Berufsforschung, BeitrAB 186, pp. 258–267. Nuremberg: Institut für Arbeitsmarkt- und Berufsforschung der Bundesanstalt für Arbeit.

Gieseke, Wiltrud (1994) Weiterbildung in den neuen Bundesländern, in Arnim Kaiser, Jörg Feuchthofen & Rainer Güttler (Eds) *Europahandbuch Weiterbildung*, article 25.30.220. Berlin: Luchterhand.

Greinert, Wolf-Dietrich (1994) *The 'German System' of Vocational Education. History, Organization, Prospects*. Series: Studien zur Vergleichenden Berufspädagogik. Baden-Baden: Deutsche Gesellschaft für Technische Zusammenarbeit.

Groothoff, Hans-H. (Ed.) (1964) *Das Fischer Lexikon Pädagogik*. Neuausgabe. Frankfurt a. M.: Fischer.

Heimerer, Leonhard (1995) Die Berufsschulen – sind besser als ihr Ruf, *Die berufsbildende Schule. Zeitschrift des Bundesverbandes der Lehrer an beruflichen Schulen*, 47, pp. 166–170.

Her Majesty's Inspectorate (HMI) (1995) *Post-16 Vocational Education and Training in Germany. International Report*. London: Further Education Funding Council.

Holldack, Egon, Manning, Sabine & Thomas, Rudolf (1996) Konzeptionelle Positionen, in Wissenschaftsforum Bildung und Gesellschaft e.V. (WIFO) (Ed.) *Bildung im Wandel zwischen Ostdeutschland und Westeuropa. Erkenntnisse aus Forschungsprojekten*, pp. 3–13. Berlin: WIFO.

Horn, Manfred (1992) Berufsausbildung in der DDR, in Bundesinstitut für Berufsbildung (BIBB) (Ed.) *Neue Länder – neue Berufsausbildung? Prozess, Probleme und Perspektiven des Übergangs der Berufsausbildung in den neuen Bundesländern; ein Reader mit Beiträgen aus Forschung, Wissenschaft und Praxis*, pp. 51–64. Berlin: BIBB.

Hörner, Wolfgang (1996) Das deutsche Bildungswesen zwischen Ost und West, in Erich Geissler & Sylvia Huber (Eds) *Pädagogik im sich einigenden Europa*, pp. 49–57. Frankfurt am Main: Lang.

Jordan, Sigrid (1992) Bildungsprogramme der Europäischen Gemeinschaft und die neuen Bundesländer, in Bundesinstitut für Berufsbildung (BIBB) (Ed.) *Neue Länder – neue Berufsausbildung? Prozess, Probleme und Perspektiven des Übergangs der Berufsausbildung in den neuen Bundesländern; ein Reader mit Beiträgen aus Forschung, Wissenschaft und Praxis*, pp. 503–519. Berlin: BIBB.

Jordan, Sigrid (1996) Das EU-Förderprogramm PETRA in Deutschland in seiner Wirkung auf das nationale Berufsausbildungssystem, in Wissenschaftsforum Bildung und Gesellschaft e.V. (WIFO) (Ed.) *Bildung im Wandel zwischen Ostdeutschland und Westeuropa. Erkenntnisse aus Forschungsprojekten*, pp. 99–121. Berlin: WIFO.

Keune, Saskia & Zielke, Dietmar (1992) Individualisierung und Binnendifferenzierung: eine Perspektive für das duale System? *Berufsbildung in Wissenschaft und Praxis*, 21(1), pp. 32–37.

Kloas, Peter-Werner (1994) 10 Thesen zur Modernisierungs- und Differenzierungsfähigkeit des dualen Berufsausbildungssystems, in Sabine Liesering, Karen Schober & Manfred Tessaring (Eds) *Die Zukunft der dualen Berufsausbildung. Eine Fachtagung der Bundesanstalt für Arbeit*. Series: Beiträge zur Arbeitsmarkt- und Berufsforschung, BeitrAB 186, pp. 136–

147

142. Nuremberg: Institut für Arbeitsmarkt- und Berufsforschung der Bundesanstalt für Arbeit.

Kloss, Günther (1985) Vocational Education: A Success Story? in Günther Kloss (Ed.) *Education Policy in the Federal Republic of Germany 1969–1984*, pp. 100–114. Manchester: Department of Language and Linguistics, University of Manchester Institute of Science & Technology (reprinted in David Phillips [Ed.] [1995] *Education in Germany. Tradition and Reform in Historical Context*, pp. 161–170. London: Routledge).

Kutscha, Günter (1992) 'Entberuflichung' und 'Neue Beruflichkeit' – Thesen und Aspekte zur Modernisierung der Berufsausbildung und ihrer Theorie, *Zeitschrift für Berufs- und Wirtschaftspädagogik*, 88, pp. 535–548.

Kutscha, Günter (1993) Modernisierung der Berufsausbildung im Spannungsfeld von Systemdifferenzierung und Koordination, in Friedrich Butler, Reinhard Czycholl & Helmut Pütz (Eds) *Modernisierung beruflicher Bildung vor den Ansprüchen von Vereinheitlichung und Differenzierung*. Series: Beiträge zur Arbeitsmarkt- und Berufsforschung, BeitrAB 177, pp. 40–62. Nuremberg: Institut für Arbeitsmarkt- und Berufsforschung der Bundesanstalt für Arbeit.

Kutscha, Günter (1995) *General and Vocational Education and Training in Germany – Continuity amid Change and the Need for Radical Modernization*, <http//:www.uni-duisburg.de/FB2/BERU/download/vocation.zip> (55KB).

Kutscha, Günter (1996) *Berufsbildungssystem und Berufsbildungspolitik*, <http//:www.uni-duisburg.de/FB2/BERU/download/berufpol.zip> (183KB).

Kutscha, Günter (1998) Ausbildungsordnungen unter dem Einfluß der Internationalisierung und Pluralisierung von Industrienormen, in Dieter Euler (Ed.) *Berufliches Lernen im Wandel – Konsequenzen für die Lernorte? Dokumentation des 3. Forums Berufsbildungsforschung 1997 an der Friedrich-Alexander-Universität Erlangen-Nürnberg*. Series: Beiträge zur Arbeitsmarkt- und Berufsforschung, BeitrAB 214, pp. 265–284. Nuremberg: Institut für Arbeitsmarkt- und Berufsforschung der Bundesanstalt für Arbeit.

Lemke, Dieter (1992) *Bildungspolitik in Europa – Perspektiven für das Jahr 2000. Eine Analyse europäischer Bildungssysteme*. Hamburg: Hamburger Buchwerkstatt.

Lüth, H. (1991) Das berufsbildende Schulwesen in den Schulgesetzen der neuen Länder, *Wirtschaft und Berufserziehung*, 10, pp. 300–303.

Manning, Sabine (1992) EG-Förderprogramme für Bildung und Beschäftigung im Überblick, in Bundesinstitut für Berufsbildung (BIBB) (Ed.) *Neue Länder – neue Berufsausbildung? Prozess, Probleme und Perspektiven des Übergangs der Berufsausbildung in den neuen Bundesländern; ein Reader mit Beiträgen aus Forschung, Wissenschaft und Praxis*, pp. 495–502. Berlin: BIBB.

Manning, Sabine (1993) Die Rolle der EG-Bildungsprogramme in den neuen Bundesländern, *Bildung und Erziehung*, 46, pp. 61–72.

Manning, Sabine (1994) Bildungsprogramme der EG in den neuen Bundesländern, in Klaus Schleicher & Wilfried Bos (Eds) *Realisierung der Bildung in Europa. Europäisches Bewußtsein trotz kultureller Identität?* pp. 137–150. Darmstadt: Wissenschaftliche Buchgesellschaft.

Max-Planck-Institut für Bildungsforschung (Arbeitsgruppe Bildungsbericht) (1994) *Das Bildungswesen in der Bundesrepublik Deutschland. Strukturen und Entwicklungen im Überblick*. Reinbeck: Rowohlt.

Mitter, Wolfgang (1990) Educational Reform in West and East Germany in European Perspective, *Oxford Review of Education*, 16, pp. 333–341.

Müller, Karlheinz & Schaarschuch, Andreas (1996) Das Entwicklungspotential des dualen Systems, *Berufsbildung in Wissenschaft und Praxis*, 25(3), pp. 9–12.

Münk, Dieter (1997) Berufsausbildung in der EC zwischen Dualität und 'Monalität' – eine Alternative ohne Alternative? *Berufsbildung*, 45, pp. 5–8.

Neubert, Renate (1999) Ausbildende Fachkräfte in Ostdeutschland, in Brigitte Schmidt-Hackenberg (Ed.) *Ausbildende Fachkräfte – die unbekannten Mitarbeiter*, pp. 95–107. Berlin and Bonn: Bundesinstitut für Berufsbildung.

Neugebauer, Wolfgang (Ed.) (1992) *Schule und Absolutismus in Preussen. Akten zu preußischen Elementarschulwesen bis 1806.* Series: Veröffentlichungen der Historischen Kommission zu Berlin, vol. 83. Berlin: Walter de Gruyter.

Noah, Harold J. & Eckstein, Max A. (1988) Business and Industry Involvement with Education in Britain, France and Germany, in Jon Lauglo & Kevin M. Lillis (Eds) *Vocationalizing Education*, Comparative and International Education Series, vol. 6, pp. 45–68. Oxford: Pergamon Press.

Parmentier, Klaus, Schober, Karen & Tessaring, Manfred (1994) Zur Lage der dualen Berufsausbildung in Deutschland. Neue empirische Ergebnisse aus dem IAB, in Sabine Liesering, Karen Schober & Manfred Tessaring (Eds) *Die Zukunft der dualen Berufsausbildung. Eine Fachtagung der Bundesanstalt für Arbeit.* Series: Beiträge zur Arbeitsmarkt- und Berufsforschung, BeitrAB 186, pp. 7–47. Nuremberg: Institut für Arbeitsmarkt- und Berufsforschung der Bundesanstalt für Arbeit.

Phillips, David (1999) Das 'Zusammenwachsen' Deutschlands in Bereich des Bildungswesens. Perspektiven und Probleme aus britischer Sicht, in Wolfgang Hörner, Friedrich Kuebart & Dieter Schulz (Eds) *'Bildungseinheit' und 'Systemtransformation'. Beiträge zur bildungspolitischen Entwicklung in den neuen Bundesländern und im östlichen Europa.* Schriftenreihe der Deutschen Gesellschaft für Osteuropakunde, vol. 41, pp. 51–59. Berlin: Berlin Verlag Arno Spitz.

Phillips, David & Economou, Anastasia (1999) Conducting Research into EC Education and Training Policy: some theoretical and methodological considerations, *Compare*, 29, pp. 303–316.

PRESTiGE (Problems of Educational Standardisation and Transitions in a Global Environment) (Ed.) (1998) *Newsletter*, 1, June (Stockholm: PRESTiGE).

Pritchard, Rosalind, M.O. (1999) *Reconstructing Education. East German Schools and Universities after Unification* (New York: Berghahn Books).

Rothe, Georg (1995) *Die Systeme beruflicher Qualifizierung Frankreichs und Deutschlands im Vergleich. Übereinstimmung und Besonderheiten in den Beziehungen zwischen den Bildungs- und Beschäftigungssystemen zweier Kernländer der EU.* Series: Beiträge zur Arbeitsmarkt- und Berufsforschung, BeitrAB 190. Nuremberg: Institut für Arbeitsmarkt- und Berufsforschung der Bundesanstalt für Arbeit.

Schmidt, Hermann (1996) Flexibilisierung der Berufsausbildung – Flexibilisierung als Organisationsprinzip? *Berufsbildung in Wissenschaft und Praxis*, 25(4), p. 1ff.

Schöngen, Klaus & Tuschke, Heidrun (1999) Nach der Ausbildung fehlt die Arbeit. Beschäftigungssituation und Berufsverlauf von Ausbildungsabsolventinnen und -absolventen aus den neuen Bundesländern, *Berufsbildung in Wissenschaft und Praxis*, 28(1), pp. 12–16.

Schwengler, Barbara (1998) Ausbildungsverhalten von Betrieben in West- und Ostdeutschland. Ergebnisse des IAB-Betriebspanels 1997, *Berufsbildung in Wissenschaft und Praxis*, 27(6), pp. 14–17.

Siemon, Günter (1991) Die kaufmännische Berufsausbildung in der DDR, in Martin Twardy (Ed.) *Duales System zwischen Tradition und Innovation*, pp. 269–277. Köln: Botermann Verlag.

Simons, Diane (1966) *Georg Kerschensteiner. His Thought and Its Relevance Today*. London: Methuen.

Sloane, Peter F.E. (Ed.) (1993) *Transnationale Ausbildung im Handwerk*. Cologne: Carl.

Sloane, Peter, F.E. (1994) 'Innenansichten' zum Transformationsprozeß der Erziehungswissenschaft, in Adolf Kell (Ed.) *Erziehungswissenschaft im Aufbruch. Arbeitsberichte*, pp. 197-221. Weinheim: Deutscher Studien-Verlag.

Sloane, Peter F.E. (1997a) Modularisierung in der beruflichen Ausbildung – oder: Die Suche nach dem Ganzen, in Dieter Euler& Peter F.E. Sloane (Eds) *Duales System im Umbruch. Eine Bestandsaufnahme der Modernisierungsdebatte*, pp. 223–245. Pfaffenweiler: Centaurus-Verl.-Ges.

Sloane, Peter F.E. (1997b) Alte Theorie – neue Praxis – neue Theorie? 'Innenansichten' von Berufsschullehrern und Ausbildern, in Adolf Kell & Jan-Hendrik Olbertz (Eds) *Vom Wünschbaren zum Machbaren. Erziehungswissenschaft in den neuen Bundesländern*, pp. 351–372. Weinheim: Beltz.

Tessaring, Manfred (1996) Qualifikationsentwicklung bis 2010. Welche Trends bestimmen die langfristige Entwicklung unter besonderer Berücksichtigung von Aus- und Weiterbildung? in Peter Diepold (Ed.)*Berufliche Aus- und Weiterbildung. Konvergenzen/Divergenzen, neue Anforderungen/alte Strukturen. Dokumentation des 2. Forums Berufsbildungsforschung 1995 an der Humboldt-Universität zu Berlin*, Series: Beiträge zur Arbeitsmarkt- und Berufsforschung, BeitrAB 195, pp. 277–288. Nuremberg: Institut für Arbeitsmarkt- und Berufsforschung der Bundesanstalt für Arbeit.

Thyssen, Simon (1954) *Die Berufsschule in Idee und Gestaltung*. Essen: Girardet.

Ulrich, J.G. & Westhoff, G. (1994) Die Ausbildung absolviert, den Umbruch auch? *Berufsbildung in Wissenschaft und Praxis*, 23(4), pp. 16–21.

Uthmann, Karl-Josef (1991) Vocational Education and Training in Germany after Unification, *European Journal of Education*, 26, pp. 15–12.

Voigt, Birgit (1995) Zur Situation von Mädchen und jungen Frauen auf dem Ausbildungsstellenmarkt – Probleme und Handlungsbedarf, in Friedrich-Ebert-Stiftung (Ed.) *Berufsausbildung in den neuen Bundesländern*. Gesprächskreis Arbeit und Soziales Nr.42. Eine Tagung der Friedrich-Ebert-Stiftung am 27. Oktober in Halle/Saale, pp. 83–91. Bonn: Forschungsinstitut der Friedrich-Ebert-Stiftung.

Wagner, Peter (1991) Science of Society Lost: on the failure to establish sociology in Europe during the 'Classical' period, in Peter Wagner, Björn Wittrock & Richard Whitley (Eds) *Discourses on Society. The Shaping of the Social Science Disciplines*, pp. 219–245. Dordrecht: Kluwer.

Walden, Günter (1996) Berufliche Bildung in den neuen Bundesländern, in Peter Diepold (Ed.) *Berufliche Aus- und Weiterbildung. Konvergenzen/Divergenzen, neue Anforderungen/alte Strukturen. Dokumentation des 2. Forums Berufsbildungsforschung 1995 an der Humboldt-Universität zu Berlin*, Series: Beiträge zur Arbeitsmarkt- und Berufsforschung, BeitrAB 195, pp. 171–178. Nuremberg: Institut für Arbeitsmarkt- und Berufsforschung der Bundesanstalt für Arbeit.

Walter, H. & Höpfner, Hans-Dieter (1994) Erreichtes in der Ausbildungsentwicklung – Was ist weiterhin zu tun? in Bundesinstitut für Berufsbildung (BIBB) (Ed.)

Ausbildungsentwicklung in den neuen Bundesländern – ein verbindendes Transferprojekt, pp. 134–145. Berlin: BIBB.

Waterkamp, Dietmar (1985) *Das Einheitsprinzip im Bildungswesen der DDR. Eine historisch-systemtheoretische Untersuchung.* Bildung und Erziehung, Beiheft 3. Köln/Wien: Böhlau.

Waterkamp, Dietmar (1987) *Handbuch zum Bildungswesen der DDR.* Berlin: Arno Spitz.

Weissflog, Ingrid (1992) Ostdeutsche Berufsausbildung im Übergangsprozeß – Probleme, Standpunkte und Lösungsansätze zu ausgewählten Sachfragen, in Bundesinstitut für Berufsbildung (BIBB) (Ed.) *Neue Länder – neue Berufsausbildung? Prozess, Probleme und Perspektiven des Übergangs der Berufsausbildung in den neuen Bundesländern; ein Reader mit Beiträgen aus Forschung, Wissenschaft und Praxis*, pp. 105–119. Berlin: BIBB.

Werner, Rudolf (1992) Struktur der Ausbildungsberufe vor und nach der Wende, in Bundesinstitut für Berufsbildung (BIBB) (Ed.) *Neue Länder – neue Berufsausbildung? Prozess, Probleme und Perspektiven des Übergangs der Berufsausbildung in den neuen Bundesländern; ein Reader mit Beiträgen aus Forschung, Wissenschaft und Praxis*, pp. 215–232. Berlin: BIBB.

Wilde, Ulrich (1991) Ausbildung von Industriekaufleuten. Erfahrungen bei der Umsetzung neuer Ausbildungsordnungen in den Berufsschulen, *Berufsbildung in Wissenschaft und Praxis*, Sonderheft, pp. 9–13.

Wilson, David N. (1997) The German Dual System of Vocational Education and Training: a comparative study of influence upon educational policy in other countries, in Christoph Kodron, Botho von Kopp, Uwe Lauterbauch, Ulrich Schäfer & Gerlind Schmidt (Eds) *Vergleichende Erziehungswissenschaft: Herausforderung, Vermittlung, Praxis. Festschrift für Wolfgang Mitter zum 70*, pp. 437–447. Geburtstag. Köln: Böhlau Verlag.

Wordelmann, Peter (1992) Zwischenbilanz des Übergangs der Berufsausbildung in den neuen Bundesländern, in Bundesinstitut für Berufsbildung (BIBB) (Ed.) *Neue Länder – neue Berufsausbildung? Prozess, Probleme und Perspektiven des Übergangs der Berufsausbildung in den neuen Bundesländern; ein Reader mit Beiträgen aus Forschung, Wissenschaft und Praxis*, pp. 11–28. Berlin: BIBB.

Christian Schools and Religious Education in the New *Bundesländer*

ROSALIND M.O. PRITCHARD

The Problem

East Germany was one of the most atheistic countries in Europe by the time the Berlin Wall fell, yet it had once been the heartland of Lutheranism, the epicentre of the Reformation, and a bastion of religious faith. It was there that Martin Luther was born, exercised his priestly functions, published his 95 theses and worked on his translation of the New Testament (Bainton, 1955). In 1949, the overwhelming majority of the East German population had belonged to a form of organised religion (over 90% Protestant) but by 1992, two-thirds had no religious affiliation at all (Evangelische Kirche Deutschland [EKD], 1994). After unification, the German Basic Law, permitting the establishment of church schools and religious education, was extended to the New *Bundesländer* in a social· context which was largely atheistic and unreceptive to Christianity. By this stage, there was widespread ignorance about religious matters, and many young people had never entered a church. Yet, by common consent, a values vacuum was acknowledged to exist: Marxism-Leninism had become discredited and it was felt imperative to give children some form of moral education with which to replace it. In the circumstances, faith-based schools and religious education assumed considerable importance and were of widespread public interest.

This chapter seeks answers to the following questions.

- How did the attitude of the state socialist authorities towards Christianity impact upon the churches in the pre-*Wende* epoch and, in view of the GDR's doctrinaire atheism, how was the Protestant Church able to assume a leadership role contributing substantially to the Peaceful Revolution? What became of its salient profile after unification had been accomplished?
- What efforts are now being made by the two great Christian churches, Protestant and Roman Catholic, to establish faith-based schools? How do their policies differ denominationally in relation to the foundation of such schools?

- What efforts are being made to offer religious education in the New *Bundesländer* and, in cases where it is not accepted by the school-going population and their parents, what alternatives are being offered?
- Is it likely that developments relating to religious and moral education in the New *Bundesländer* will have implications for the Old *Bundesländer*? If so, why and what might these be?

Religion in a Socialist State

The official position of Marxism-Leninism was that churches and religion were the 'opium of the people', a mere 'cult' and a potential foe to be handled cautiously. They were regarded as a form of institutionalised superstition, which, according to scientific socialist atheism, would die away. Church membership was strongly stigmatised and often actively sanctioned; church communities were systematically infiltrated by the Secret Police, and every effort was made to integrate them into totalitarian structures and to 'differentiate' their members. 'Differentiation' meant deliberate subversion and division into 'progressive', 'loyal' and 'reactionary' categories: people and groups estimated as potentially 'useful' were dissociated from those assessed as 'troublesome' by methods such as systematic discreditation of reputation, rumour-mongering, setting people up for personal and professional failure, fomentation of conflict, mutual suspicion and mistrust, formation of groups 'loyal' to the GDR, etc. (Wagner, 1994; Schäfer, 1999, p. 127). The numbers of GDR church people diminished greatly under socialism, but a hard core remained which did not die away. The fact that this core was obviously capable of reproducing itself was displeasing to the ideologists of Marxism-Leninism, but eventually accepted as a fact of life.

Under the GDR constitution religions had the right to exist and were formally granted freedom of worship but with certain reservations: in the 1968 constitution (Article 39[2]), the churches' autonomy was only guaranteed in so far as it was 'compatible with the constitution and the legal provisions of the GDR'. By systematic discrimination and harassment, and by insisting that the churches organise according to the laws of the GDR, the Party was able to push the Protestant East German churches towards separation from the West, and in 1969 this was formalised in the Federation of Protestant Churches *(Kirchenbund)*.

Although the GDR constitution gave the appearance of tolerance and religious freedom, constitutions in Communist countries had a different status and function from those in democratic states. They could be more easily changed, were more ephemeral, and sometimes more honoured in the breach than in the observance. The fact that some Articles could be relatively easily abrogated undermined their authority. It is true that in keeping with the formal guarantee of religious liberty, the state made certain 'tokenistic' positive gestures like permitting some Christian children to do their school-leaving certificates, thus qualifying for university entrance, but the reality was that GDR priests and laity suffered heavy discrimination, and the religious education of the young was deliberately rendered as difficult as possible. For example, in 1955, the *Jugendweihe* was (re)introduced as a secular alternative to church confirmation, and in 1958 the Lange Decree was passed to make religious education within schools more difficult: it was not allowed to be taught until 2 hours after school had ended, and its teachers had to apply every 4 months for permission from their school principal to continue courses. Nevertheless, the churches had a constitutional right to exist, and were the only bodies which had the legal right to print and distribute newsletters marked for church use. These two factors gave them a special position in the GDR and were conducive to their exercising a role beyond the spiritual. The Protestant Church in particular acted as a 'fig leaf' for oppositional groups, and gave them support.

The Roman Catholic Church

The Protestant Church assumed a much greater role than the Roman Catholic Church in GDR opposition to socialism, and it is necessary at the outset to explain how this came about. The Roman Catholic Church faced much the same difficulties as the Protestant Church under socialism, but it was much smaller in terms of its congregation: by the time of the *Wende*, only about 5.9% of the East German population belonged to it compared with 27% adhering to the Protestant denomination (EKD, 1994). It could not have survived without financial support from the West (neither could the Protestants), and its quasi diaspora status may have attenuated its influence. More important than size as a determinant of political force, however, was its own attempt to preserve its organisational integrity: the relatively negative attribute of political passivity had to be balanced against church unity, which for some Roman Catholic church authorities took precedence over opposition to an anti-Christian regime. The more the Church adopted an oppositional stance, the more heavily the state would be likely to come down upon it and force it towards an East German identity, split off from the West. The SED (Socialist Unity Party) assumed that a division would help to profile the GDR internationally as a legitimate independent state. It suffered from a serious legitimacy deficit which it sought by every possible means to overcome, for example, by aspiring to specifically East German international sporting success or to its 'own' churches within its political boundaries (though of course in the last resort it did not want organised religion at all).

The relative merits of church unity versus opposition to the socialist state had to be carefully weighed, and various Roman Catholic bishops adopted different policies in relation to these values. Pope Paul VI was clearly much readier to conciliate the GDR regime than his successor John Paul II and, closer to the grass roots, there was much disagreement between church people as to how far they should adapt to socialist reality by accommodating to the SED and how far they should stand out for Christian principles by publicly resisting the SED. In the early post-Second World War years, the Bishop of Berlin, Konrad Graf Preysing, had been a firm opponent of National Socialism and after the War also opposed the socialists. He resided in the American sector of Berlin and ran his operations from that base, more or less consistently opposing the SED regime. However, his successor, Wilhelm Weskamm (Bishop of Berlin from 1951), avoided such confrontation, and pursued a policy of detachment (*Abgrenzung*) from the state. With the foundation of the Berlin *Ordinarienkonferenz* (*BOK*) in the context of the Fulda Bishops' Conference, the Vatican gave East German Catholicism a distinctive organisational structure which might have been the beginning of a structural division, although it was actually intended to ensure the continuation of an efficient ecclesiastical jurisdiction in the east (Schäfer, 1999, pp. 58–59).

Weskamm's successor, Julius Döpfner, reverted to earlier policies and came into renewed conflict with the state. For example, as the Bishop of Berlin, he preached a sermon on 22 September 1957 in which he inveighed against the powers of godlessness (read the GDR state), hell, devils and Satan regarded by the authorities as very provocative and brought down sanctions (Schäfer, 1999, p. 130). During his period of office, Döfpner consistently overestimated the aggressive potential of the Roman Catholic Church, and this led him into a political cul-de-sac, with the result that the Vatican moved him to Munich in 1961 (Schäfer, 1999, p. 456).

His successor was Cardinal Alfred Bengsch who came into office immediately after the construction of the Wall (1961). Although he rejected Communism, his overriding objective was to preserve the unity of the Roman Catholic Church in Germany, even at the cost of political abstention which was reinstigated under his leadership. The Roman Catholic Church no longer protested publicly against the SED regime, and maintained silence in public about the building of the Berlin Wall (*Deutscher Bundestag*, 1995, p. 932). With the Church not posing much of a challenge to the GDR state, contacts and cooperation between the GDR and the Vatican intensified, and the Church enjoyed a much more favourable position in the GDR than in any of the other eastern bloc states (Schäfer, 1999, p. 310). In 1973, the bishops of Erfurt, Magdeburg and Schwerin were nominated administrators '*permanenter constituti*', directly responsible to the Vatican, thereby suspending the formal jurisdiction of the West German bishops (Schäfer, 1999, p. 315). This rapprochement between the GDR and the Vatican, and the fact that the Vatican wanted to develop diplomatic relationships with the GDR, met with sharp criticism on the part of many German bishops. Rome, however, was concerned to retain the concessions of the diplomatic status quo, and wanted to avoid endangering them by inflexibility; it also desired to use its improved contacts with the GDR as a basis for making diplomatic progress in the whole eastern bloc of countries.

In 1976, an independent Berlin bishopric (*Berliner Bishofskonferenz [BBK]*) was founded, apparently heralding establishment of East German dioceses, and hence the possible separation of East from West German Roman Catholicism. The Vatican prepared to establish Apostolic Administratures, and the GDR ambassador, Klaus Gysi, was despatched to Rome to help execute the arrangements, but on 6 August 1978, Pope Paul VI died and was replaced by the Polish Pope John Paul II. The new Pope had grown up under a Communist regime and was vigilant in relation to it: commenting on his accession, the Secret Police declared that the shift in the balance of power was 'not in favour of the GDR's interests' (Schäfer, 1999, p. 319). Pope John Paul was anti-Communist, wary of making too many concessions to the GDR and did not want to split the German

Roman Catholic Church. At the last moment, the arrangements for the Administratures were cancelled, and a further rapprochement or possible split between the East and the West German Roman Catholic churches was averted. Not long afterwards, Cardinal Bengsch died, and high-status clerical presence at his funeral was widely, and correctly, perceived as Rome's endorsement of his work in preventing division of the German Roman Catholic Church.

However, this unity was at the cost of political oppositional involvement, and the Roman Catholic Church gave little support to the protest groups of the late 1980s and the Peaceful Revolution of 1989 (Besier, 1997, pp. 63–64). As Schäfer dispassionately puts it:

> *The relationship between the state and the Catholic church was characterised by a certain distance, but it was an amalgam of conflicts and pragmatic co-operation, of irreconcilable opposites and convergences. Between apparently polar opposites there arose in the course of GDR history reciprocities which in the end were to lead to a certain routine. (1999, p. 453)*

In the end, loyalty to the regime (in the form of political abstinence) was traded for the unity of the bishopric of Berlin.

The Protestant Church

Whereas the Roman Catholic Church in Berlin discouraged pluralism emanating from individual self-conviction (Schäfer, 1999, p. 458), the essence of Protestantism was to follow the dictates of reason and individual conscience rather than ancient ecclesiastical authorities with their pre-structured world-view. This naturally gave rise to institutional fragmentation. It was incumbent upon Protestants to self-structure their own existence and try to give it meaning by service and good works. Inacker (1997, pp. 12–13) believes that this freedom simultaneously represented opportunity and risk. On the one hand, Protestants contributed enormously to modernisation and political progress, but on the other, their tendency to adapt to the spirit of the age, combined with lack of a firm system of norms and institutions, made them vulnerable to 'metaphysical opportunism' and can explain their lack of support for democracy in the years up to 1945 (see Thierfelder, 1998; Novak, 1998). In Inacker's view, for too long after the War the East German Protestant churches clung to the hope of being able to bring about change in socialism and the representatives of the state, ignoring the fundamental incompatibility between Christian belief and a totalitarian ideology (Inacker, 1997, pp. 22–23).

This, however, is a harsh verdict which fails to do sufficient justice to the role of the Protestant Church under socialism. After 1945, its *Diakonie* (the charitable arm of the church for social welfare) was very active in rebuilding the society and limiting human misery. Some of its workers were arrested, its institutions confiscated, and its *Bahnhofsmissionen* (railway missions) closed down (Neukamm, 1998). Despite such harassment, the work of the *Diakonie* continued, facilitated by transfers of money from the West – which in a state hungry for Western currency was welcome to the SED and gave both Christian churches an important internal function. The SED did not pass on all this money to the churches: by adjusting the exchange rate and by other chicanery, the Party contrived to 'harvest' large sums of money which went into technical equipment for the Secret Police or into an account manipulated by Erich Honecker personally, for example, to relieve scarcity or to help brother states in need (Schäfer, 1999, p. 324). However, the Protestant Church's most serious political problems arose from the fact that it was unwilling to accept a curtailment of its role to spirituality and to 'good deeds', no matter how useful. A number of its bishops believed that they should not eschew political relevance, and this naturally set Church and state on a collision course. There were many subjects of conflict between the Protestant Church and the regime: Stalinist policies such as the collectivisation of agriculture and the socialist transformation of industry, abortion, human rights, the education of clergymen and of their children, the ecological environment and socialist militarism.

The Protestant Church confronted the SED particularly sharply over educational matters. Indeed, it would be true to say that education was the most bitterly contested issue dividing Church and state, because it was the key to forming the outlook and value system of the young. The state claimed a total monopoly on education and used this monopoly to promote the goals of the SED. Schools, colleges, universities, institutions, both formal and informal, and the laws of the land – all these were made to serve the ideological monism of Marxism-Leninism. No private schools were permitted, and the Church was not accepted as a partner in policy-making or in shaping the curriculum. The state authorities defended this stance by pointing out that to give the Church a consultative role of this type would be to contravene the principle of strict separation of Church and state. The SED's Eighth Congress (June 1971) declared anew that the socialist personality was atheist and Marxist-Leninist, and in 1975, courses on scientific atheism were introduced into universities and colleges. Atheistic propaganda material was reincorporated into the study programme of Party members in 1977/78 (Railton, 1986, pp. 79–81).

These legal prescriptions had direct consequences for GDR teachers. Hundreds of Christian teachers lost their posts and many young Christians were expelled from secondary schools and universities. It was made clear to those that remained that if they gave courses in religious education, their chances for promotion would disappear and they might be transferred to another locality (Railton, 1986, pp. 70–71). Christian youth groups were declared illegal organisations, and the sole newspaper for Christian youth, *Die Stafette* (1947–53), was prohibited, supposedly because of a paper shortage. The Youth Dedication Ceremony was promoted as a secular alternative to confirmation and, by 1985, 97.4% of all 14 year-olds participated in it (*Jugendweihe*, 1989). It was, therefore, an almost universal experience, and failure to take part in it seriously jeopardised one's chances of entering the upper forms of secondary school (*Erweiterte Oberschule* [*EOS*]) which prepared pupils for university entrance.

Of course, it was Christians, especially clergymen's children, who tended to abstain from the *Jugendweihe* and thus were penalised. Even if they had excellent academic records and outstanding academic achievements, they were rarely granted prizes or distinctions. Of all the hardships to which Christians were subjected at school, the most serious was the difficulty of gaining entry to the *EOS*. By 1966, parents were required by law to cooperate with the principles of socialist morality, and married couples were obliged to reject religion as the basis of their marriage (Railton, 1986, pp. 78, 159). The parents of Christian children were not acceptable as members of Parents' Committees because they were considered unreliable in supporting the *Jugendweihe*. Christian symbols and practices were outlawed, and Christian pupils were not allowed to talk about their beliefs inside school buildings. As a result of the Lange Decree (1958) mentioned earlier, religious education could not be taught during normal school hours, and the Protestant and Catholic Churches therefore developed their own structures for Christian instruction at parish level with a well-laid-out curriculum and trained catechists to carry out the task. By 1976, discrimination against Christians had reached such a pitch that Pastor Oskar Brüskewitz committed suicide by burning himself to death. This caused such a crisis in Church-state relations that in 1978 a meeting took place between Erich Honecker and the head of the *Kirchenbund*, Bishop Schönherr, as a result of which the Church was granted certain rights making life more bearable for its members.

This was the sombre, dangerous background against which the oppositional activities of the Protestant Church took place. The Church was of major service to dissidents, both members and non-members. Peace seminars, environmental protection campaigns, children's church days and book fairs were all popular with GDR youth who were disillusioned with GDR society, bored with official ideology or had problems with their family and housing. Such young people longed for freedom to express their feelings and wanted to be taken seriously. The Church had the merit of addressing deep personal and spiritual questions, and the Party was aware of this strength. To help counter church influence, the SED brought out its own literature about the meaning of life: *Wozu lebe ich?* (Kosing, 1983) and *Vom Sinn unseres Lebens* (1983). Religion was the only sphere of private activity permitted by the SED, and newsletters could be legally printed and distributed if intended for church use. This was one reason why the Church played such a salient role in the peaceful protests leading up to the fall of the Wall.

The rhetoric of the SED about ecological issues was that its government was founded on 'scientific laws' which would bring prosperity to all and solve environmental problems; yet data on air pollution were kept secret because they indicated that the air quality was damaging people's health (Maaz, 1992, p. 61). The rhetoric–reality gap did not fail to impact on socialists who observed pollution and environmental degradation all around them. It was the Church which formed a front for protest about the environment, and when the Government forbade the publication of environmental data in 1982, church-affiliated groups disseminated it themselves (Hager, 1992).

From 1981 onwards, the Protestant Church began its *Friedensdienst* with 10 days of prayer to culminate in a service to be held on 18 November 1981 in the Church of St Nicholas, Leipzig. It was not until early 1988 that such prayers became overtly oppositional. Their effect was intensified by the attendance of people who had nothing to lose because they had already applied for permission to leave the GDR and had therefore alienated themselves from the state and the Party. At first, church leaders did not really intend to bring about reforms but rather to hold on to the concessions wrung out of Honecker in the summit meeting of 1978 (Wagner, 1994, p. 20). However, the Monday Prayers formed a burning glass for political protest. Their regularity ensured that the issues raised would not be dropped and forgotten the next day; they formed a point of repose which was a preliminary to movement on the streets. On 30 October 1989, more than 300,000 people participated in demonstrations in Leipzig, and on 4 November, up to a million people in Berlin. On 6 November, another demonstration estimated at about half a million participants took place in Leipzig, and on 9 November, the Wall fell.

Of course, not all the demonstrators were Christians, and it was not just the activities of the Church which brought down the SED regime. The situation was much more complex than that, and sometimes the Church even acted to contain and 'manage' discontent in the interests of avoiding bloodshed; but, as Wagner (1994) points out, the spiritual impetus behind the Prayer Movement was not to be underestimated and formed a real force for moral resistance. He regards the Prayers as a kind of 'Wailing Wall' (1994, p. 32), constituting a catalyst and a decisive symbol of the GDR revolution. The authorities of the Church of St Nicolas point out that for years their congregations were infiltrated by members of the Secret Police who in the line of their duty were thus involuntarily exposed to the word of God. Being church people, they believe that it was the power of the Holy Spirit which acted to ensure that the GDR revolution was peaceful rather than bloody. Maaz (1992) pays tribute to the courage of the Protestant Church which for decades was the only oppositional force in the GDR, and provided a forum for alternative ways of thinking or feeling, whilst simultaneously addressing the profound questions of human existence.

Religion in the United Germany

Once the downfall of the SED regime was achieved, loyalty to the East German churches faded, and support for them was not sustained at the white-hot, pre-*Wende* level. There were many reasons for this. In a more open society with multiple possibilities of free speech, the Church's former privileged role as practically the only forum for open expression no longer applied. The numbers participating in the Monday Prayers had been swelled by people who were not Christians and who wished to leave the GDR; many other options opened to them after unification. The churches, previously accustomed to financial support from the West, were now expected to sustain themselves materially, and found this quite difficult. The unification tax was almost the same proportion of income as the church subscription, and this coincidence, together with the financial hardship experienced by many people, led to loss of membership. Above all, the churches faced unaccustomed competition after the *Wende*. For decades, they had been in a special situation in the GDR: they were non-state-sponsored bodies which did not share the values of the Party and yet were officially, even constitutionally, tolerated. As such, they represented for many people a precious and unique forum for communication and expression. The pluralism of East German society, long covertly under development, suddenly almost overnight became overt. The Church was now only one option among many, whereas during the GDR's existence it had been the only available legal alternative to the state world-view. It had to compete with other attractions for the attention of the population. After unification, it lost ground to television, computers, travel, new hobbies and many other activities. There was, too, the revelation that some church people were politically 'tainted' by collaboration with the Party and the Secret Police; this unpleasant fact discouraged membership in some quarters.

The Establishment of Church Schools

The Legal Basis

The basis of acceptance in East German society was rather narrow when it came to religious education and church schools, but pockets of people existed who were passionately keen to see voluntary schools established after the fall of the Wall and there was more demand for them than the Roman Catholic and Protestant Churches could satisfy financially. The Basic Law (Article 7) provided the legal basis for their establishment, and specified four important points.

(1) The whole school system is under the control of the state.

(2) The parents or guardians have the right to decide on the participation of the child in religious education.

(3) Religious education is a normal full school subject in public schools with the exception of non-denominational schools. Without prejudice to the supervisory right of the state, religious education is to be taught in keeping with the principles of the religious communities. No teacher may be forced to teach religious education against his or her will.

(4) The right to the establishment of private schools is guaranteed. Private schools as a substitute for public schools require the permission of the state and are subject to the laws of the Länder. *Permission may be granted if the private schools are not inferior to public schools in their learning aims and arrangements, and in the academic education of their teaching staff; they should not promote a division of pupils according to the financial circumstances of the parents. Permission is to be denied if the economic and legal situation of the teaching staff is not sufficiently well assured.*

Article 141 mitigated part of Article 7, and stated that:

Article 7, paragraph 3, sentence 1 does not apply in a Land *in which on 1 January 1949, another* Land *regulation applied.*

These Articles of the Basic Law owed much to the Weimar constitution of 11 August 1919. After 1918, the education sector was regarded as a means of overcoming crisis, and there was intense debate in relation to it. On 16 November

1918, the Minister of Education, Adolph Hoffmann, ordered the separation of church and state; 13 days later, he forbade religious festivals in school, and made religious education an optional subject. All of this unleashed a storm of protest in churches and communities, as a result of which the decisions were rescinded. However, controversy surrounded the '*Kampf um die Schule*' for the duration of the Weimar Republic (Schreiner, 1996). In the constitution of 19 August 1919, the right to establish denominational schools was conceded, and religion was allowed to remain a normal school subject. However, according to Article 144 of the Weimar constitution, the whole school system, including the private sector, came under the supervision of the state, and the churches were granted a supervisory right only for religious education. This arrangement meant the dissolution of the synthesis between Christianity, culture, school and education (Schreiner, 1996, p. 208) and assured the separation of throne and altar. As Schreiner (1996, p. 241) points out, it gave the state unrestricted power over the nation's schools. Mette (1997), however, highlights the fact that religious education is in fact better secured by means of Article 7 than any other subject, and that the churches have the right to agree the syllabus.

Article 141 of the Basic Law is the so-called 'Bremen Clause', which is important in the context of this chapter. It provided a legal basis for Brandenburg and Berlin to instigate a pattern of religious or moral education deviating from that in other New *Bundesländer*. This possibility arose as the result of a historical accident. In 1949, when the Basic Law was introduced, Berlin (at that time Berlin-Brandenburg) and Bremen already had their *Länder* law in place, and they were given an exemption from the religious education regulations applying to all other *Länder*: they could enact different legislation. After German unification, the education authorities in Brandenburg argued that:

- the New *Bundesland* of Brandenburg was in legal continuity with the *Land* of Brandenburg as it had existed prior to 1949 when East and West Germany were divided;
- on the basis of this continuity argument, Brandenburg (like Bremen) was not subject to Article 7(3) of the Basic Law concerning denominational religious education;
- Brandenburg was therefore legally empowered to introduce a model of religious and/or moral education diverging from that prevailing in other *Länder* which were clearly subject to Article 7(3) of the Basic Law.

As we shall see, Brandenburg did in fact follow this road both in the position which it accorded to religious education and in the development of a new curricular syllabus for the teaching of ethics.

Protestant and Catholic Schools

The right to establish private schools had never existed in the GDR, so the Basic Law opened up new opportunities to found them. For the first time since the Second World War, East Germans were accorded the right to freedom of conscience, the free unfolding of the individual, and parental power over the education of their children. The possibility of developing schools in the New *Bundesländer* gave a great stimulus to both Catholic and Protestant providers. It is difficult to count school numbers so that the two denominations are comparable. As a result of the demographic decline, mergers and sharing of accommodation have become commonplace; in the present study, general school types co-existing under one roof (e.g. *Grundschule* and *Gymnasium*) have been counted as one institution; furthermore, vocationally-related school types with closely-related specialisms taught in one location (e.g. *Fachschule für Krankenpflege* and *Fachschule für Altenpflege*) have also been counted as one. Bearing these rationalisations in mind, the most recent figures obtainable are as shown in Tables I and II.

School type	General	Vocationally-related	Special
Berlin	0	0	0
Brandenburg	3	9	5
Mecklenburg-Vorpommern	3	5	5
Sachsen	12	10	10
Sachsen-Anhalt	4	14	4
Thüringen	7	6	12
Total	29	44	36

Table I. Protestant schools in the New *Bundesländer*. Source: *Schulen in Evangelischer Trägerschaft*. Münster: Comenius Institute, March 1999.

School type	General	Vocationally-related	Special
Berlin	2	1	0
Brandenburg	3	0	3
Mecklenburg-Vorpommern	2	0	0
Sachsen	5	2	2
Sachsen-Anhalt	3	2	0
Thüringen	2	2	1
Total	17	7	6

Table II. Roman Catholic schools in the New *Bundesländer*. Source: data provided at the author's request by *Zentralstelle Bildung der Deutschen Bishofskonferenz*, Bonn.

Parents sending children to these faith-based schools usually pay fees, samples of which are shown in Table III.

Grundschulen	DM 40,00
Haupt- and *Realschulen*	DM 60,00
Gymnasien and *Fachschulen*	DM 80,00

Table III. Sample monthly fees for Roman Catholic schools in Berlin. Source: leaflet published by *Erzbischöfliches Ordinariat* Berlin, 1997. No author's name given.

It is interesting to note that both Protestant and Catholic schools have mixed religious compositions, and so it is not unusual to find a Protestant school with a sizeable minority of Catholics or vice versa. Both denominations accept children who have no religious affiliation, provided their parents broadly endorse the aims of the school.

In the establishment of denominational schools, the Roman Catholic Church made vigorous use of the legislation, and gained an early start in establishing an extensive network of faith-based schools. By 1996, it had 31 general and health-related schools compared with only 12 for the Protestant Church (data provided by the appropriate church authorities; see Pritchard, 1999, p. 100). The Catholics therefore were quicker off the mark in the establishment of new schools than the Protestants. The reasons for this disparity seem to be as follows: the Protestants experienced more difficulty than the Catholics in relation to the financing of their faith-based schools, both in West and in East Germany, sometimes to the point where schools had to be transferred to a public provider, as happened in the case of the Dietrich-Bonhoeffer-Gymnasium in Ahlhorn. They were divided among themselves about policy, uncertain whether it was wise to put substantial resources into schools, and tended instead to put their energies into assuring religious education as a normal school subject (Schreiner, 1996, p. 336). There were many intra-church factions, some of which believed that, given increased religious liberty, they could bear witness to their faith throughout the education system rather than setting up their own distinctive schools. In effect, therefore, they endorsed a permeation model, which they believed to be more suited to a pluralistic, multicultural society.

The Catholics, on the other hand, tended towards the view that if they were to have the desired influence, they needed to concentrate their religious witness. They therefore gave more priority to the establishment of their own schools than did their Protestant counterparts. This is in line with developments in the Federal Republic of Germany as a whole where the Roman Catholic denomination has about a quarter of a million children in its schools, whereas the Protestants have only about 60,000 (Klemm & Krauss-Hoffmann, 1999, p. 62). In relation to provision of faith-based schools, Klemm & Krauss-Hoffmann (1999) allude to the difficulty of obtaining firm data from the Protestant side, and to the incomplete and contradictory figures which they were given. However, it seems that the Protestants are now laying greater stress on their schools, and the increased seriousness with which the matter is being taken is evinced by the publication of the recent compendious *Handbuch Evangelische Schulen* (Scheilke & Schreiner, 1999) and of Schreiner's *Im Spielraum der Freiheit* dealing with Protestant schools since the Reformation (1996). Große (1999, p. 390) admonishes the Protestants not to squander what they have created: 'The fact that before the *Wende*, democratic structures and processes were kept up almost exclusively in the Protestant churches lays upon us a special duty to bring this heritage into the formation of East Germany's future'.

Religious and Moral Education in State Schools

Religious Education

In the Old *Bundesländer*, ethics has been offered as an alternative to religious education since 1974/75. Normally ethics cannot be featured without religious education because ethics is viewed as an *alternative*, which logically presupposes a first option, in this case religious education. In the New *Bundesländer*, however, less than 4% of the school-going population is Roman Catholic and less than 18% is Protestant (Degen, 1999). In deference to this fact, ethics (or an equivalent) is offered in its own right rather than as an 'alternative'. Religious education is offered too: in Berlin, for example, about 126,000 pupils studied Catholic and Protestant religion in the school year 1997/98 (Evangelische Kirche in Berlin-Brandenburg/Erzbistum Berlin [EKiBB/EB], 1998) The take-up rate varies from about 3% in Saxony-Anhalt to 20% in Thuringia. In church circles, a potential figure of 20% is often regarded as about the maximum which can be achieved. Obviously, teachers need to be trained before religious education can be offered, and this takes time. An empirical study by Hanisch & Pollack (1995) shows that religious education (as distinct from Christian instruction) is positively received in Saxony – and not just by those who come from church backgrounds. Almost 50% of the sample of 1500 pupils had no relationship with the Church, but 81% believed in God at least 'sometimes'. Degen too (1999, p. 29) notes that when voluntary religious education is in competition with a compulsory moral education subject, religious education by no means necessarily loses out.

The East German churches were at first sceptical about school religious education because they did not (and do not) want to abandon their own Christian instruction: in the Protestant Church of Berlin-Brandenburg, for example, 30,344 children in forms 1–6 took such classes in 1995/96. The ultimate purpose is confirmation into the Church, but some of those in Christian instruction classes have never been baptised and belong to no church. Curiously, commitment to the *Jugendweihe* has not died out in the New *Bundesländer*. Since 1990, more than a quarter of a million *NBL* youths – that is about half of all 14 year-olds – have taken part in the ceremony (Mohrmann, 1996, p. 197). This is very probably an assertion of a distinctively East German identity, and also an indication that parents so enjoyed their own *Jugendweihe* that they wish to pass on a pleasant experience to their offspring.

The Special Case of Life Skills–Ethics–Religion: 'LER'

The most distinctive and controversial innovation in the field of moral education has taken place in Brandenburg. One day before German unification on 3 October 1990, the Modrow government recommended the introduction of a subject called *Life Skills, Ethics, Religion* (LER), which had been nurtured and developed in GDR times, and was thus a home-grown product (Brandenburg Ministerium für Bildung, Jugend und Sport [BB MBJS], 1996, pp. 7–8). The first Minister of Education in Brandenburg was Marianne Birthler who had been a Protestant catechist and took a particular interest in the proposed subject. Under her leadership, a decision was made to pilot LER carefully, and to have an academic evaluation done to establish whether it should be offered throughout the entire *Land*. LER was to be non-denominational and was intended for all pupils. The experiment ran from 1992 to 1995 in 44 post-primary schools. A concurrent analysis was conducted by Achim Leschinsky, from 1992 professor at the Humboldt University, Berlin, and prior to that at the Max-Planck-Institute, Berlin. Assisted by colleagues, he produced a book with the title *Vorleben oder Nachdenken?* (1996) in which he analysed the advantages and disadvantages of LER in action.

A crucial feature of LER was the life skills component which addressed itself to the real existential problems of young people. Indeed, the balance of the three components was strongly skewed in favour of the first element. The study of ethics encouraged pupils to consider their dilemmas in moral terms but without preaching to them. Religion was intended not just to teach them 'about' it, but also to acquaint them with real religious experience by bringing them face to face with teachers who had spiritual belief as well as cognitive knowledge. This aspect of the course required the active participation of the churches: the Protestant Church was involved for the duration of the experiment, but the Roman Catholic Church refused to take part because the status of religious education was never defined to its satisfaction.

There were many sources of tension for the Protestant church workers taking part in the pilot study. They felt that they took second place to the normal class teachers, and regretted the fact that there were no marks for LER to help motivate the pupils and make them take it seriously. There were organisational and structural difficulties, and – it had to be admitted – not all of the 'authentic representatives of religion' were equally good pedagogues. Though many were excellent, some church workers were not used to handling whole classes of lively, questioning pupils. In the end, the church workers did not feel accepted by the class teachers as full partners, and by the time the pilot study ended, some had become disillusioned with the scheme and had withdrawn.

In a demanding in-service training programme, teachers were gradually trained to deliver the subject (or more accurately 'subject cluster'). By the end of the third year, the Ministry produced Guidelines (*Hinweise*) setting out objectives and content. The Protestant Church drafted a report on the pilot study; the Brandenburg Institute for In-Service Teacher Education (PLIB) also reported, as of course did Leschinsky (1996), who had been specially commissioned to do so. It became clear that, whereas the churches had perhaps expected more of an opportunity to inculcate faith, parents and pupils valued the social and personal aspects of LER, and viewed it as a very suitable vehicle for moral education in a secular society. On the basis of the pilot study results and the predominantly positive reception of LER by the 'users', the Brandenburg government decided to introduce the subject into its schools, in the first instance at post-primary level. Values education, however, was now taken to be the task of *all* teachers – not just church people – and normal class teachers were encouraged to treat questions of religion and faith in their lessons (BB MBJS, 1996).

The Brandenburg Ministry decisively backed its new subject with words and deeds. It was to become compulsory, to be taught to all pupils, and its title was to be slightly amended: the R for religion now came to stand for Religion*skunde* which implied teaching *about* religion rather than actually teaching *religion* itself. By 1998/99, the number of classes doing LER had risen to 1665. That year, in the new intake to the first form of secondary school, almost 23,000 pupils in 895 classes had begun LER (about 60% of the whole age cohort). The drop-out rate was miniscule, about 2.2%, and the overall indicators of success were so positive that additional pilot studies were commissioned so as to prepare for offering the subject in primary school (hitherto it had only been offered in secondary school). LER therefore seemed buoyant, and the intention was to extend it ever further until it reached the whole school population (data from SchulVerwaltung MO, 1999).

The Roman Catholic Cardinal, Georg Sterzinsky, declared, however, that pupils of his faith would not take part in LER. Conflict arose between the Brandenburg Ministry and the major Christian churches over LER and the place of religious education. Both Berlin and Brandenburg had decided to make use of the Bremen Clause (Article 141 of the Bonn constitution) and refused to make religious education a 'normal school subject' within the curriculum. It was merely an option offered within the school by church people, whereas LER was compulsory in Brandenburg. From one point of view, the authorities' stance seemed understandable given the predominantly atheistic nature of the school-going population, but it infuriated the churches. Both the Protestant and the Roman Catholic Churches (as well as certain other interested bodies) resorted to legal action designed to test whether Brandenburg was in fact justified in its decision to marginalise religious education in favour of LER. They brought a case before the Constitutional Court in Karlsruhe, which, at time of writing, has not yet been resolved, and which turns on two main issues. 1. Can the churches insist that religion does indeed have to be a normal school subject under Article 7 of the Basic Law? 2. Is Brandenburg truly entitled to make use of the Bremen Clause for the purpose of diverging from Article 7? To be justified in doing so, it needs to prove beyond dispute that it is in legal continuity with the Brandenburg state which existed before 1949. The case raises issues of whether Church and state are indeed separate in Germany, and whether concessions to Christianity under the constitution contravene the principle of the state's neutrality in religious matters. The Constitutional Court in Karlsruhe has not yet delivered its verdict on the case.

In the meantime, Bishop Wolfgang Huber of the *Evangelische Kirche in Berlin-Brandenburg* and Cardinal Georg Sterzinsky of the *Erzbistum Berlin* are making common cause in interdenominational statements and publications about religious education and LER. They cannot argue for the abolition of LER, but they do call for a halt to its development at least until the Constitutional Court's verdict has been delivered. They reject LER as a state-sponsored, compulsory subject for all pupils, and see therein the danger of an exclusive state claim to religious education and training. They believe that in a pluralistic society, there have to be various, clearly-profiled offerings of moral and religious education, and that religious education has a right to its place within the curriculum. They propose a new subject cluster of their own which would include Protestant and Catholic religion, as well as ethics or philosophy, and possibly Judaism and Islam – all subjects within the cluster to have equal status – and are attempting to popularise this cluster in Berlin (EKiBB/EB, 1998).

Conclusion

The roles played by Roman Catholic and Protestant church people during the days of socialism differed strikingly at a political and institutional level. Both Churches suffered greatly but had different ways of dealing with the agents of that suffering: the GDR state, the SED and the Secret Police. The Protestant Church was used as a front by people who had no other vehicle for protest, and when freedom came, with all its diverse possibilities, those who were not genuinely committed to it melted away. In a sense, this is disappointing, but not altogether surprising. It is perhaps more difficult to understand why the Protestant Church was at first slow to realise the importance of denominational schools which could serve as beacons in a secular society after the *Wende*. The Roman Catholic Church has developed an education network which will serve it well in any attempt at the 're-evangelisation' of the former GDR.

The extension to East Germany of the Bonn constitution after the GDR's 40 years of atheism has created opportunities for the establishment of voluntary schools and the teaching of religious education which are very welcome to the religiously-affiliated. However, Brandenburg's acceptance of LER and marginalisation of religious education may have far-reaching consequences for west as well as for east German churches, if the verdict of the Constitutional Court goes against them. As Degen (1999) says:

> *Even if at first LER appeared to some observers, especially those from the West German religious education tradition, a marginal, short-lived exotic phenomenon, this model may nevertheless establish itself Land-wide ... and have consequences reaching beyond Brandenburg's borders into West German educational environments.*

If the churches definitively lose the battle for religious education's curricular position in the New *Bundesländer*, then *ipso facto*, their position will be lost in the Old *Bundesländer* too. Religious education may be taken out of state control and become purely a matter for the churches – tantamount to a return to the GDR Christian instruction. It will be interesting to see what justification the Constitutional Court gives for its verdict, whatever it may turn out to be, and how that verdict is accepted in various quarters. If the Court finds against the case for religious education as a normal school subject, it will be a victory for secularism, and a recognition too that Germany has become a very different place since the days of the Weimar Republic. The accession of East Germany with its own traditions and values has contributed decisively to that difference, and has forced difficult decisions in relation to moral education. Without unification, it might have been many years before these problematic questions gained the urgency with which they resonate at present.

References

Bainton, R.H. (1955) *Here I Stand*. New York: Mentor.

Basic Law. See *Grundgesetz*.

Brandenburg Ministerium für Bildung, Jugend und Sport (BB MBJS) (1996) *Abschlußbericht zum Modellversuch 'Lernbereich Lebensgestaltung- Ethik- Religion'*. Potsdam: MBJS.

Besier, G. (1997) Die Kirchen und die Wiedervereinigungsdiskussion, in C. Lenhartz (Ed.) *Evangelische Kirche Demokratie Stasi-Aufarbeitung*, pp. 25–64. Bergisch Gladbach: La Colombe.

Degen, R. (1999) Das Schulfach LER: Eine Momentanaufnahme gegenwärtiger Entwicklungen und Fragen, *Pastoraltheologische Informationen*, 19, pp. 25–37.

Deutscher Bundestag (1995) 'Katholische Kirche', in 'Rolle und Selbstverständnis der Kirchen in den verschiedenen Phasen der SED-Diktatur', in *Materialien der Enquête-Kommission 'Aufarbeitung von Geschichte und Folgen der SED-Diktatur in Deutschland'*. Bonn: *Deutscher Bundestag*, Nomos and Suhrkamp Verläge, Band VI/2.

Evangelische Kirche Deutschland (EKD) (1994) *Kirchenzugehörigkeit in Deutschland: 'Was hat sich verändert?' Evangelische und katholische Kirche im Vergleich*. Statische Beilage Nr. 89 zum Amtsblatt der EKD, Heft 10 vom 15. Oktober. Hannover: EKD.

Evangelische Kirche in Berlin-Brandenburg/Erzbistum Berlin (EKiBB/EB) (1998) Religionsunterricht in Berlin: Schulisches Unterrichtsfach in einer Fächergruppe (leaflet). Berlin: EKiBB/EB.

Große, L. (1999) Wider Marx und McDonald: Perspektiven von Schulen in kirchlicher Trägerschaft – vorzugsweise in Ostdeutschland, in C.T. Scheilke & M. Schreiner (Eds) *Handbuch Evangelische Schulen*, pp. 388–391. Gütersloh: Gütersloher Verlagshaus.

Grundgesetz für die Bundesrepublik Deutschland (1998) Bonn: Bundeszentrale für politische Bildung.

Hager, Carol J. (1992) Environmentalism and Democracy in the Two Germanies, *German Politics*, 1, pp. 95–108.

Hanisch, H. & Pollack, D. (1995) Der Religionsunterricht im Freistaat Sachsen: eine empirische Untersuchung zur Akzeptanz eines neuen Unterrichtsfaches, *Zeitschrift für Evangelische Ethik*, 39, pp. 243–248.

Inacker, M.J. (1997) Die Ideologieanfälligkeit des deutschen Protestantismus, in C. Lenhartz (Ed.) *Evangelische Kirche Demokratie Stasi-Aufarbeitung*, pp. 11–24. Bergisch Gladbach: La Colombe.

Jugendweihe (Zeitschrift für Mitarbeiter und Helfer), 6, 8 November 1989. The entire issue is devoted to the history of the *Jugendweihe* in the GDR.

Klemm, K. & Kruass-Hoffmann, P. (1999) Evangelische Schulen im Spiegel von Selbstdarstellung und Elternurteil, in C.T. Scheilke & M. Schreiner. (Eds) *Handbuch Evangelische Schulen*, pp. 60–80. Gütersloh: Gütersloher Verlagshaus.

Kosing, A. (1983) *Wozu lebe ich?* Berlin: Akademie der Gesellschaftswissenschaften beim ZK der SED.

Lange, G. (1993) *Katholische Kirche im sozialistischen Staat DDR*. Berlin: Bischöfliches Ordinariat.

Leschinsky, A. (1996) *Vorleben oder Nachdenken?* Frankfurt am Main: Diesterweg.

Maaz, H-J. (1992) *Der Gefühlsstau*. Munich: Knaur.

Mette, N. (1997) Das umstrittene Konfessionsprinzip, *Neue Sammlung*, 37, pp. 207–230.

Mohrmann, Ute (1996) Festhalten am Brauch: Jugendweihe vor und nach der '*Wende*', in W. Kaschuba, T. Scholze & Leonore Scholze-Irrlitz (Eds) *Alltagskultur im Umbruch*, pp. 197–213. Weimar: Böhlau.

Neukamm, K.H. (1998) Das Netzwerk kirchlich-diakonischer Hilfen der deutschen Teilung, in U. Röper & C. Jüllig (Eds) (n.d. assumed 1998) *Die Macht der Nächstenliebe: Einhundertfünfzig Jahre Innere Mission und Diakonie 1848–1998*, pp. 266–273. Berlin: Deutsches Historisches Museum and Diakonisches Werk der Evangelischen Kirche in Deutschland.

Novak, K. (1998) Eugenik, Zwangssterilisation und 'Euthanasie', in U. Röper & C. Jüllig (Eds) (n.d. assumed 1998) *Die Macht der Nächstenliebe: Einhundertfünfzig Jahre Innere Mission und Diakonie 1848–1998*, pp. 236–249. Berlin: Deutsches Historisches Museum and Diakonisches Werk der Evangelischen Kirche in Deutschland.

Pritchard, R.M.O. (1999) *Reconstructing Education: East German Schools and Universities after Unification*. Oxford: Berghahn.

Railton, N.M. (1986) *Youth and the Church in East Germany*, unpublished PhD thesis, University of Dundee.

Schäfer, B. (1999) *Staat und katholische Kirche in der DDR*. Köln: Böhlau.

Scheilke, C.T. & Schreiner, M. (Eds) (1999) *Handbuch Evangelische Schulen*. Gütersloh: Gütersloher Verlagshaus.

Schreiner, M. (1996) *Im Spielraum der Freiheit*. Göttingen: Vandenhoeck & Ruprecht.

SchulVerwaltung MO (1999) Erhebung zur LER, no. 4. No author's name given.

Thierfelder, J. (1998) Zwischen Anpassung und Selbstbehauptung, in U. Röper & C. Jüllig (Eds) (n.d. assumed 1998) *Die Macht der Nächstenliebe: Einhundertfünfzig Jahre Innere Mission und Diakonie 1848–1998*, pp. 224–235. Berlin: Deutsches Historisches Museum and Diakonisches Werk der Evangelischen Kirche in Deutschland.

Vom Sinn unseres Lebens (1983) Berlin: Zentraler Ausschuß für Jugendweihe in der Deutschen Demokratischen Republik. (No author's name given.)

Wagner, H. (1994) Introduction to *Freunde und Feinde: Dokumente zu den Friedensgebeten in Leipzig zwischen 1981 und dem 9. Oktober 1989*, ed. C. Dietrich & U. Schwabe. Leipzig: Evangelische Verlagsanstalt.

Notes on Contributors

NINA ARNHOLD completed her MSc in Comparative Education in the Department of Educational Studies at the University of Oxford in 1996. After teaching in Poland for a year, she returned to the University of Oxford where she is now a doctoral student in the Department of Educational Studies. Her research interests include: higher education in Europe, education for reconstruction and processes of transition in education.

HUBERT ERTL is currently working at the Institute for Vocational Education (Institut für Wirtschafts- und Sozialpädagogik) at the University of Munich, where his research is concerned with EU policies for vocational education and training. The research for the chapter in this volume was conducted during his time as Research Officer at the Department of Educational Studies, University of Oxford. More specifically, the chapter resulted from involvement in the EU-funded project PRESTiGE (Problems of Educational Standardisation and Transitions in a Global Environment). His book *Modularisation of Vocational Education in Europe: NVQs and GNVQs as a model for the reform of initial training provisions in Germany?* will be published by Symposium Books in 2000.

KAREN GALTRESS-HÖRL is an English teacher at Munich's Institute for Foreign Languages and at the Department of English of Munich University; she is also a CELTA teacher trainer. During the period 1992–96 she was involved with the retraining of language teachers in Güstrow, eastern Germany.

E.J. NEATHER, until recently Senior Lecturer in Education at the University of Exeter, was a frequent visitor to the GDR from the early 1970s onwards and was Visiting Professor in the Education Department of the Technical University of Dresden in 1992. His publications include 'Streitfall Lehrerbildung' in F. Busch (Ed.) *Tradition und Erneuerung in der Erziehungswissenschaft* (TU Dresden, 1993); and 'Education in the New Germany', in D. Lewis & J. McKenzie (Eds) *The New Germany: social, political and cultural challenges of unification* (University of Exeter Press, 1995).

DAVID PHILLIPS is a Fellow of St Edmund Hall and Professor of Comparative Education in the University of Oxford. His main research interest is in education in Germany, and he has published many books and articles in this area. He is Editor of the *Oxford Review of Education* and served during 1998–2000 as Chair of the British Association for International and Comparative Education.

ROSALIND M.O. PRITCHARD is Professor of Education at the University of Ulster with particular responsibility for postgraduate programmes in Teaching English to Speakers of Other Languages. She is interested in problems relating to foreign countries and cultures, and has developed particular expertise in the field of German education. She is the author of *The End of Elitism? The Democratisation of the West German University System* and of *Reconstructing Education: East German Schools and Universities after Unification.* She is joint editor with Eva Kolinsky & Christopher Flockton of *The New Germany in the East: policy agendas and social developments since unification.*

BERNHARD THOMAS STREITWIESER completed his PhD in Comparative and International Education at Teachers College, Columbia University. His area of specialisation is eastern German secondary school education and the educational transition process of former GDR teachers since unification. His other interests include issues of European educational policy and school reform.

STEPHANIE WILDE completed her doctorate at the University of Oxford Department of Educational Studies. She is now undertaking research into education for citizenship, based at the Max-Planck Institute for Educational Research in Berlin. She has been awarded the Theodor Heuss Fellowship and is a Research Fellow of the Oxford Department.

NEW FROM SYMPOSIUM BOOKS

Learning from Comparing: new directions in comparative educational research
Volume 1. Contexts, Classrooms and Outcomes
Edited by ROBIN ALEXANDER,
PATRICIA BROADFOOT & DAVID PHILLIPS
ISBN 1 873927 58 4 (published 1999)
Volume 2. Policy, Professionals and Development
Edited by ROBIN ALEXANDER,
MARILYN OSBORN & DAVID PHILLIPS
ISBN 1 873927 63 0 (due 2000)

Globalisation, Educational Transformation and Societies in Transition
Edited by TEAME MEBRAHTU, MICHAEL CROSSLEY
& DAVID JOHNSON
ISBN 1 873927 78 5 (due 2000)

Doing Comparative Education Research: issues and problems
Edited by KEITH WATSON
ISBN 1 873927 83 5 (due 2000)

Monographs in International Education
Operation Blackboard: policy implementation in Indian elementary education
CAROLINE DYER
ISBN 1 873927 88 6 (due 2000)

Modularisation of Vocational Education in Europe: NVQs and GNVQs as a model for the reform of initial training provisions in Germany?
HUBERT ERTL
ISBN 1 873927 98 3 (due 2000)

Reschooling and the Global Future: politics, economics and the English experience
JAMES PORTER
ISBN 1 873927 53 3 (published 1999)

For the full contents of all Symposium books, their prices and an order form, please see www.symposium-books.co.uk

SYMPOSIUM BOOKS PO BOX 65 WALLINGFORD OXFORD OX10 0YG   UNITED KINGDOM
Voice: +44 (0) 1491-838 056 Fax: +44 (0) 1491-834 968 orders@symposium-books.co.uk

Oxford Studies in Comparative Education

Series Editor: Professor David Phillips, University of Oxford

Published recently

Education in Germany Since Unification
Edited by David Phillips
ISBN 1 873927 73 8

Education Systems of the United Kingdom
Edited by David Phillips
ISBN 1 873927 73 8

Comparing Standards Internationally:
research and practice in mathematics and beyond
Edited by Barbara Jaworski & David Phillips
ISBN 1 873927 68 1

Processes of Transition in Education Systems
Edited by Elizabeth A. McLeish & David Phillips
ISBN 1 873927 48 7

Education for Reconstruction: the regeneration
of educational capacity following national upheaval
Nina Arnhold, Julia Bekker, Natasha Kersh,
Elizabeth A. McLeish & David Phillips
ISBN 1 873927 43 6

Education and Privatisation in Eastern Europe and the Baltic Republics
Edited by Paul Beresford-Hill
ISBN 1 873927 38 X

Education and Change in the Pacific Rim: meeting the challenges
Edited by Keith Sullivan
ISBN 1 873927 33 9

For full contents of these titles and others in
this series see *www.symposium-books.co.uk*

SYMPOSIUM BOOKS, PO BOX 65, WALLINGFORD
OXFORD OX10 0YG, UNITED KINGDOM
Voice: +44 (0) 1491-838 056 Fax: +44 (0) 1491-834 968 orders@symposium-books.co.uk

NEW FROM SYMPOSIUM BOOKS

Learning from Comparing: new directions in comparative educational research

Volume 1. Contexts, Classrooms and Outcomes
Edited by ROBIN ALEXANDER,
PATRICIA BROADFOOT & DAVID PHILLIPS
ISBN 1 873927 58 4 (published 1999)

Volume 2. Policy, Professionals and Development
Edited by ROBIN ALEXANDER,
MARILYN OSBORN & DAVID PHILLIPS
ISBN 1 873927 63 0 (due 2000)

Globalisation, Educational Transformation and Societies in Transition
Edited by TEAME MEBRAHTU, MICHAEL CROSSLEY
& DAVID JOHNSON
ISBN 1 873927 78 5 (due 2000)

Doing Comparative Education Research: issues and problems
Edited by KEITH WATSON
ISBN 1 873927 83 5 (due 2000)

Monographs in International Education
Operation Blackboard: policy implementation in Indian elementary education
CAROLINE DYER
ISBN 1 873927 88 6 (due 2000)

Modularisation of Vocational Education in Europe: NVQs and GNVQs as a model for the reform of initial training provisions in Germany?
HUBERT ERTL
ISBN 1 873927 98 3 (due 2000)

Reschooling and the Global Future: politics, economics and the English experience
JAMES PORTER
ISBN 1 873927 53 3 (published 1999)

For the full contents of all Symposium books, their prices and
an order form, please see www.symposium-books.co.uk

SYMPOSIUM BOOKS PO BOX 65 WALLINGFORD OXFORD OX10 0YG   UNITED KINGDOM
Voice: +44 (0) 1491-838 056 Fax: +44 (0) 1491-834 968 orders@symposium-books.co.uk

Oxford Studies in Comparative Education

Series Editor: Professor David Phillips, University of Oxford

Published recently

Education in Germany Since Unification
Edited by David Phillips
ISBN 1 873927 73 8

Education Systems of the United Kingdom
Edited by David Phillips
ISBN 1 873927 73 8

Comparing Standards Internationally:
research and practice in mathematics and beyond
Edited by Barbara Jaworski & David Phillips
ISBN 1 873927 68 1

Processes of Transition in Education Systems
Edited by Elizabeth A. McLeish & David Phillips
ISBN 1 873927 48 7

Education for Reconstruction: the regeneration
of educational capacity following national upheaval
Nina Arnhold, Julia Bekker, Natasha Kersh,
Elizabeth A. McLeish & David Phillips
ISBN 1 873927 43 6

Education and Privatisation in Eastern Europe and the Baltic Republics
Edited by Paul Beresford-Hill
ISBN 1 873927 38 X

Education and Change in the Pacific Rim: meeting the challenges
Edited by Keith Sullivan
ISBN 1 873927 33 9

For full contents of these titles and others in
this series see *www.symposium-books.co.uk*

SYMPOSIUM BOOKS, PO BOX 65, WALLINGFORD
OXFORD OX10 0YG, UNITED KINGDOM
Voice: +44 (0) 1491-838 056 Fax: +44 (0) 1491-834 968 orders@symposium-books.co.uk